THE LAND CARRIES OUR ANCESTORS

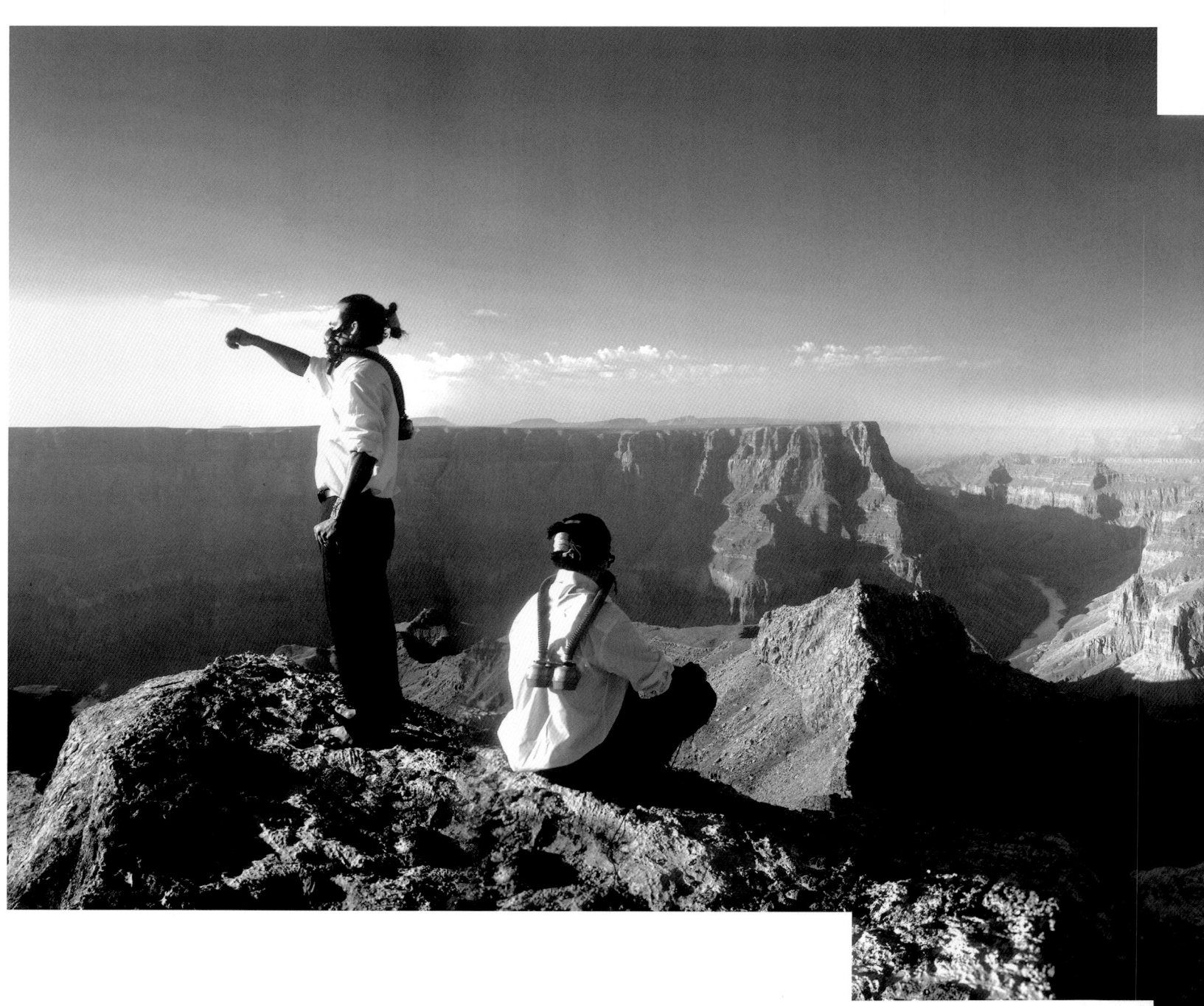

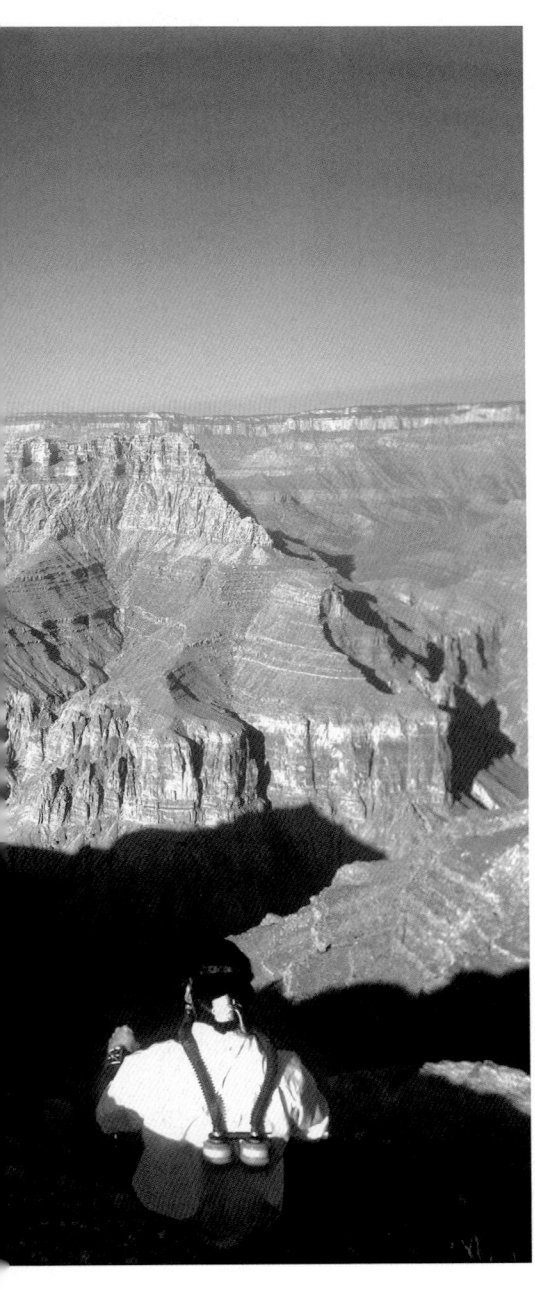

THE LAND CARRIES OUR ANCESTORS
CONTEMPORARY ART BY NATIVE AMERICANS

Jaune Quick-to-See Smith

Joy Harjo
heather ahtone
Shana Bushyhead Condill

National Gallery of Art, Washington
in association with Princeton University Press,
Princeton and Oxford

CONTENTS

FOREWORD AND ACKNOWLEDGMENTS

It is a great honor for the National Gallery of Art to present *The Land Carries Our Ancestors*, an exhibition celebrating contemporary works of art by Native Americans who visualize a rich array of land-based knowledge systems shared by Indigenous peoples across millennia, addressed in the present, and looking to the future. The framework for including work by living Native artists was determined by Jaune Quick-to-See Smith (Citizen of the Confederated Salish and Kootenai Nation), guest curator for the exhibition. She counters notions of Native Americans as existing only in the historical past and emphasizes the presence and creative innovations of Indigenous nations across the United States today. Two of the artists, Gail Tremblay (1945–2023, Onondaga/Mi'kmaq descent) and Jim Denomie (1955–2022, Lac Courte Oreilles Ojibwe, Ajijaak Clan), sadly passed on after their work was chosen. Jaune wished to retain their work to honor their considerable creative spirits, giving meaningful dimension to the word "ancestors" in the exhibition title. We join her in our respect for their remarkable contributions.

This intergenerational, diverse group of artists from all over the United States illuminates the symbiotic relationship between Native American culture and the natural environment. Such reciprocity is seen in the great variety of mediums and creative expressions by the exhibition's some-50 artists representing a vast field of tribal affiliations. Each artist honors their visual sovereignty in keeping with respective individual, regional, and cultural identities. At the same time, the Indigenous beliefs shared by the artists reflect a holistic worldview informed by common reverence and stewardship for the land. We are indebted to these artists for making their vital knowledge visible and for generously participating in this exhibition for the great benefit of all audiences. It is our hope, and expectation, that *The Land Carries Our Ancestors* will create the conditions to consider and engage with the messages of strength, vitality, and resilience these works impart.

The National Gallery of Art is deeply grateful to Jaune Quick-to-See Smith for curating this exhibition, which powerfully voices the care of the natural environment by Indigenous peoples. At every turn, the works reveal inspiring social and cultural practices by focusing on the relationship between humans and nature and the devotion necessary for a mutually sustainable future. *The Land Carries Our Ancestors* is a testament to Jaune's work over the past 40 years to bring the art of her fellow Native Americans into full view. Not only an acclaimed artist and the subject of a major retrospective this year organized by our colleagues at the Whitney Museum of American Art, Jaune has also led the field through her curatorial activity, having organized over 30 Native art exhibitions.

Since 2019, when the National Gallery began the process of acquiring Jaune's painting *Target* (1992), we have been in a constant state of learning. Jaune's background as an educator is clear in her pedagogical approach to her work. After she accepted our invitation to curate this exhibition, Jaune generously shared her stories, histories, and abundant resources with our staff, who continue to benefit from her keen knowledge. We will take this gift forward as we expand our work on Native American art.

The National Gallery has presented seven exhibitions of Indigenous art since the museum opened in 1941. *The Land Carries Our Ancestors* is the first show since *Art of the American Frontier: The Collecting of Chandler and Pohrt*, cocurated by David Penney and George P. Horse Capture (1937–2013, A'aninin) in 1993.[1] As the nation's art museum, we have a responsibility to highlight and foster greater understanding of the rich artistic traditions of the first inhabitants of this land. This exhibition is therefore one step on a journey to developing and sustaining meaningful relationships with Native peoples, increasing Native representation on our staff, engaging in honest dialogue with Indigenous community members, and centering the work by Native artists in our collections and programs.

As part of the National Gallery's mission to represent all people of this country, it is especially important to honor the Indigenous peoples from the land on which the United States is situated. Our colleagues at the National Museum of the American Indian, Smithsonian Institution (NMAI), remind us of this need in their website accompanying their critically important exhibition *Americans*, which leads with a set of facts, followed by a question. It says, "Indians are 1 percent of the population. Yet images and names of Indians are everywhere. How is it that Indians can be so present and so absent in American life?"[2]

As we endeavor to answer this prompt, we recognize the rich and complex histories in the field of Indigenous art and its changing place in museums, and we are most fortunate to have benefitted from the expert scholarship, leadership, and gracious counsel of our many colleagues at NMAI, our neighbors across the National Mall. Without the advice of its director, Cynthia Chavez Lamar; generous support from curator Anya Monteil as

well as associate director of museum scholarship David Penney; and curators Paul Chaat Smith and Rebecca Head Trautmann, along with the generous assistance with the loan of a pair of works in their care, this exhibition would not have been possible. It has been a great professional pleasure for our staffs to collaborate on this show of mutual interest.

Shana Bushyhead Condill (Eastern Band of Cherokee Indians), executive director of the Museum of the Cherokee Indian, North Carolina, has served as an invaluable advisor and interlocutor from the beginning of this project. She began significant work before she departed the National Gallery and continued long thereafter as she consulted with Jaune in hours of conversation and wrote about the works of art for the catalog. In addition, an essay by heather ahtone (Choctaw/Chickasaw Nation), director of curatorial affairs at the First Americans Museum in Oklahoma City, provided key Native art historical perspectives, placing these artworks within the larger context of American visual art. As a capstone, Joy Harjo (Muscogee [Creek] Nation), twenty-third US poet laureate, shared her poem "Once the World Was Perfect."

This publication was overseen by chief content officer and publisher Emiko Usui. Deborah Littlejohn (Eastern Band of Cherokee Indians descent) designed the book with great care and thoughtfulness in collaboration with design manager Brad Ireland. Christina Wiginton and Jasmine Lee, with the assistance of Anne Levine, oversaw the images and production of the book. Mariah Shay, Peggy Martin, Isabella Bulkeley, Nicola Wood, and many others in the department of content strategy, publishing, and branding saw to the myriad details that went into creating the publication. We also thank our publishing partner Princeton University Press, and in particular Michelle Komie, Annie Miller, and Ruthie Rosenstock, for supporting this project.

For her initiative, I thank Molly Donovan, curator of contemporary art at the National Gallery, who identified and acted on the inclusion of contemporary Native artists in the collection and proposed this exhibition. Joining her in working on all aspects of the show has been an outstanding core team of National Gallery colleagues, including Paige Rozanski, curatorial associate, who lent her organizational skills to the project, corresponded with artists and coordinated artworks, and managed object information; Lawrence Hyman, exhibition officer, and Elizabeth Dent, exhibition associate, who attended to every loan detail, contract, internal coordination, and external communication; Nancy Eickel, catalog editor and publication project manager, who liaised with each artist and author; and Rachel Trinkley, interpretation manager, who ensured the respectful treatment that the words and ideas of every artist deserve. This group worked diligently over the past two-plus years to move this project forward, and their efforts to bring this show to our audiences have my deepest appreciation.

The elegant exhibition design owes much to the thought and skill of Michael Lapthorn, chief of design; Donna Kirk, senior architect and designer; Brian Sentman, designer; Jane Grigg, head of graphic design; Lisa Farrell, graphic designer; Rachel Schechtman, design assistant; Drew Watt, supervisory exhibit specialist; and Evan West, production coordinator. The seamless presentation created by this group enables the remarkable art in *The Land Carries Our Ancestors* to be seen at its very best.

For expertly handling the complicated task of safely shipping the art, I thank Melissa Stegeman, associate registrar for exhibitions, and Bethann Heinbaugh, senior conservator. Once at the National Gallery, the preparation of the works of art was attended to with utmost care by Caroline Danforth, matting and framing specialist; Michelle Facini, works on paper conservator; Jay Kreuger, senior paintings conservator; and Katy May, objects conservator.

Great attention was given to presenting the exhibition content for the benefit of our various audiences of every age, near and far. The department of learning and engagement, headed by Damon Reaves, with head of interpretation Joanna Marsh and deputy head of interpretation Lynn Matheny, worked diligently to clearly present the voices of the artists and curator. Head of public programs Grace Murray, academic programs head Ali Peil, and education assistant Rachel Tanzi organized a remarkable set of public lectures and programs, while Danielle Hahn, head of music programs, offered a complement of Native music, an integral component of Indigenous culture. Joanna Raczynska, head of film programs, organized an essential time-based presentation to augment the exhibition beyond the exhibition space.

The Land Carries Our Ancestors benefitted from the sincere efforts of every division leader at the National Gallery, including Luis Baquedano, secretary and general counsel; Kate Haw, executive officer for collections, exhibitions, and programs; Sheila McDaniel, administrator, and her successor, Laura Lott; Eric Motley, deputy director; Steven Nelson, dean of the Center for Advanced Study in the Visual Arts; and E. Carmen Ramos, chief curatorial and conservation officer. I am grateful to work with this amazing team in support of our mission. Special thanks go to Mikka Gee Conway, chief diversity, inclusion, and belonging officer and EEO director; Carolyn Greene McKee, associate general counsel; Anabeth Guthrie, chief of communications; Scott Keiner, head of the production studio; Paula Lynn, head of planning and evaluation; and Chelsea Souza, head of special events, for playing critical roles in the successful outreach initiatives accompanying this remarkable exhibition.

Countless colleagues outside the National Gallery offered assistance and advice at many points in the exhibition's organization. Garth Greenan and Hugh O'Rourke from the Garth Greenan Gallery, together with Chris Barton, Julian Corbett, Niki Hunt, and Rachel Garbade, were key partners from the exhibition's beginning. Neal Ambrose-Smith was a tremendous help on countless fronts in lending an able hand. Our National

Gallery curatorial team benefitted from conversations with colleagues Wanda Nanibush, curator of Indigenous art at the Art Gallery of Ontario; Steven Loft, vice president of Indigenous ways and decolonization, National Gallery of Canada; Elizabeth Rule, assistant professor of critical race, gender, and culture studies, American University; Sasha Scott, associate professor and director of art history and graduate studies, Syracuse University; and Gabrielle Tayac, associate professor of history and art history, George Mason University.

As *The Land Carries Our Ancestors* looks to the future, it is fitting that it travels to a second venue. Following its debut in Washington, the exhibition is presented at the New Britain Museum of American Art. Thank you to our colleagues Brett Abbott, director and chief executive officer, Lisa Williams, curator, and Keith Gervase, collections manager, for their interest in and support of this show.

On behalf of the National Gallery and the New Britain Museum of American Art, I extend my gratitude to the lenders who so graciously agreed to part with the works in their care so that additional audiences may see them. Many public collections, including Crow's Shadow Institute of the Arts; Davis Museum at Wellesley College; Eiteljorg Museum of American Indians and Western Art; Hirshhorn Museum and Sculpture Garden; Hood Museum of Art, Dartmouth College; National Museum of the American Indian; Nerman Museum of Contemporary Art; Plains Art Museum; Stark Museum of Art; Rubell Museum; and the Art Museum of West Virginia University, worked to make the art in their collections available. In addition, many of the artists lent their work, including Gerald Clarke Jr., Joe Feddersen, Nicholas Galanin and Merritt Johnson, Edgar Heap of Birds, John Hitchcock, Luzene Hill, Linda King, George C. Longfish, Cannupa Hanska Luger, Mario Martinez, Rose Powhatan, Cara Romero, Kay WalkingStick, and Will Wilson, and those who wish to remain anonymous. For assistance with these and other loans, we thank Blue Rain Gallery, Bockley Gallery, Peter Blum Gallery, Chiaroscuro Contemporary Art,

Charles Froelick Gallery, Garth Greenan Gallery, Hales Gallery, K Art, Kouri + Corrao Gallery, Sherry Leedy Contemporary Art, PDX Contemporary Art, Sikkema Jenkins & Co., Jack Shainman Gallery, Jessica Silverman Gallery, and Andrew Smith Gallery. Private collectors and foundations who graciously enabled us to borrow works — Steven Campbell and Christina Ziegler Campbell, Jerry Cowdrey, John and Susan Horseman, RJ and Anne Grissinger, Tia Collection, Travois, Sasha and Charlie Sealy, Mark and Amy Spencer, and Christy Vezolles — entrusted the art in their holdings to us for a time. We are grateful for the major support provided for the exhibition by the Robert and Mercedes Eichholz Foundation and for the additional funding provided by the Director's Circle and the Tower Project of the National Gallery of Art.

By sharing the works of these Native artists from across the United States, we hope visitors will bring what they learn from this vibrant Native American contemporary art forward to enrich future generations.

Kaywin Feldman
Director, National Gallery of Art

ONCE
THE WORLD WAS
PERFECT

Joy Harjo   Muscogee (Creek) Nation

Once the world was perfect, and we were happy in that world.
Then we took it for granted.
Discontent began a small rumble in the earthly mind.
Then Doubt pushed through with its spiked head.
And once Doubt ruptured the web,
All manner of demon thoughts
Jumped through —
We destroyed the world we had been given
For inspiration, for life —
Each stone of jealousy, each stone
Of fear, greed, envy, and hatred, put out the light.
No one was without a stone in his or her hand.
There we were,
Right back where we had started.
We were bumping into each other
In the dark.
And now we had no place to live, since we didn't know
How to live with each other.
Then one of the stumbling ones took pity on another
And shared a blanket.
A spark of kindness made a light.
The light made an opening in the darkness.
Everyone worked together to make a ladder.
A Wind Clan person climbed out first into the next world,
And then the other clans, the children of those clans, their children,
And their children, all the way through time —
To now, into this morning light to you.

SKY AS PLACE, LAND AS BODY, LANDSCAPE AS SPIRITUAL COMPASS

heather ahtone　　　Choctaw/Chickasaw Nation

Landscape art has been a practice of expression since the earliest humans documented their relationship to the natural environment. Those artists preserved their knowledge of animal migrations in the drawings and paintings at the Chauvet Cave in southeastern France and their understanding of meteorology and cosmological cycles in the architecture at Chaco Canyon in present-day New Mexico, among other significant sites. This way of heralding the distinctly localized knowledge of places and spaces continues on every human-occupied continent. Landscape art remains a critical lens through which we humans express and comprehend our relationships to the natural environment.[1]

The visual devices that artists use to express this knowledge shift in each pair of creative hands, reflecting the cultural epistemology of each maker. What is evident when viewed as a whole is that across time our human relatives have cultivated unique social relationships to the land upon which we have lived in common, responding to a variety of cultural and social values and priorities. We foster relationships with the land where we live; we both shape the land and become shaped by it. This dynamic of reciprocating response is, broadly put, a product of the philosophical worldview of our cultures and society. To understand how landscapes in art express our relationships to the land and how the concept of landscape is subject to the philosophical foundation from which it emerges, we need only look comparatively at the genesis stories that guide the artist's hand.

Euro-American traditions of landscape art are commonly recognized on this side of the world, so this discussion begins there. The Euro-American social concept of landscape painting is defined through a perspectival view of a deep landscape with the endless sky above. In Europe, Titian, Rembrandt van Rijn, and Paul Cézanne taught us how to read the land through color, light, and form. Thomas Cole, Winslow Homer, Thomas Moran, and Georgia O'Keeffe constructed a corpus of knowledge about the American landscape, often visually advancing the rhetoric of the "West" as being vacant, untamed, sensual, and waiting to be conquered. The forces of earth, sky, and water in a constant dance of verticals and diagonals, light and shadow, stand as a challenge to human capacities for control and domination. These artists, and so many others, undoubtedly helped translate for viewers a passionate love for the energy and vibrancy of the spaces depicted. That awe continues to be felt by audiences who encounter these works in museums and see them in books. That passion drives people to travel to these locations to "escape" the restrictive corridors associated with (sub)urban spaces, where we safely live in organized neighborhoods that rely on civic improvements, such as sidewalks and traffic control signals.

Such awe of the landscape can be taught in the classroom, as I learned as a graduate student at the University of Oklahoma two decades ago. I distinctly remember Professor Victor Koshkin-Youritzin lamenting over Albert Bierstadt's work, "Do you see the mountains licking the sky?" (fig. 1).[2] His descriptive phrasing drew my attention to the sharp edges of the mountains protruding against the ethereal blue sky. For me, the mountains stand as a monument to earthly powers, and the sky is the visual and metaphorical domain wherein lies the "heavenly father." It is no accident that the landscapes of the 18th and 19th century so often show our continent as a vast wilderness. In a manner of thinking, this visual state of being manifested what was divinely granted in the biblical story of Genesis: for man to have dominion over the earth.

In a synthesized version of the biblical origins story, God creates the heavens and the earth, all the animals, and then man. God grants to man dominion over the earth and all that inhabit it, including the animals. Forgive the grossly simplistic synthesis, but the larger key philosophical concepts of Christianity are found in this story. In fact, within this story are planted the seeds for colonialism and capitalism. Man has been

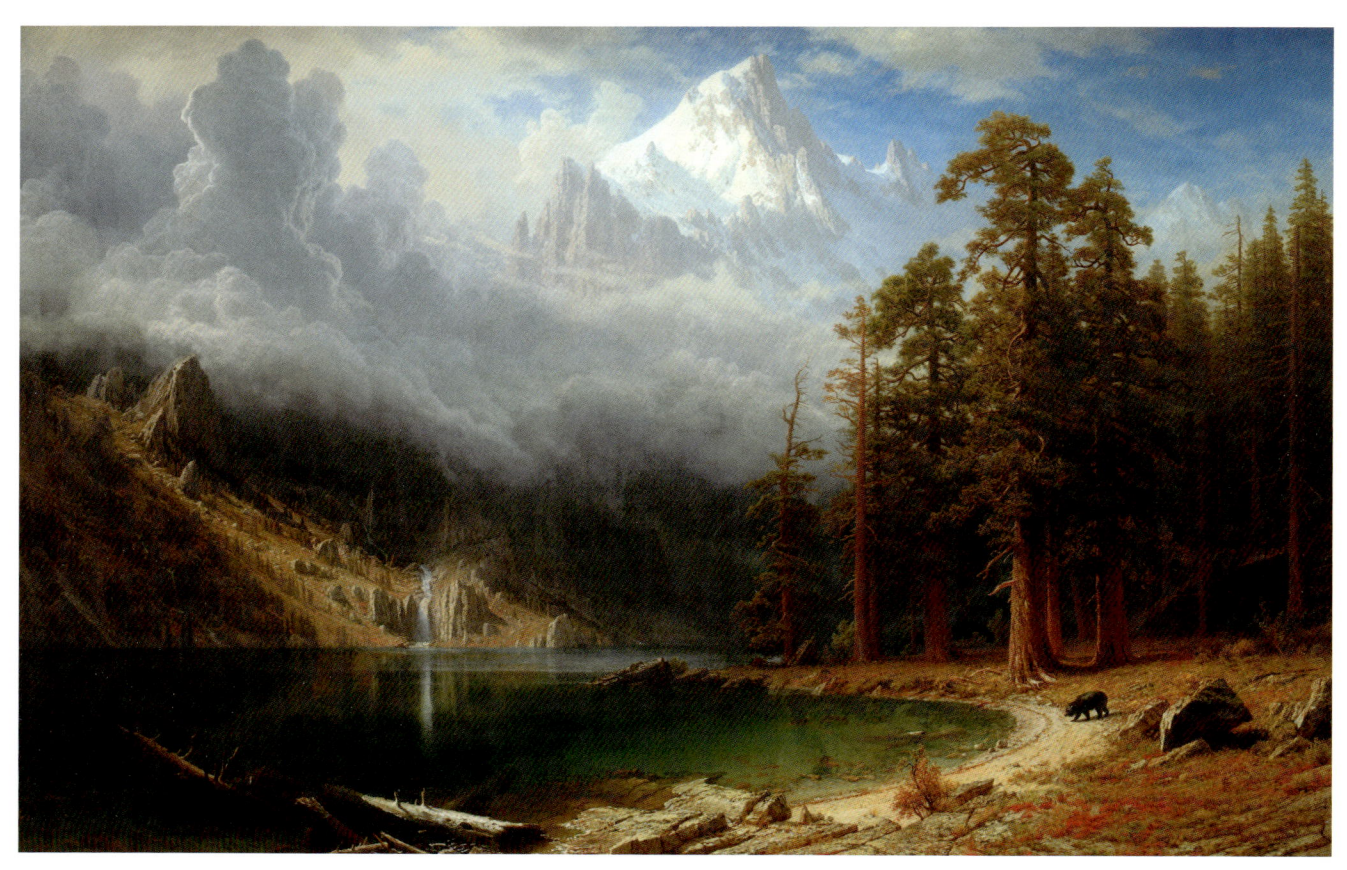

FIG. 1
Albert Bierstadt, *Mount Corcoran*,
c. 1876–1877, oil on canvas. National
Gallery of Art, Washington. Corcoran
Collection (Museum Purchase,
Gallery Fund), 2014.79.4

given dominion over the earth and, thereby, the admonition to carry these responsibilities to the four corners of the earth. Under man's dominion, the earth is transformed from a site of creation into an asset, private property monetized with the emergence of capitalism. The story facilitates a direct relationship between God and Man, with the assignment of rights to control (and name) passing from the divine to the human who carries this directive as a personal foundation.

This concept, fundamental to Christian philosophy, is the underpinning of Western culture's expansion during the Age of Discovery. It becomes interwoven with the teachings of the ancient Greek philosopher Aristotle (and Plato, to some extent), who positions all non-Greeks as *others*, as barbarians who are subject to political dominance or, more specifically, to slavery or extinction. Aristotle was particularly interested in identifying Persians as barbarians to justify their enslavement by the Greek patriarchy. As Christianity converged with the ever-expanding Roman Empire, this origins story was weaponized by an insatiable appetite for the advocation of Christian domination of the world (read as all non-Romans). Many people today never question where this idea originated, but this particular genesis story is widely believed to be related to Mesopotamian mythology.[3] It is a twist of power to steal the genesis story of ancient Persian cultural people in Mesopotamia, adopt it through Christianity, and then use it to subdue and oppress people on all continents.

This is another simplification of a history that took centuries to enact in Europe, where tribal people had their own genesis stories erased. The appetite for dominion, control, and greed eventually led to the biblical story in Genesis arriving on the shores of the continents now known as the Americas. The advancement of colonialism stood boldly on the shoulders of capitalism as it raced to dominate all the continents in a hungry lust for more land and assets in partnership with a Christian righteous fervor that measured civility on the capacity to convert and adopt this origins story. For the 18 million souls that were already on the North American continent, however, we have long understood that this land was made by the Creator, and we were placed here with responsibilities to protect it, to guard it and all that live with us on it, in a system of reciprocity and respect.[4]

The stark contrast of these philosophical worldviews cannot be overstated. It remains a challenge for understanding contemporary landscape art by Indigenous American artists. We must keep in mind that thousands of cultural groups, each with its own genesis story, were likely organized within the borders known today as the United States. Even with the almost 600 federally recognized tribes that remain in the United States today (with the additional state-recognized tribes and those that continue to resist cultural extinction as unrecognized tribes), if any light shines through the darkness, we can be grateful for all the sacrifices made by our ancestors, who carried our knowledge into the 21st century. Indigenous people, to the best of our ability against the onslaught of colonialism and capitalisms, have fervently held on to and protected our knowledge across generations. For so many of us, it is a fact that we still have our genesis stories. Further, our artists continue to express our cultural relationships to the land that are found in the philosophies of our genesis stories. The philosophical conflict between Western and Indigenous worldviews, however, has left the work of Indigenous artists who are exploring concepts of landscape as part of their visual expression conceptually inaccessible to the broader public who view it through a Euro-American cultural lens.

To understand how these worldviews conflict, let us consider Indigenous genesis stories. Indigenous people originated by dynamic and complex primal forces that reflect the Creator's appreciation for diversity, perhaps as a way to keep it all interesting. My own Choctaw people, we believe, were born of the earth, and we know the site of the cave from which we emerged, very

Being born from the earth and acknowledging our relationship to the land as her children, we honor and protect the earth as any human would shelter the person who has nurtured, fed, and provided for them.

near the mound where our ancestors are buried. These two locations remain sacred to us. My ancestors and relatives suffered to protect that land, which we call our mother.[5] The common reference to our Mother Earth comes from a relationship to the land upon which we all share a dependency as a source of power and of nurturing and life-sustaining energy. Our Choctaw genesis story, again simplified, is one of a migration that brought us from within the earth, born into this land. The Creator placed us in community with the animals from which we learned to be human. Our stories are recorded in the stars, with constellations helping us to remember the divine source of our cultures. I have often thought of the genius of our ancestors for reading our stories in the sky, far away from the threat of human erasure and the vulnerable knowledge held in books.[6] In the 21st century these genesis and animal stories remain the regular fodder by which we raise our children with the values and worldviews passed to us from the Creator, as has been done across uncountable generations.

Being born from the earth and acknowledging our relationship to the land as her children, we honor and protect the earth as any human would shelter the person who has nurtured, fed, and provided for them. We return to the earth, with each generation metaphorically and cyclically caring for the next. This relationship positions humans as having a responsibility to the earth that is not simply nostalgic or transactional. We exist because the earth exists. Our survival is intertwined with the care and protections we provide her. While our tribal nations have been forced to participate in the capitalistic market economy, one of our most profound political actions has been to engage in a process of purchasing parcels of land that were given to us by the Creator and then stolen by the US federal government and settler populations. We are resuming our culturally guided responsibilities to the land by protecting and praying for it. Even for my relatives who, like myself, live on land that is far from our original homelands, we recognize that all land was made by the Creator and that the earth must be cared for everywhere. We can rebuild the protections where we live, even in urban spaces, for this whole continent is Indian Country. We can see the earth responds to our prayers and the care we give to the land, no matter the suffering we share in common under the subjective rule of capitalism.

Each tribal nation has had to manage this complex history and relationship in its own best manner. Some tribes have been radical in the fight to protect the land. I think of the water protectors who stood against the physical onslaught of the energy companies in 2016 and 2017 in Standing Rock in the Dakotas. Protected by private militia and brutal police, oil companies facilitated the raping of the earth and threatened the life-sustaining waters with which the people's survival was intertwined. Other tribes have been subversive in their quiet participation in the open market, purchasing plot after plot to assume direct responsibility for large parcels of land, even in urban spaces. Those tribes have used the laws that protect private ownership to shift property into their care and management, employing the very dictates of capitalism to ensure this land is not stolen again.

For Indigenous people, our relationships to the land are informed by our cosmological stories, the contemporary responsibilities of living in the United States, and the respect we have for those animate forces with which our survival is interdependent. We often see the animals as our teachers and the rivers and landforms as markers of our history and identity. Understanding that our complex relationships and philosophies form a kincentristic energy that binds our life forms together is key to looking at Indigenous landscape art.[7] Kincentricity describes the Indigenous perspective of the interdependency that exists between Indigenous people with animate and inanimate life forms and forces, including the clouds, rain, animals, plants, and earth.

Our ancestors, well aware of our interdependency with these varied life forms, often abstracted kincentristic life forces into graphic motifs and designs that remain in use today. We need only look at Plains beadwork, Pueblo pottery, Plateau baskets, and Anishinaabe embroidery to see the long history of this practice. Each tribal community incorporated the complexity of our knowledge into cultural aesthetic systems that have been carried across time. A singular cardinal direction, a seasonal shift, and migratory patterns not only have been overlaid with philosophical understanding about the responsibilities that humans carry, but they also have been reduced to representation by a particular mineral color, such as the sky-blue color in Cheyenne beadwork or the walnut-dyed black in Navajo ceremonial baskets. These colors are often tied to the natural palette of the cultural homelands, which is, of course, a product of our ancestors' genius to use what they have and to extend its service as multivalent signifiers.

This practice has complicated the canonization of our knowledge under the homogenized term Native American. While the racialization of our Indigenous people into a single group made it easier for others to manage us politically, this simplification denies the uniqueness by which each tribe has undertaken its own wholistic approach to visualize a philosophical paradigm. The same color or motif used by one tribe, for example, can represent far different knowledge from another tribe, perhaps even a neighboring one. Throw in creative artistic license, and the same color may simply be a pleasing visual accent. We can only imagine how this complicated diversity must have overwhelmed the earliest European explorers who could not apply their Western logic to our complex cultural ways of knowing and expressing our worldviews. For them, it was easier to discount us as uncivilized and to disregard our humanity and our beautiful ways of knowing philosophy, science, and the Creator.

For all these reasons, and perhaps more, fully exploring contemporary Indigenous perspectives on landscape art becomes difficult. Artists combine their own tribal knowledge system with their expressive personal style. To start the conversation, Jaune Quick-to-See Smith has brought together artists whose works share the beauty of this diversity. Smith introduces artists whose works express their love for the land as a place, the sky as a space, the cosmos as a home, and the landscape as a spiritual compass for our humanity. Our cultures have prayed for, danced on, and cared for the land for millennia.[8] These deep ties are difficult to translate into English, which, like Western culture, is temporally myopic. We have understood through our genesis stories that we survive because the earth survives. We are connected to the moment of genesis through a continuum of creation. We are

Smith introduces artists whose works express their love for the land as a place, the sky as a space, the cosmos as a home, and the landscape as a spiritual compass for our humanity.

often reminded that we are as close to the past as we are to the future. Our gratitude for this connection provides a path for our continued efforts to prepare for the future — and to understand the land is not ours to exhaust.

Among those whose love for the land and all our relationships to it is Marwin Begaye (Diné), whose large-scale woodblock prints and lithographs honor the birds that are messengers and carriers of blessings in his communities in Navajo country and in Oklahoma. Similarly, James Lavadour (Walla Walla) constructs gestural portraits of the peaks and valleys found in the Cascade Mountains and the Plateau prairies. As Indigenous artists participate in their cultures, live in their local communities, and pray for Mother Earth, their devotion and regard are evident in their continued processes of creating images.

Sometimes it takes only a single color to connote that affection. The exuberant blue of *Fog Bank* (2020) by Emmi Whitehorse (Diné) expresses the energy and gratitude she feels with the arrival of fog, as water vapor condenses to form droplets resembling clouds kissing the earth (p. 133). Water is sacred in all forms, including fog. This core tenet activates every tribal community in defending its rights to natural resources. For many, this belief in water's sacredness is a significant component of annual ceremonies. Water not only supports the life of humans, plants, and animals alike, but it is also an expression of love given by the Creator. Whitehorse refers to all of these ideas with gestural abstract marks, yet many of these marks stand as synecdoche for a lush and robust life

cycle, one generated by the arrival of clouds and moisture to the thirsty desert. The delicacy of these marks speaks to the interdependency and frailty with which we all live.[9]

Water is a life force. It is often figured into tribal genesis stories as a woman who gently brings the community what it needs to carry on. Sometimes water arrives in the form of a male storm filled with anger and greed that sweeps across the landscape causing destruction. These figures teach us not simply about the world as a gendered space (though more than the binary) but also that we humans as much as nature can be a force for good or bad. Such stories instruct us to make appropriate choices in how we honor our relationships to our Mother Earth and to one another.

Personal and communal human responsibilities are often at the core of our creation stories. We learn that our decisions have impacts, generally irreversible ones, beyond ourselves. Animal stories teach us that all choices have repercussions. Decisions made for the good remind us that we sometimes have to make personal sacrifices for the well-being of all. Other choices may have lasting consequences that extend beyond our own known time and hurt future generations. The reason why these genesis stories are so critical is that, despite contemporary circumstances, their lessons resonate. We can still rely on the teachings gifted at creation to guide us to be caring, responsible human beings today. Many of us have been taught this means being "good ancestors."

Artists use their creative voices to serve as harbingers of long-term human impacts that hurt the land. Their works address the comprehensive doom we all face as climate change becomes acutely focused in hyper-shifting weather systems and the gross negligence by which we are bringing about the sixth mass extinction in the history of the planet. The same animals that taught us in the creation stories are also many of the same ones that are being exterminated by our actions.

The land is our mother, and Indigenous people will do whatever is needed to protect her.

Such grim messages are equally important to explore in our relationships to the landscape.

Numerous artists possess the courage to address these dark topics. Athena LaTocha (Keweenaw Bay Ojibwe/Standing Rock Lakota) and John Hitchcock (Comanche/Kiowa/European descent) directly confront the petroleum and military industries, respectively, in their works. Fearless in how they push the boundaries of defining beauty, they build surfaces that reflect the chaos and fervor with which these industries violate all that is sacred today. Other artists look to the future and ask us to consider how our decisions impact those yet unborn.

The premise of the *Auto-Immune Response* series by Will Wilson (Diné) acutely challenges our ambitions and our measures for progress against the costs that must be paid (p. 135). He utilizes the Navajo story of the Hero Twins, Monster Slayer and Born for Water, the children of Changing Woman and the Sun. The twins prepared the earth for humans to live in peace, harmony, and balance, concepts embedded in the philosophy of *hózhó*. Transforming the Hero Twins found in the Navajo genesis story into contemporary figures, Wilson examines the remains of a postapocalyptic world. He positions these Hero Twins in known and specific spaces to anchor their inquiry into the world in which we actively live and play. In Wilson's photographs the twins survey the earth and seek out the monsters that make it uninhabitable. They reveal the consequences of choices we have made in neglected uranium mines and heavily drought-stricken deserts. Through this futuristic romp we participate as active antagonists (or not), depending on the choices we make today. We might even surmise from his images that we, as Americans, have become the monsters. Using the lens of photography to aggravate our discomfort, Wilson looks at the landscape by using the familiar perspectival vantage point and by forcing us to see our footprints, even before we've made them.

Even in Wilson's photography, LaTocha's cascading petroleum glaciers, and Hitchcock's militant installations, the love that these Indigenous artists have for their homes, the land, and their cultures is evident. They remain steadfastly passionate about their relationships to their cultural homelands and to the earth in general. Though some of these artists work in urban spaces (Andrea Carlson in Chicago) and others are far from their homelands (Teri Greeves in New Mexico), their ties to Mother Earth are rooted in the teachings of our cultures. Jaune Quick-to-See Smith has brought together works that are both a survey of Indigenous landscape art and a compilation of love letters to the land. On behalf of the earth, these works entreat us to remember our planet is not merely a resource or an asset over which humans have been given dominion. The land is our mother, and Indigenous people will do whatever is needed to protect her. She carries the spirits of the Creator, our ancestors, and each of us. May we be blessed to extend our gratitude and return the care she has given us so generously.

LAND/LANDBASE/ LANDSCAPE

Jaune Quick-to-See Smith   Citizen of the Confederated Salish and Kootenai Nation

A Short History of America

Snow White came from Europa.
She kissed the Frog
Who turned into
A Ledger Book Prince.
She converted corn
Into Fritos
And soon
She put everything
Up for Sale.

When I was a kid, I traveled with my father for horse trading. Part of the time we lived on other reservations, like the Hoopa in northern California, the Muckleshoot near Seattle, and the Nisqually near Olympia in Washington state. I experienced first-hand how important salmon was for our survival. Nisqually peoples are Salish and speak a dialect of my Salish tribal language. My father was a Salish speaker, so in many ways it was like living with relatives. Also, our drinking water came from a hand pump fed from the river and was shared by the tribal peoples in their log cabins. This experience helps me understand the dire situation at Standing Rock, with the proposed oil pipeline threatening the water in the Missouri River reservoir. That impasse is still not resolved.

Nearly every day my email is filled with articles and reports on fracking, new drilling sites on Native lands, and record-setting storms besetting us everywhere. The myriad of articles and reports I receive might also include heartbreaking news about tribes whose culture for thousands of years was built upon salmon, but now they must import frozen salmon for their communities' sustenance needs and ceremonies. All food is connected to the Sacred and the ceremonial.

Then again, I might read an article on various reservation cancer rates, such as at Hanford, Washington, where radioactive waste is slowly poisoning the Cayuse, Walla Walla, and Umatilla tribes. That's one of the world's largest toxic waste cleanup sites. Also, New Mexico harbors over 500 abandoned uranium mines on land of the Navajo Nation, causing Navajo peoples to have one of the highest cancer rates in the nation. Bits of the uranium slag heaps piled since World War II blow in the wind and leach into the groundwater, poisoning the sheep and eventually the tribal members. Radioactive waste from 272 abandoned mines also leaches into the Cheyenne River in South Dakota and poisons the Lakota peoples there as well as their hunting and fishing areas, domestic animals, and family agriculture. More than 50 uranium mills were allowed to process ore all over the West, almost always on or near Native peoples' lands. So much of this news has been reported only since 1991.

That year, I curated an exhibition centered around landscape. Titled *Our Land, Ourselves*, the exhibition traveled to several venues across the country and included a catalog with important works by 30 Native American artists. Since that time, a lot has changed in contemporary Native arts. So many more artists are working successfully in the mainstream today, but often they are not recognized as Native unless they have names like Halfmoon, Heap of Birds, or Quick-to-See Smith (an old family name). Like other peoples, most of our names originally came from the natural world, as do a lot of our artworks. I certainly could see a trajectory of that exhibition I curated in 1991 to the time we live in now, with the ever-changing dynamics hurled upon our Mother Earth, whether it be a pipeline that runs across sacred land and threatens to pollute the only safe and clean drinkable water for miles around or mining that threatens the integrity of land, sky, and water for millennia.[1]

LANGUAGES AND PICTURES

Our languages are tied to our landbase, to the natural world. We named everything around us, the animals, birds, insects, rivers, trees, vegetation, our foods, all our geography, even the weather and our astronomical world. Our origin stories are tied to our natural worlds, our worldview, our philosophy, our epistemology, our metaphysics,

Our languages are tied to our landbase, to the natural world. We named everything around us, the animals, birds, insects, rivers, trees, vegetation, our foods, all our geography, even the weather and our astronomical world.

our values, our astronomical world, and even the recitation of our history. "Indian Time" is based upon the cycles of the natural world, such as the seasons, the wild harvests, and astronomy.

In my case, in my Salish homeland, Coyote named every mountain peak, every river, every creek with stories about what took place there. Our Coyote recitations are stories that describe how we came to be, what foods we eat, how our dance regalia is made. Coyote is a trickster figure. Many Indigenous societies have trickster figures who cover a broad realm of behaviors. Some tricksters are binary in terms of good and evil; others deal with questions about our origins. As Leroy Little Bear (First Nations Blackfoot), professor emeritus at the University of Lethbridge, Alberta, states, "The trickster is about chaos, the unexpected, the 'why' of creation, and the consequences of unacceptable behaviour."[2] Our trickster stories guide us with humor and tell us how to behave. These lessons in living are not a binary of right or wrong, like the Christian Bible, nor did we have guilt, which causes dysphoria and a feeling of isolation. Our tribal stories are guides and make us feel part of something larger. There is comfort and spiritual strength in that. This causes many Indigenous peoples today to dump the urban life and return to their homelands for a more spiritual and community-based life.

The Salish Cultural Committee in the Salish Qlispe Long House at Saint Ignatius Mission, Montana, has been recording the oral history of our elders from past decades through to today. The elders' epistemological recitations match up with the findings of Anglo scientists, who document the natural world as far back as 15,000 years or more. This is phenomenal to me, that our elders can orally retain history that far back. Our languages describe a world that is 15,000 years old but likely extends thousands of years before that, since the Creation Time. Radical changes in the past 100 years are producing a shift that could make our languages antiquated, much like Shakespeare's English is to today's English. For those of us who were forbidden to speak our own languages because our families were kidnapped and forced into boarding schools, we have suffered a psychological trauma. It is said that for three generations, even when we are not Native-language speakers, we use the same breath sounds, fricatives, and placement of nouns, verbs, and adjectives that our traditional languages afforded us. It is lodged in our right-leaning brains, where visual imagery, patterning, and dreams are located. I believe our languages come from the right side of the brain, not the left side. We image our language before we speak. I know I have to visualize numbers before I can do math. This is exactly how we use our languages to visualize our natural world around us. It isn't abstract to us. We make pictures in our heads.

Our Native languages carry thousands of years of actual history. The English language has no relationship to our natural world or to our cultural, epistemological, or metaphysical worlds. When English came to us, it had already parted ways with nature and was a capitalist, industrialized language, always seeking resources to exploit. Colonial genocide sought to take knowledge from us: to take our land, our food, our culture, our stories, our oral history, our children and grandchildren, and our encyclopedic languages that name and describe the natural world and how we interact with it, all the plants, animals, insects, trees, mountains, and waterways.

To destroy our languages is cultural genocide. It bankrupts our tribal Nations and strips our identity from us. The idea that this is integration or assimilation is, simply put, murder — but murder on a grand scale. It is genocide. It is assimilate or eradicate. I personally see this as giving us a cultural lobotomy.

A KINCENTRIC WORLD

Our metaphysical world is a part of our ancestral memory. This is our relationship between mind and matter, which the hegemony of the settler-colonial prerogative, that is, Christianity, has strived to destroy completely.

Uruguayan journalist Eduardo Galeano writes in *We Say No: Chronicles 1963–1991*, that "four years after Christopher Columbus first set foot on the beaches of America, his brother Bartholomew inaugurated a crematorium in Haiti. Six Indians, found guilty of sacrilege, were burned at the stake. The Indians had buried a few little drawings of Jesus Christ and the Virgin Mary. But they had buried them so that these new gods would make their plot of corn more fruitful, and they felt not the slightest twinge of guilt for such a mortal offense."[3] The explanation is that they did not know guilt. They were logically using what they saw as spiritual power to make the corn grow — nothing more and nothing less.

Too often, Christianity has ignored the natural world. From the beginning in the Bible, human beings hold a central position. The first chapter of the book of Genesis, verse 28, states that God told Adam and Eve to "have dominion over the fish of the sea and over the birds of the air [heavens] and over every living thing that moves [up]on the earth." This value system differs from the holistic view of nature held by Indigenous peoples.

The destruction of our mystical and spiritual guideposts equates to mass murder in the assimilation process. It tries to take Indigenous peoples into the totally alien world that was so long ago bankrupted by industrialization and greed that it mows down everything in its path. Today we see that major agricultural companies already control much of the world's agricultural seeds. Once they own all of the food seeds, get ready. They will control all of the world's food supplies.

Dan Wildcat, Yuchi citizen of the Muscogee Nation of Oklahoma, is my friend, a scholar, an intellect, and professor at Haskell Indian Nations University. He included a chart in *Power and Place: Indian Education in America*, which he cowrote with Vine Deloria Jr. (Standing Rock Sioux). Wildcat compares how Aristotelians or Westerners and Natives see human beings.[4] He purports Westerners see human beings as an entity at the top of a hierarchical world, but we Natives see ourselves in union with nature. We are in kinship with animals, plants, and the physical features of nature. This is animism, which means all things are moving all the time, the cosmos, the earth, and everything in it. Everything is alive, nothing is static. Wildcat identifies an ecosystem as a model of society for Natives. Further, he says Natives' greatest goods are respect and ecosystem sustainability, whereas Westerners believe individual liberty and utilitarianism are the greatest goods.

Leroy Little Bear asserts in his essay "Jagged Worldviews Colliding" that colonialism is a process that seeks to maintain a singular social order by means of force and cultural genocide. It leaves no space for diversity and only leaves a disjointed human worldview.[5] In a sense, this is reminiscent of Aldous Huxley's dystopian novel *Brave New World*, where people who refuse to take their soma pill to have blissful numbness are called savages. Hmmm, this has a familiar ring to it.

The corporate world is all about short-term financial gain by acquiring and selling goods, property, and resources with no regard for the natural world, its inhabitants, or the workers who must employ corporate tactics. I'm saying, too, that our corporate world has never reckoned with our tribal societies that have definable commu-

Our collective strength is not only shared community with family and Native nations but also with all our relations, from that of the insects and plants to the animal world.

nities and share similar cultural components. Natives of the Americas live in a holistic world without a horizon line. We are partners with the natural world; it is our kin. We live in a kincentric world. Sacred space is not a spot someplace. No, sacred space is everything around us, from the land to the sky. It is a holistic circular world. This is the reason why you sometimes don't see a horizon line in our artwork because this belief is part of our epistemology.

The Sacred is not something that hangs around our neck or is inside a building, nor is it a monument in a plaza. It is the space between land and sky, the whole enchilada and all Her inhabitants both living and thought to be inert. Nothing is inert. This is the Mothership, the Tierra Madre, our Mother Earth. Her life force goes through everything. Everything is in constant flux and is of value, every rock, every maggot, every bird, every animal, and every human.

The Peruvian poet César Vallejo described love for his homeland this way: "Go where I may, I will never forget the land I belong to, because I wear her, I walk with her, I am her."[6]

Remember the traditional Haudenosaunee (Iroquois) saying, "Our faces come from beneath the ground." We return from there to become part of life again. Our dust, our DNA, contributes to the salmon, the heron, the corn, the dragonfly, the cedar, the blue jay, and beaver. This is Native science from thousands of years of study.

Joy Harjo, Muscogee (Creek) Nation citizen, prestigious twenty-third US poet laureate, and our first Native in this role, has written,

What joins the original cultures of these lands is a shared belief system in which we are not separate from the land, or from the consequences of the stewardship of these lands. These lands aren't my lands. These lands aren't your lands. We are the land. Together we move and have moved about with the knowledge that we are not at the top of a hierarchy, rather, we are part of an immense field of knowledge and beingness, and human contribution, though crucial, is not the most important. All have a place. What use do humans have in this bio system? Are we necessary to earth ecology?[7]

I personally think the answer is a resounding No! Chief Crowfoot (Isapo-Muxika) might have responded to Harjo this way. He was a warrior of the Siksika First Nation and a profound leader who advocated peace. He said, "What is life? It is the flash of a firefly in the night. It is the breath of a buffalo in the wintertime. It is the little shadow which runs across the grass and loses itself in the sunset."[8]

Was Crowfoot a visionary? Could he have seen that our earth, our Tierra Madre, is suffering? She is presently in the middle of the sixth mass extinction, the Anthropocene, in which all living species, including ourselves, are at risk of total extinction due to destructive human activities.

ANYWHERE WE WALK
Eons of time and study have taught us that our survival is dependent upon the seen as well as the unseen. Our collective strength is not only shared community with family and Native nations but also with all our relations, from that of the insects and plants to the animal world.

We have thousands upon thousands of years of scientific study of nature in the Americas. Passed down orally through our families and through glyph writing, quipus, or other mnemonic devices, codices or other forms of recordkeeping, much of it has been destroyed in the Great Invasion (my term) — in the world's worst human holocaust.

Depending on a tribe's geographical location, unique plants, animals, trees, fish, and other living creatures of the natural world offer sustenance and life to those who participate in that locale. One stupendous example is the tribal communities that interact and live in kinship with a relation, like the western red cedar tree. From this tree come blankets, housing, fishing nets, clothing, rain hats, ropes, shoes, canoes, ceremonial objects, food, medicine, and many other important items. This tree remains vitally important to multiple tribes even today, as it has offered sustenance and life for thousands of years.

The belief is that there must be propitiation of the tree's spirit, including supplication of the surrounding trees. Over a decade ago Agnes Vanderburg, a Salish elder who I revered and who has walked on, taught all of us who would listen that we must always give thanks before taking the life of a plant, a fish, a tree and that living in union with our natural world would ensure that it would survive for our future generations. The Haudenosaunee remind us that we need to think ahead seven generations when making decisions. This flies in the face of our short-term world of making a fast buck and not looking to the future in the short-sighted consumer world we inhabit.

The life force flows through all things, living and static, which is an animistic view of the natural world. Also important is seeing ourselves as guardians, as caretakers of our surroundings. This is the antithesis of the Christian worldview, where there is a disconnect between the living world and the hierarchical status of the human world. It implies that we are not connected to this planet, not dependent on Her. To assuage this ideology, we must be encased in a steel box at death, and possibly float into outer space after the war mongers blow up our Mother Earth with nuclear bombs, or we poison what's left of the natural world, whichever comes first.

Native ideology insists that we are part of the sacred, from the solar dust on this planet as well as our bodies recycling with the ancestors and all other living things. We believe that anywhere we walk, and especially in our homelands, we have been here so long that we stir the DNA of our ancestors.

Dr. Rina Swentzell, an important Santa Clara Pueblo Native who was an artist, author, and scholar, writes she is "egocentric, that Pueblo peoples do live at the center of the universe." Certainly, this might be said for all of us. We often return to our original names because they were taken away from us by the white invaders who gave us names like Big Earrings or Blackfeet, Big Bellies or Flatheads. Nearly all of us named ourselves, the first peoples, the original peoples: We, the people, as in the preamble to the US Constitution. Remember, centuries ago it was the whites who were fleeing religious and societal persecutions as well as enslavement by kings and the feudal systems in Europe. Dr. Swentzell goes on to say that "the purpose of life . . . is to be intimately united with nature, intimately connected with everything in the natural world."[9] This is true for all our Indigenous peoples, whether we come together at a powwow, a conference, an encampment, or a meeting. When our elders pray for us in our Native languages, they will pray to the four directions plus upwards to the sky and downwards to the earth. Then they will pray to the insects, the ripples in the water, and so on. They express that everything is connected, and we are connected to everything. Dr. Swentzell says that after constructing an adobe house, it is "fed" cornmeal so it will have a good life.

I've been reading that every place on earth will be impacted by climate change, especially near the equator. Some places are already uninhabitable due to heat, impoverished by drought, or cause severe illnesses, especially in children and elders. This is happening right now. What about 50 years

We believe that anywhere we walk, and especially in our homelands, we have been here so long that we stir the DNA of our ancestors.

from now? People will need to move north, possibly to Canada, and further inland, away from our current coastal waters, and to higher altitudes. Fires and their dangers will further impact forests. We don't have to wait 50 years to see what happens. It is here. Our brothers and sisters at the southern US border are climate-change refugees, and this diaspora will only increase.

Vine Deloria Jr., noted citizen of the Standing Rock Sioux, writes in *God Is Red: A Native View of Religion* that sometime in the early 1930s Chief Luther Standing Bear (Sicangu and Oglala Lakota) commented on the strange inability of the white man to come to grips with the reality of American existence. "The white man does not understand America. He is too far removed from its formative processes. The roots of his tree of life have not yet grasped the rock and soil. . . . The man from Europe is still a foreigner and an alien. And he still hates the man who questioned his path across the continent. But in the Indian the spirit of the land is still vested. . . . Men must be born and reborn to belong. Their bodies must be formed of the dust of their forefathers' bones."[10]

So how do we move forward? Where do we go from here? The respected scholar Joseph M. Pierce (Cherokee Nation) writes that a land acknowledgment is not enough to appease Native Americans for what we have lost over generations. He qualifies this by saying it must be followed by meaningful action. The land has been stolen and desecrated, therefore confirming its existence

is not enough. It requires that people should reciprocate, steward the land, and provide the care it needs. In other words, people must see the land is a relative, a body that sustains other bodies. We have a responsibility, Pierce says, to enact an ongoing engagement of reciprocity. That would be meaningful action.[11]

What meaningful action can we take? When I envisioned this exhibition, it became clear to me that these diverse works of art are so much more than beautiful objects on display in a museum. While they might not fit into the mainstream of Euro-American perceptions of landscape, they do represent our enduring connection to land. For us, Native definitions of land/landbase/landscape are always and forever; it is the sacred land of our ancestors. We know that no matter where we go, the dust of the land carries our ancestors.

Chant with Me
I am a drop of rain
I am the mist in fog
I am the glint on wood tick
I am a grain of manoomin
I am a hair on grizzly
I am a scale on salmon
I am a thread of black moss
I am the yellow eye of the coyote
I am the pollen on corn silk
I am a bract of bitterroot
I am the shaft of a feather
I am the whisker of wolf
I am the sphagnum in muskeg
I am the wattle on a tom
I am the calyx on a serviceberry
I am the speckle on magpie egg
I am the stick and mud of beaver
I am the keratin of elk horn
I am related
I am related
I am related
I am related

THE DUST ON OUR FEET

Shana Bushyhead Condill   Eastern Band of Cherokee Indians

The scope of *The Land Carries Our Ancestors* has always been epic. How do you curate an exhibition about contemporary Native art in the United States? There are close to 600 tribes in this country alone, and every nation and culture is unique. Jaune Quick-to-See Smith wants to highlight that exact point — the vastness and diversity of Native artists working today. She intentionally chose works by artists from a variety of regions, ages, genders, and mediums. We, as Native people, are not monoliths. We do, however, all share a connection to the land.

In recent years I've had the pleasure of getting to know Jaune and to listen to her perspective. I've long admired her work and especially her activist voice. Jaune's contribution to the growing field of scholarship about Native art and art history cannot be denied, and I know she sees more work needs to be done. An active artist herself, she still dedicates much of her time and resources to adding to Native scholarship. I have witnessed Jaune's desire to both correct and continue the conversation. *The Land Carries Our Ancestors* is one step in achieving that goal.

This drive reminds me of my grandpa's story. Like many others in our communities, he experienced boarding school, where he was punished for speaking Cherokee. He made a conscious and intentional decision not to teach his children Cherokee, which of course resulted in a loss of language in our family. When I was around 12 years old, I remember him suddenly immersing himself in figuring out how to teach the Kituwah dialect of Cherokee that Eastern Band folks speak. He enlisted the help of my Aunt Jean, a teacher at the local elementary school, in creating a classroom curriculum, first on cassette tapes and later on VHS tapes. Their efforts formed the foundation for the solutions my tribe is utilizing to protect our endangered language. In a similar way, Jaune is using her knowledge and experience to ensure we have a canon of scholarship about Native art from a Native perspective.

As Jaune and I talked about this exhibition, we recognized that in many ways, landscape is an extremely useful entrée to the Native worldview. Land and place are tied to all things. History, making, ceremony, cooking, and gathering are all associated with place. For Jaune, the color blue, symbols and glyphs, animals, and the use of natural materials in art are all indicators of landscape. We also came to discern threads that weave their way throughout the exhibition. The connection to land, the trauma we have all experienced, and the humor we use as a tool all point toward hope and perseverance in the face of danger. Our very existence illustrates that truth. These recurring themes must be reconciled with our complex and often misunderstood Native identity and with our role and responsibility to our communities and this land. It is impossible and a mistake — to attempt to put each work into any one category. These works flow easily between themes.

Native people also share the disruption that occurred after the European invasion. How do we remove colonized insertions into our communities that don't align with who we are? How do we rediscover elements of our cultures that were systematically removed? And how do we create protocols and identity that accurately define who we are today?

This work is done individually but for the whole. We have a word for this in Cherokee: ᏍᏏ (*Gadugi*). The art that Jaune selected underscores how these artists bring their worldviews to their work — and offer it up to us as a gift. It's vulnerable and powerful and beautiful.

THE WORLD IS A SACRED PLACE

Everything we do is tied to the land. As Jaune explains, "A sacred place is everything around us, from the land to the sky, in all four, all six directions: the cardinal directions, up and down." In some tribes, we expand the sacred space to include center — seven directions — to mark where we are in relation to the land.

The works in this exhibition do not necessarily fit into the mainstream European definition of landscape, with a horizon line and a blue sky.

"When I'm thinking about landscape, I'm thinking about the Native American holistic approach to landscape," Jaune says. "Often in Native art you see a whole complex. There's no sky, there's no horizon line."

Jaune and I discussed an unexpected example of a landscape: *Kiowa Ah-Day*, sneakers that Teri Greeves beaded with dancers (p. 75). "When I look at these shoes," Jaune shares, "I think about people walking on the land. There are people dancing on the sides. You do a stomp dance, you do a grass dance. Everywhere we go on this land we know it carries the dust of our ancestors. We know we come from that dust and will come back to it." These shoes are a landscape because they depict the sacredness of dancing on the land. They celebrate both our world and Greeves as a mother thinking about her children leading their people into the future.

WARNINGS, DYSTOPIAN VIEWS, AND HUMOR

On the reservation in Montana where Jaune grew up, as elsewhere across the United States, treaties and negotiations, most significantly the Dawes Act of 1887, have resulted in a checkerboard pattern of land ownership. Where her tribe was once able to utilize the resources that the land provided, fence posts now mark private property. Landowners paint their fence posts orange, and if you cross a boundary, Jaune asserts, "you will be shot." These fence posts represent dishonest dealings, the withholding of resources, and a type of individual ownership that is not part of the Native worldview. They signal danger.

Such warning signs appear in numerous works here. The heavy machinery and coyote in Chris Pappan's *Atom Heart Mother (Earth)* (p. 109), the smokestacks in the background of Star WallowingBull's *Modern Day Indian* (p. 129), the solitary figure in George Alexander's *You found me, you should've never lost me* (p. 41), the tanks in John Hitchcock's *Impact vs. Influence* (p. 83), the bones in Andrea Carlson's *O Cursed Lust of Gold* 6 (p. 53), and the men wearing gas masks

in Will Wilson's *Auto-Immune Response no. 2* (p. 135) are similar to orange fence posts. They tell us to be watchful of present dangers and dystopian futures.

Jaune was talking about Diego Romero's *Girl in the Anthropocene* (p. 119) as we debated this concept over a video call with her son, Neal Ambrose-Smith, during a loud thunderstorm at my home. We discussed motherhood and the physical landscape in the work, which depicts a mother hanging laundry while her daughter looks on. Smokestacks loom in the background. As Jaune was searching for a word to describe the print, Neal said, "Foreboding." "It's dystopian," he continued, and we agreed.

What does this dystopian view mean in Native America? For us as Native people, Jaune observes, the hand we have been dealt means our cup is only half full. Humor and beauty make life survivable.

Take *Edward Curtis, Paparazzi: Chicken Hawks* as an example (p. 61). The late Jim Denomie pokes fun at the ethnologist Edward Curtis (1868–1952) and his efforts to photograph Native Americans. Denomie also adds hints of commercialism encroaching on the West, such as a Kentucky Fried Chicken sign on a covered wagon. Is his painting funny? Yes. Is it dystopian? Yes. Can it be both? Absolutely.

This concept of marrying danger (warning/struggle) with humor is also found in *A Hopi Landscape*, a photograph of a plastic cornstalk by Tom Jones (p. 87), and *Native American Art* by Gerald Clarke Jr. (p. 57). For that work, Clarke, who oversees his family's cattle ranch in California, used a branding iron to burn "native art" into a large sheet of paper (fig. 1). Julie Buffalohead takes a similar approach in *You are on Indian Land* (p. 51). Jaune describes this as being "mischievous and deadly serious at the same time," which is like many of our trickster stories. Also abruptly to the point is Edgar Heap of Birds's series of signs announcing "Today Your Host Is . . ." (p. 79). These works help us, as Native people who have been saying these things for years, to laugh at how damn blunt we

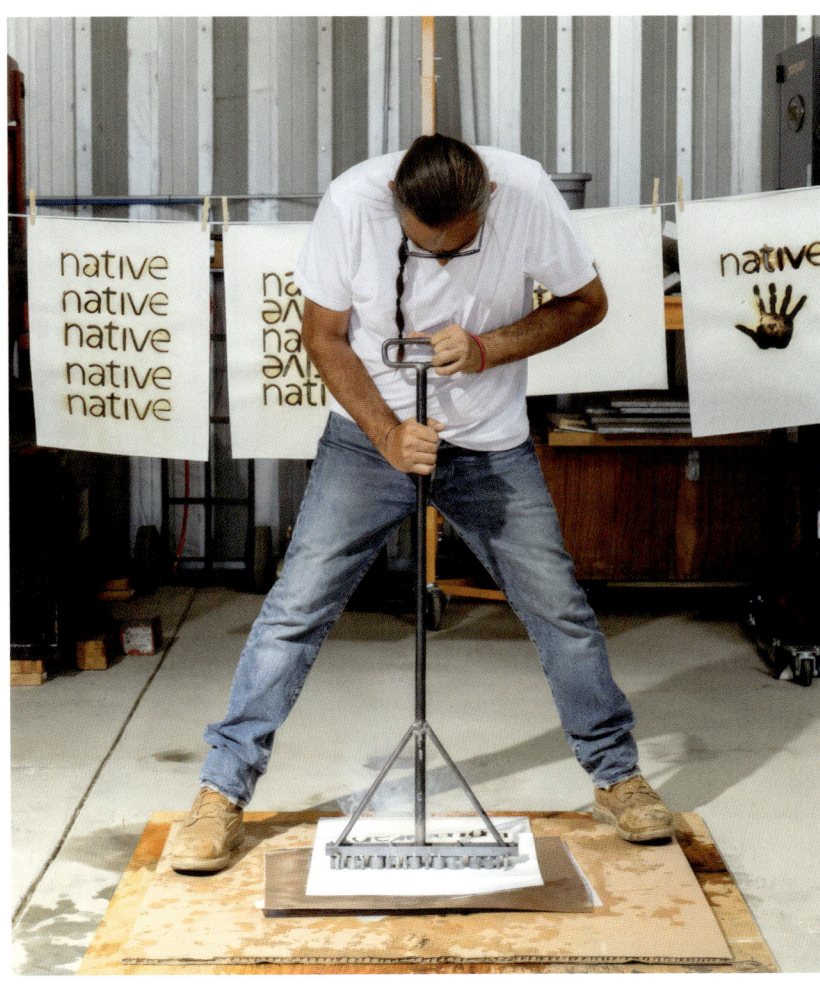

apparently need to be. This is Native art. This is Native land. This is a Native landscape.

HAUNTED BY BLUE

"The color blue was haunting me when I was looking for work for this exhibition," Jaune shares, "and it's threaded its way all the way through the show." I immediately see the thread she's describing in the shades of blue in stunning works by Emmi Whitehorse (*Fog Bank*, p. 133), George C. Longfish (*As Above So Below*, p. 97), Edgar Heap of Birds *(Neuf for Modoc*, fig. 2), James Lavadour (*Duotone 2*, p. 93), and others. *Antipodes*, which Marie Watt created with vintage Italian glass beads,

celebrates our relationship to the blue sky as it honors the Hodinöhsö:ni' ironworkers, called sky-walkers, who helped build the skyscrapers of New York City (p. 131).

Gail Tremblay incorporated blue in an unexpected way in her basket *After Global Warming, How Long Will it Take to Re-Invent a World Where Everything People Invented Depended on Snow, Frozen Food, Ice, and Digging Through it for Cold Water* (p. 125). The artist used a 16mm film that froze the Netsilik Inuit in an "ethnographic present" by depicting the colonizers as civilized and the Indigenous people as primitive. I'm struck by Tremblay's use of non-Native ethnographic

FIG. 1
Gerald Clarke using a branding iron to char a damp sheet of paper.

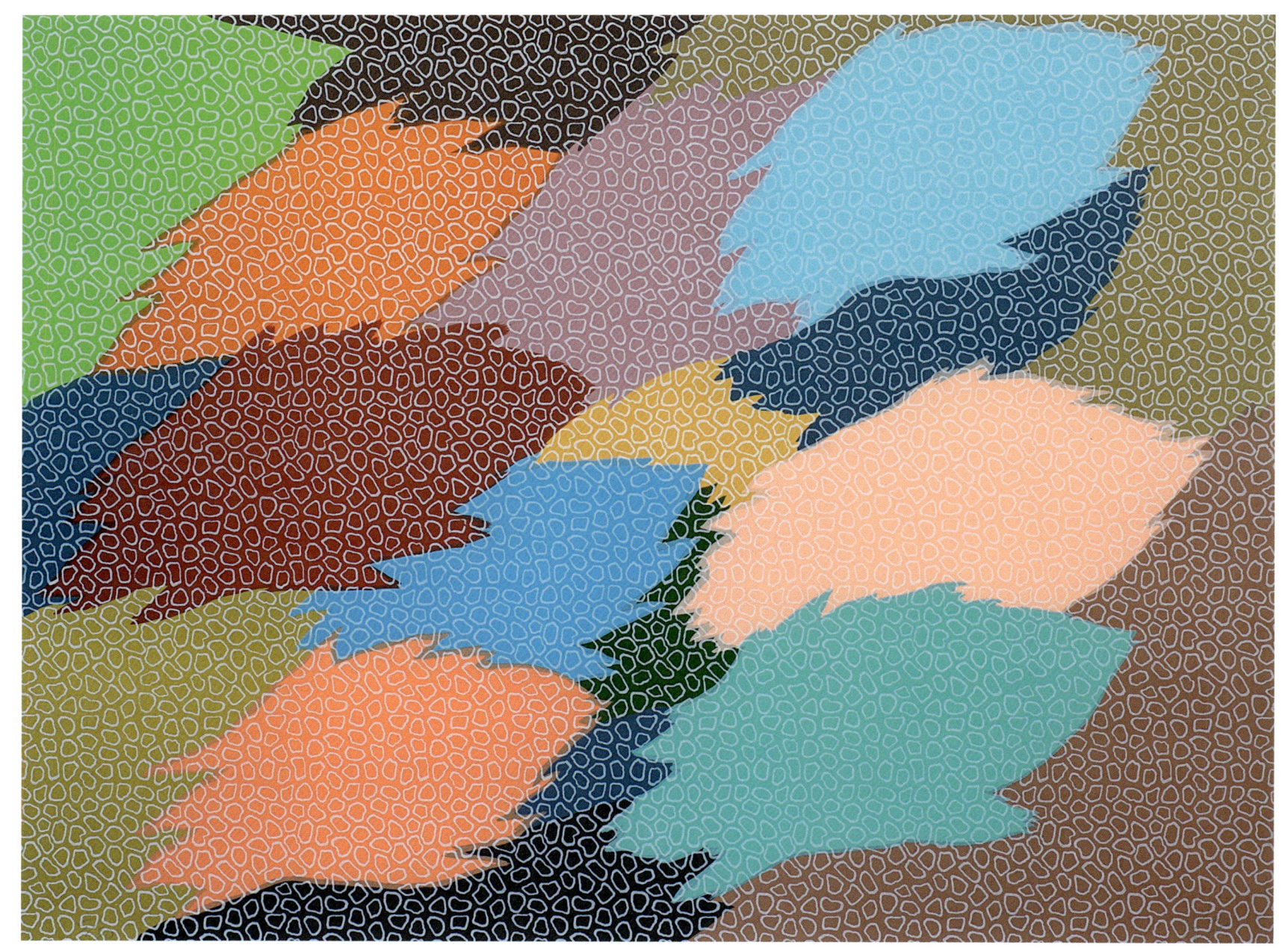

FIG. 2
Edgar Heap of Birds, *Neuf for Modoc*,
2001, 18-color lithograph on Rives BFK
white paper

material to weave a traditional basket form that reshapes the original intent of the very medium that caused harm to a tribal community.

LAND, SKY, AND WATER

Jaune sees connections between landscapes and our sacred world. For Native people, land, sky, and water are landscapes to be respected. Water is life. Water is everything. Water is everywhere. She explains, "It doesn't matter where the landscape is located, water provides the life." In his series of lithographs inspired by the Colorado and Little Colorado rivers, Duwawisioma (Victor Masayesva Jr.) honors the waters and the rains that refresh the land (p. 65). Jaune is also quick to point out that polluted water, like that found at Standing Rock, may mean the difference between life and death.

As we talk about Standing Rock, Jaune is reminded of the Tongass rainforest, the largest tract of temperate rainforest in the world. In 1996, Jaune made *Tongass Trade Canoe*, a painting that incorporates collaged images of elk, slogans, and newspaper below a shelf that holds eight brightly colored plastic bins (fig. 3). The trade canoe asks what exactly is being traded. My favorite part is the collaged phrase "Protect Endangered Loggers," an example of Jaune's sharp wit.

Much like Jaune, Cannupa Hanska Luger is not an artist who can be easily categorized. His exploration of mediums always has a connection to land, and like Jaune, is tied to activism and action. One of his most iconic works came from his time at Standing Rock. *Mirror Shield Project* is a powerful call to action (fig. 4; p. 99). Luger

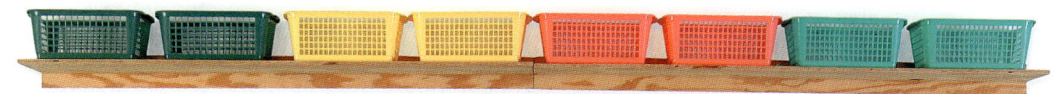

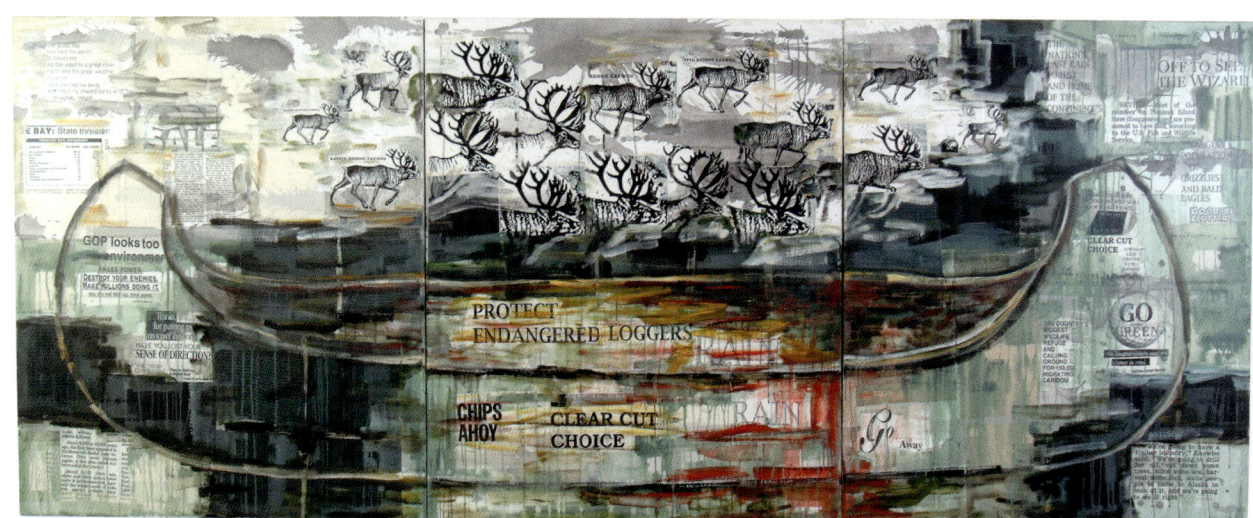

FIG. 3
Jaune Quick-to-See Smith, *Tongass Trade Canoe*, 1996, mixed media on canvas, Gift of John W. and Carol L. H. Green, Yellowstone Art Museum, Billings, Montana

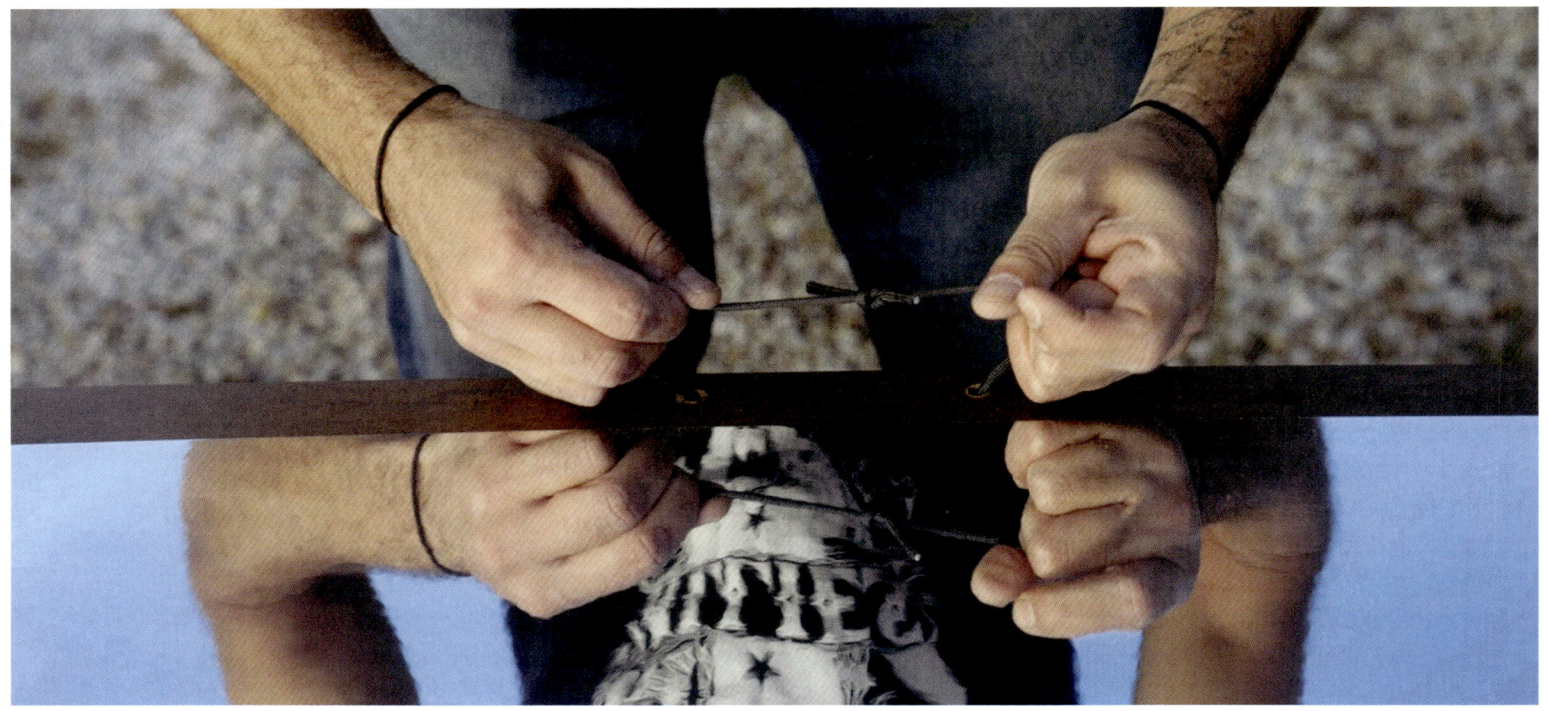

FIG. 4
Cannupa Hanska Luger constructing a
mirror shield.

says, "Whether working with institutions, communities, or the land itself, my work is inherently social and requires engagement." Connection to the land and each other is essential to his work.

Through the land we also feel a connection to feminine power and matrilineal ancestry. The protective essence of the land emerges in Nicholas Galanin and Merritt Johnson's *Creation with her Children*, which is actually made from the land, with a head carved from wood (p. 71). Rose B. Simpson's sculptural work *Tonantzin* draws attention to a pre-Hispanic Aztec mother deity (p. 121). Rose Powhatan's *Fire Warrior Woman* pays tribute to our female ancestors who fought and continue to fight for our homelands and traditional knowledge (p. 111). Luzene Hill's *Untitled* depicts "a continuum of culture" by suggesting the lines of women who have come before her and will come in the future (p. 81).

Indian Canyon, Cara Romero's photograph of a sacred landscape in Southern California, emphasizes the connection of our children with our ancestral lands (p. 117). Romero describes the young Chemehuevi as a "time-traveling apparition" who is inseparable from the landscape and from those who came before us. We walk where our ancestors walked.

Elsewhere in the landscape Native people have left enduring messages for those above, those below, and those who are yet to come. Even though we have sometimes been separated from the messages contained within symbols and glyphs, they persist. Jaune points out the painting *Ute's Homelands*, in which Kay WalkingStick has placed traditional designs directly upon the landscape (p. 127). Ka'ila Farrell-Smith shows glyphs from a sacred place of her ancestors with a solitary figure— a guide— in *G' EE' LA* (p. 67). Raven Chacon uses symbols to respond to the music inherent in the land in *For Zitkála Šá Series (For Carmina Escobar)* (p. 55), while Joe Feddersen places both modern and ancient glyphs together in *Inhabited Landscapes I* (p. 69).

We can see ourselves in Steven Yazzie's *Orchestrating a Blooming Desert* (p. 137). How are we connected? How do we heed the warnings all around us? Linda King does it by using her skill as a traditional basket maker to utilize natural materials as it has been done for generations. Her basket *Teaching of the Tree People* embodies her active reclamation of knowledge (p. 89). For Jeffrey Gibson, who created the beaded punching bag *TO FEEL MYSELF BELOVED ON THE EARTH*, our connection to land extends to our health (p. 73). He explains that we should see the elements of our natural environment as "our equal ancestors, living relatives, and as extensions of our own minds and bodies."

HÓZHÓ: WALK IN BEAUTY

It may sound simple, but it's worth noting: there is beauty through each of these works. The concept of beauty in the world around us is a Diné concept that resonates through all the work in the exhibition. And even when we see a balance of beauty with warning and heartbreak, it exists together and in tension. Both can be true.

The reality that many Indigenous people continue to live under the weight and betrayal of the settler-colonizer nation-state underlies the lithograph *No Place Like Hózhó* by Demian DinéYazhi', who contemplates Indigenous issues of detachment and longing as well as the importance of ancestral lands (p. 63). In what DinéYazhi' describes as "a hopeful and regenerative reminder of the power of Indigenous resilience," six traditional hogans encircle the word *hózhó* and emphasize its spiritual concept of beauty before us, beauty behind us, beauty around us.

Wendy Red Star applies the concept of home to houses provided by the US Department of Housing and Urban Development (HUD) stacked one upon the other, with a twister in the background, in her print *The (HUD)* (p. 113). Government housing on our homelands is a familiar sight to many of us. The threatening tornado and the potential removal from home are unsettling yet humorous. The scene is oddly comforting in the chaos.

The beauty in Peter Jemison's *Sentinels (Large Yellow)* (p. 85), Frank Big Bear's *Sunflowers in Autumn* (p. 49), and Mario Martinez's *Esoteric Vibration Landscape* (p. 103) is apparent on first view, but these artists encourage us to take a closer look. Through their works they ask us to pay attention to details, colors, shadows, the passage of time. Looking closely at Melissa Melero-Moose's *Access Denied* reveals barbed wire just below the surface, a reference to the separation of Indigenous people from resources and power (p. 105).

Like Jaune, I am attracted to beauty in the unexpected. When we were discussing this idea, we both thought of Melissa Cody's intricate weaving *World Traveler*, which Jaune says "goes beyond what we have ever seen" (fig. 5; p. 59). Athena LaTocha often salvages natural and man-made materials to add layers of depth and meaning in her landscapes (p. 91). Other examples of unexpected works that use natural materials are Eric-Paul Riege's larger-than-life earrings in *jaatłoh4-Ye'iitsoh [3 – 4]* (p. 115) and Natalie Ball's *Bang bang*, which incorporates hide, textile, and eagle imagery (p. 45). These works, as Ball writes, "disrupt mainstream definitions of Indian . . . [to] reflect the complexity of Native American lives. . . ."

Depictions of animals, and particularly birds, are integral parts of this landscape exhibition. Colorful and layered with meaning, the birds in Marwin Begaye's *Columbia River Custodian* (p. 47) and Linda Lomahaftewa's *Parrots Prayer Song* (p. 95) offer a visual contrast to *Peep*, Jamie Okuma's boots enlivened with beaded birds (p. 107), and Preston Singletary's *Raven Steals the Sun*, a trickster bird made of blown and sand-carved glass (fig. 6; p. 123). Raven Halfmoon's stoneware *lichíile (horse | Crow/Apsáalooke)* (p. 77) and Keri Ataumbi's delicate earrings in the shape of dragonflies (p. 43) stretch our concepts of the land even further.

Brenda Mallory's work is meaningful to me in the messages carried by our ancestors. Her works of "repeated rhythmic forms," such as *The Plural of Nexus* (p. 101), are familiar to me. I was excited to learn that she had proposed a residency

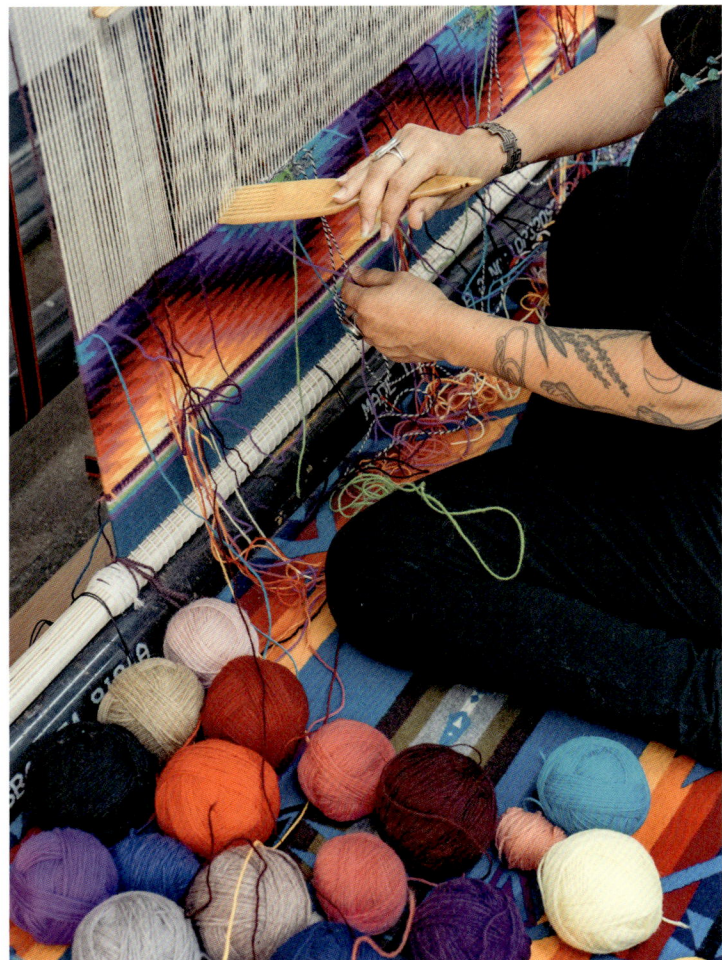

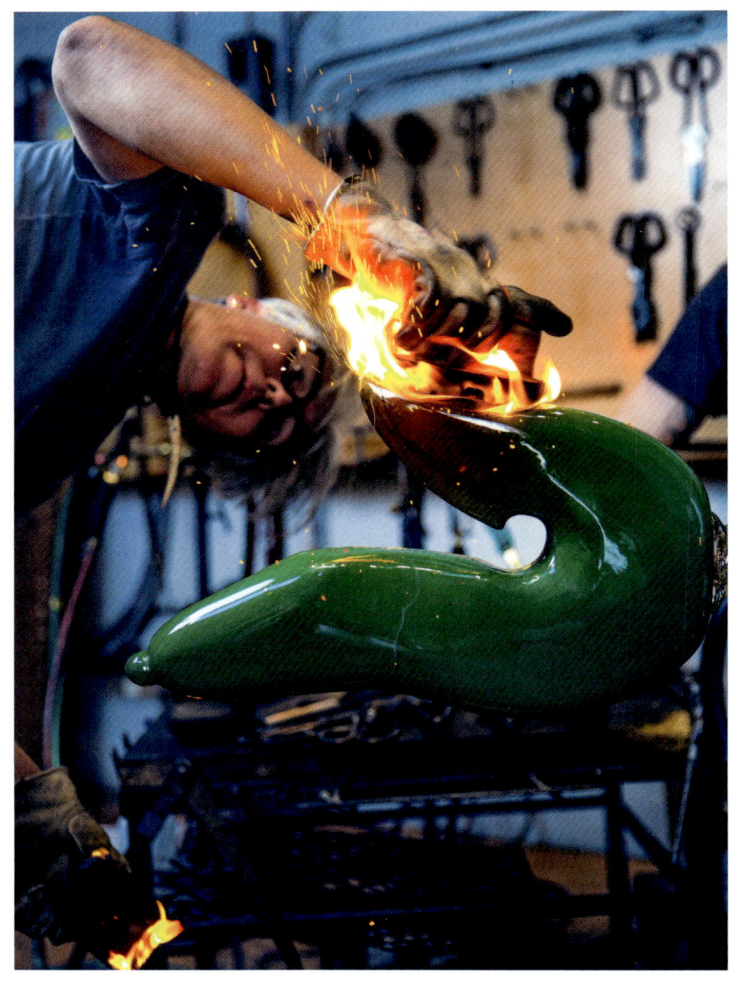

FIG. 5
Melissa Cody weaving at a traditional Navajo loom.

FIG. 6
Preston Singletary creating a glass sculpture.

for several women Cherokee artists in western North Carolina, our original homelands. Most of these women do not currently live on our ancestral homeland. Brenda, a Cherokee Nation citizen, lives in Oregon. Her ancestors were forcibly removed to Oklahoma in 1838, adding another layer of separation.

At their disposal were resources to create ceramics, and Brenda had been working on a project in clay (fig. 7). I was invited, along with Dakota Brown (Eastern Band of Cherokee Indians), the director of education at the Museum of the Cherokee Indian, to visit and see their works in progress. Dakota observed, "Those forms look like river cane." Until spending time on that land, Brenda hadn't realized how much river cane — a traditional material Cherokee people have used for centuries — had influenced her linear, repeating works. When I showed a photo of *The Plural of Nexus* to Dakota, we were all moved by the innate ancestral message Brenda Mallory was carrying inside her.

Dakota Brown refuses to say "lost" when speaking about language or songs or methods; she always says "dormant." The land is the key to unlocking the ancestral knowledge that has been removed from many of our communities and sometimes lies dormant. Connecting to the

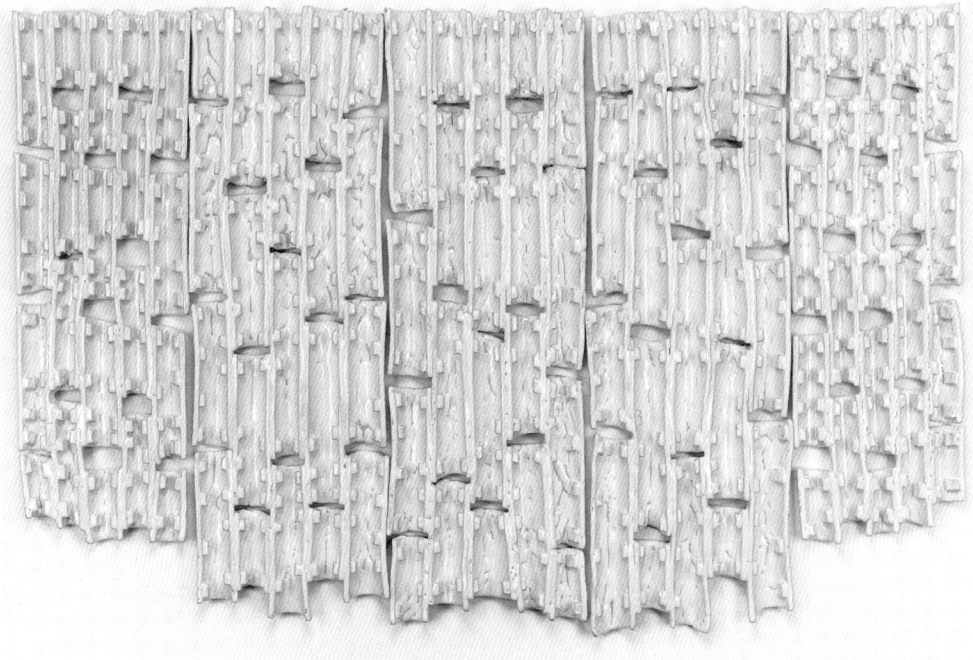

land is essential to reclaiming knowledge and, I would argue, to assisting humankind to reconnect to our planet. Jaune has spent decades sounding the alarm and holding us accountable in her work and her writing and her speaking. Her choices for each of these works are intentional. Together, they illustrate the intense power and beauty of land, the danger to it and therefore ourselves, and our unwavering hope that lies in that inter-connected love.

FIG. 7
Brenda Mallory, *Recollecting Cane*, 2021, glazed stoneware

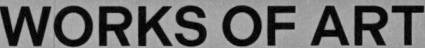

WORKS OF ART

George Alexander

Muscogee

We often use labels to identify ourselves, but it can be a double-edged sword when we use labels to create division. From the vantage point of an astronaut out in our universe, our individual differences are insignificant in comparison to the fact that we are all one species. Portraying the astronaut's perspective on Earth inspires us to challenge societal complexes from the past and work toward a future where we view ourselves as one unified culture. A lone astronaut on horseback symbolizes Humanity's timeless journey towards unity. Navigating this journey in the modern landscape, Humanity has become lost in an alley where we put trash and other relics that will eventually be forgotten. Navigating out of this place will require Humanity to adopt a new perspective.

You found me, you should've never lost me, 2022, acrylic on canvas, 101.6 × 76.2 cm (40 × 30 in.)

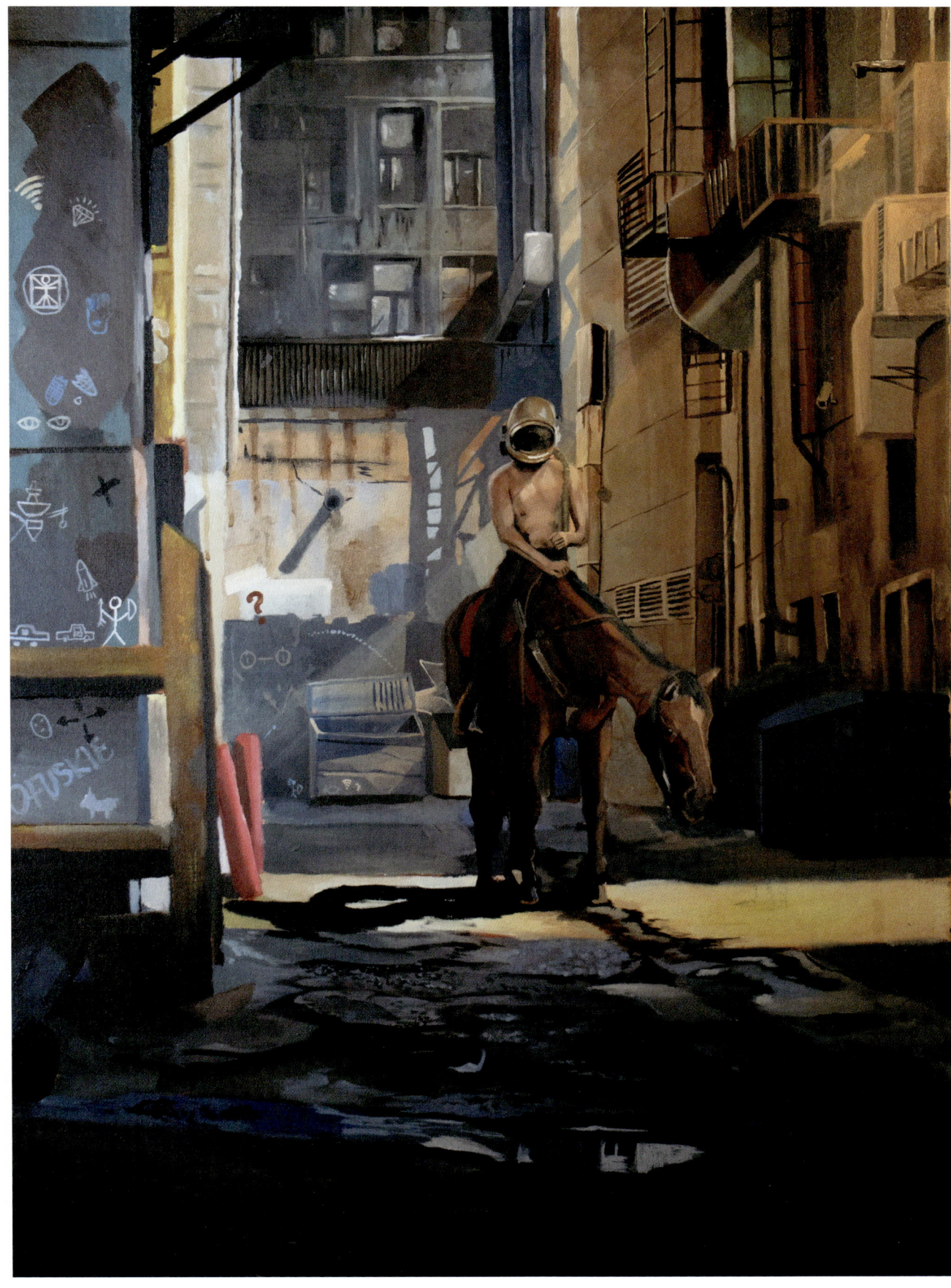

Keri Ataumbi

Kiowa

I am interested in making work that changes contemporary Native adornment as defined by objects that conform to material choices and/ or a traditional aesthetic. My work transmutes the philosophical and ceremonial continuums that are the backbone of our identities as Native Americans.

One of my sister's great-great grand-mothers was named Kientaddle. She fought in several battles alongside her husband and her father, Poorbuffalo, who was a leader or chief. Kientaddle was the last of the original Mahtahns for Ton-Kon-Gah in 1927. Ton-Kon-Gah was revived in 1958, and today my sisters, our families, and I all participate. A few years back the arena was filled with dragonflies during the women's dances. I made these earrings in honor of Kientaddle and all Kiowa women: those who came before us, those living, and those yet to be born.

Kientaddle Baygoon Gah (Dragonflies Dancing), 2021, oxidized sterling silver, 18k yellow gold, brilliant cut diamonds, each 8.9 × 4.5 cm (3 ½ × 1 ¾ in.)

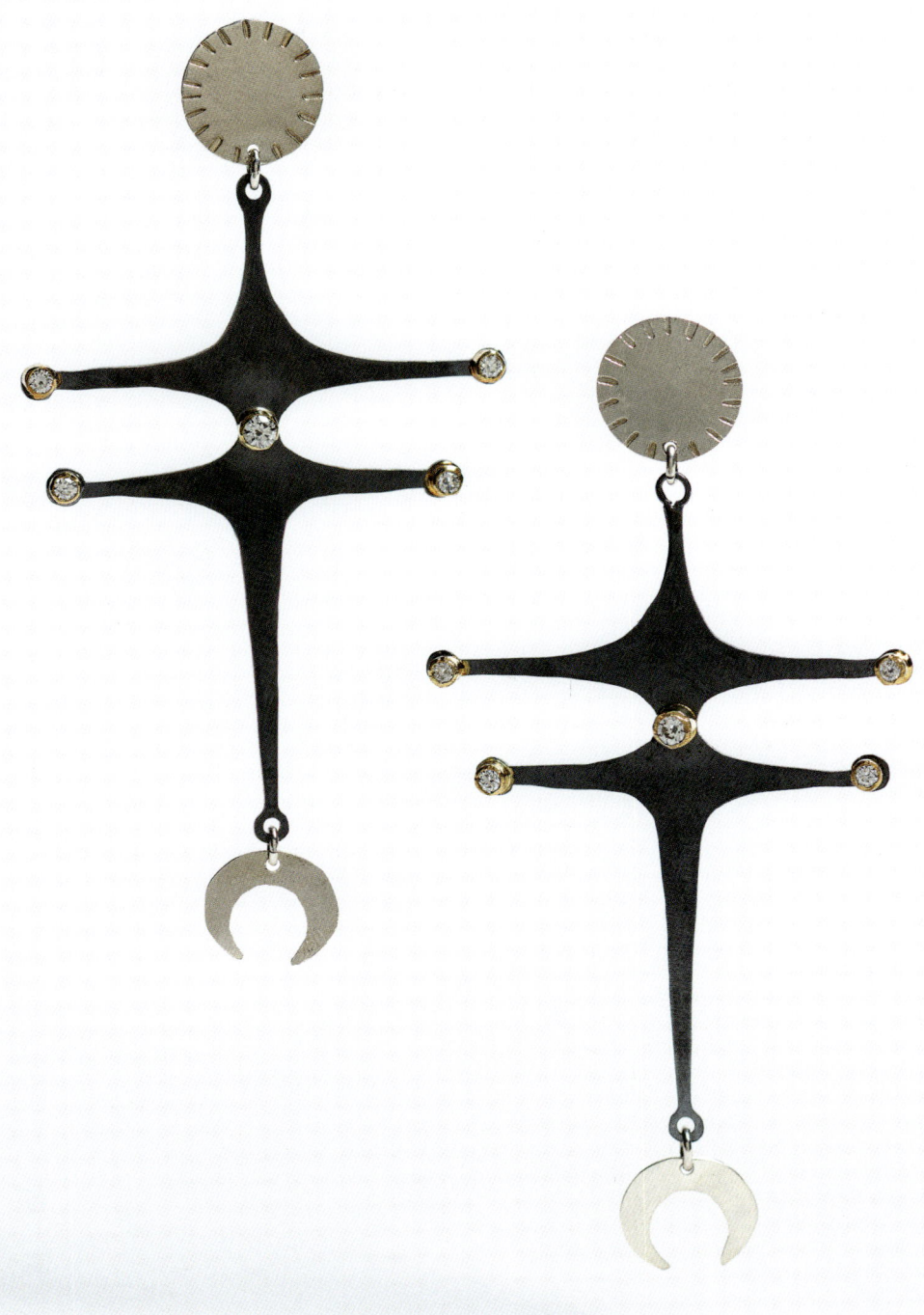

Natalie Ball

Modoc/Klamath

Through auto-ethnography, I attempt to move "Indian" outside of governing discourses to offer a visual genealogy that refuses to line up with the many constructed existences of Native Americans. I map personal and historical landscapes, allowing them to travel through generations, engaging the history of violence, dispossession, and survivance while filling in gaps and forging stories to hold space for new complex narratives to exist. To disrupt mainstream definitions of Indian with personal, community, and US histories that reflect the complexity of Native American lives, like my own, is to better understand ourselves, the nation, and necessarily our shared experiences and histories.

Bang bang, 2019, elk hide, rabbit fur, oil stick, acrylic, charcoal, cotton, and pine, 213.4 × 315 cm (84 × 124 in.)

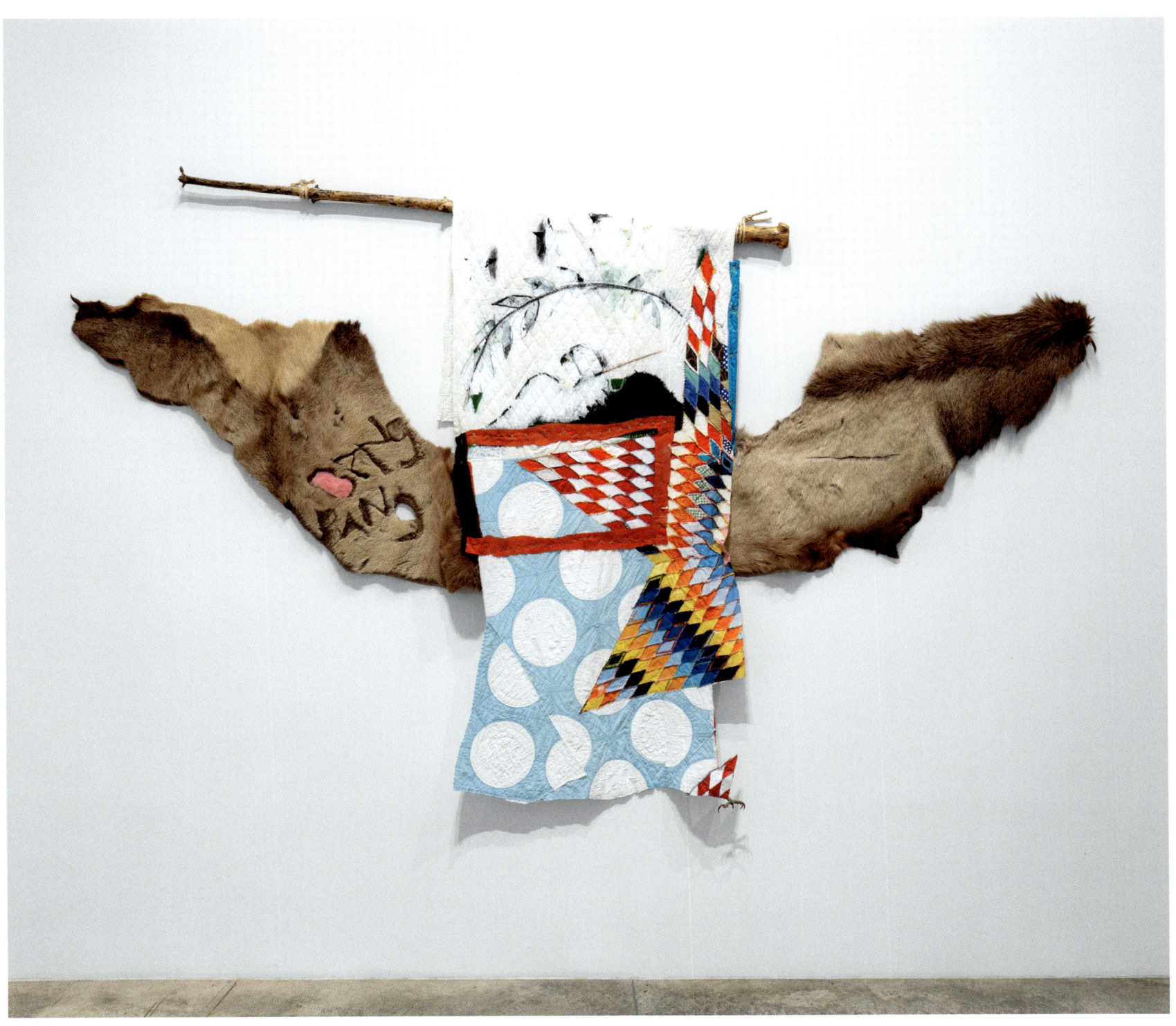

Marwin Begaye

Diné

After a lifetime of listening to cultural stories in a place upon which my ancestors have lived for millennia, my identity is interwoven with the landscape and epistemology, as expressed through songs and prayers. This results in place names and stories that mutually inform one another and trigger memories. *Columbia River Custodian* visualizes a story told by Lillian Pitt (Wasco) of when Condor convinced Eagle to help starving humans find salmon on the Columbia River. I wanted to honor the river, the salmon, the condor, and the people who have a relationship through this story.

Columbia River Custodian, 2019, lithograph, 71.8 × 56.5 cm (28 ¼ × 22 ¼ in.)

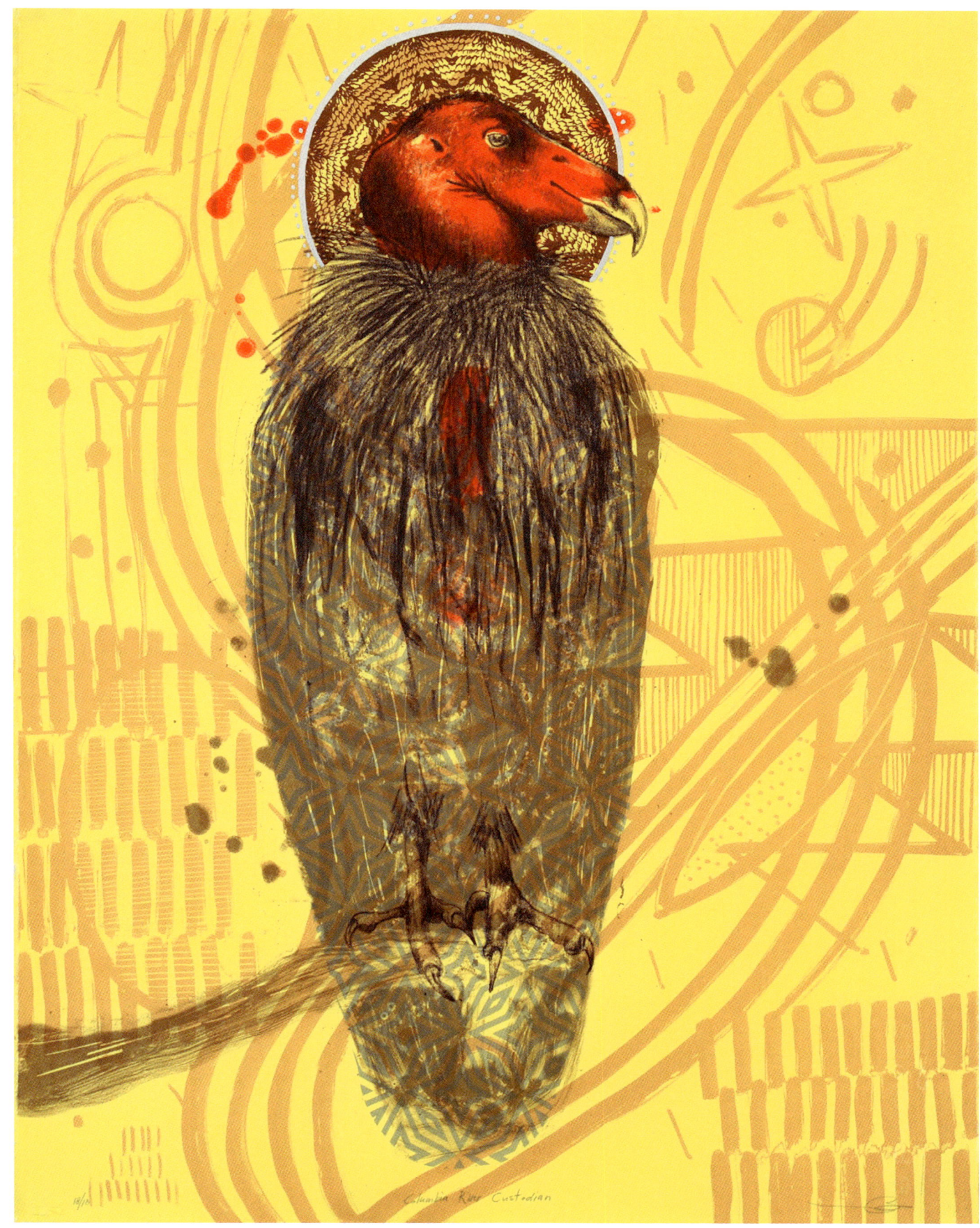

18/18   Columbia River Custodian

Frank Big Bear

Ojibwe, White Earth Nation

I have been an artist almost my whole life, since I began drawing as a young child on any material I could find. My art saved me; I wouldn't have survived without it. I was raised on Pine Point of the White Earth Reservation, and I left northern Minnesota to find work in Minneapolis when I was 14. I later went to North High School, where my art teacher, Katherine Mattson, became my mentor and friend. I attended Macalester College and the University of Minnesota, but formal education was too rigid and boring for my preference. I decided to continue my self-education by driving a cab — exchanging ideas with people from around the world for three decades — and by reading, as I still do today, about anything and everything through the Minneapolis Public Library network. Self-education is the best way for some people, like me, to learn. Being alone is very important to my creative process.

Sunflowers in Autumn, 2007, Prismacolor pencil on paper, 76.2 × 66 cm (30 × 26 in.)

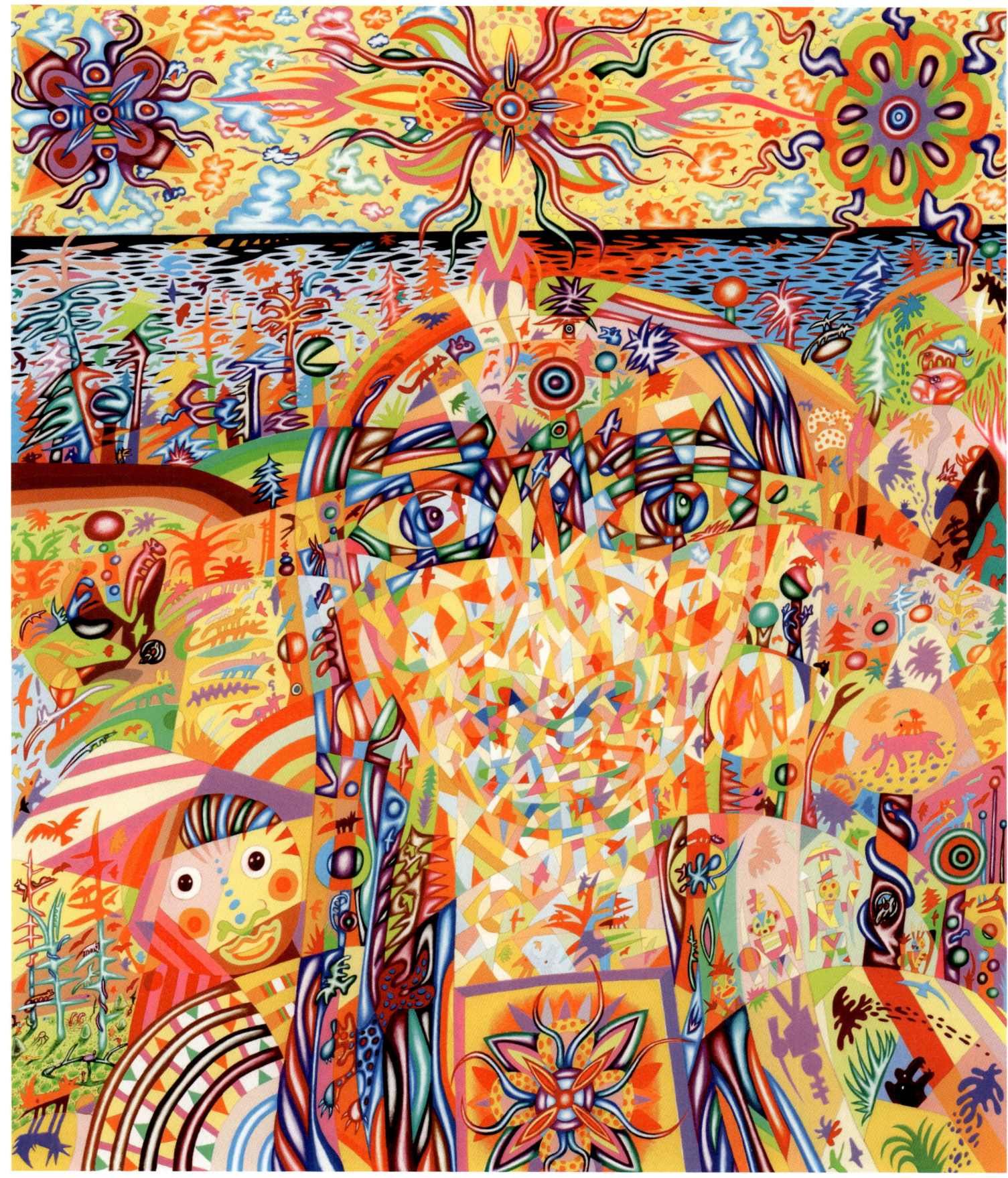

Julie Buffalohead

Ponca Tribe of Oklahoma

I endeavor to create work relating to my experience as a Native woman. Traditionally, rabbits, coyote, and deer are characters that exist in American Indian storytelling. In this work they are contextualized inside the events of the Standing Rock confrontation in 2016. A defaced concrete barrier and upside-down flag symbolize the irony that Indian sovereign nations sometimes do not control their own lands — perhaps through destruction of sacred sites, loss of mineral rights, or actions by executive order. This is a reclamation of a distinct narrative and a change of perspective that land occupied by present-day homes and businesses was obtained through genocide.

You are on Indian Land, 2017, acrylic, ink, and pencil on paper, 105.4 × 228.6 cm (41 ½ × 90 in.)

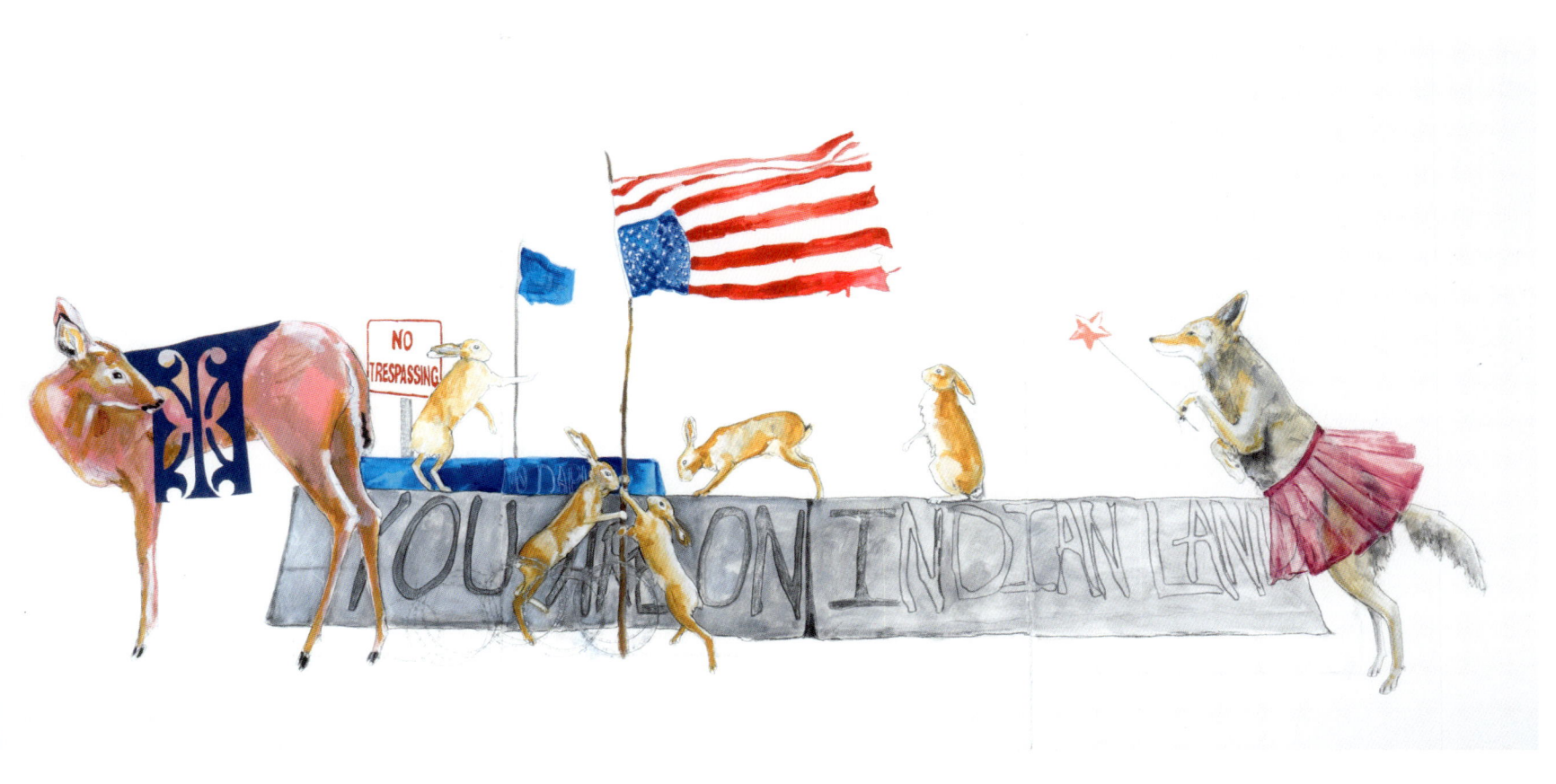

Andrea Carlson

Grand Portage Ojibwe/European descent

The shore of Lake Superior is the land represented in my paintings. It is home. I grew up walking the shores of Lake Superior in what is now northern Minnesota. Many of my ancestors have perished in the lake, but it is also a place of healing that is integral to my process. The shore has become a formula for how I arrange visual information within my work, but it is also part of my process. Walking along the shoreline is trance-inducing and hypnotic. Listening to the rhythm of the waves against the sound of my footsteps and beating heart is like listening to the oldest, universal song. If one meditates while walking along a shore, poems and stories can be pulled out of that rhythm. That is where my work begins.

O Cursed Lust of Gold 6, 2014, ink and oil on paper, 27.9 × 76.8 cm (11 × 30 ¼ in.)

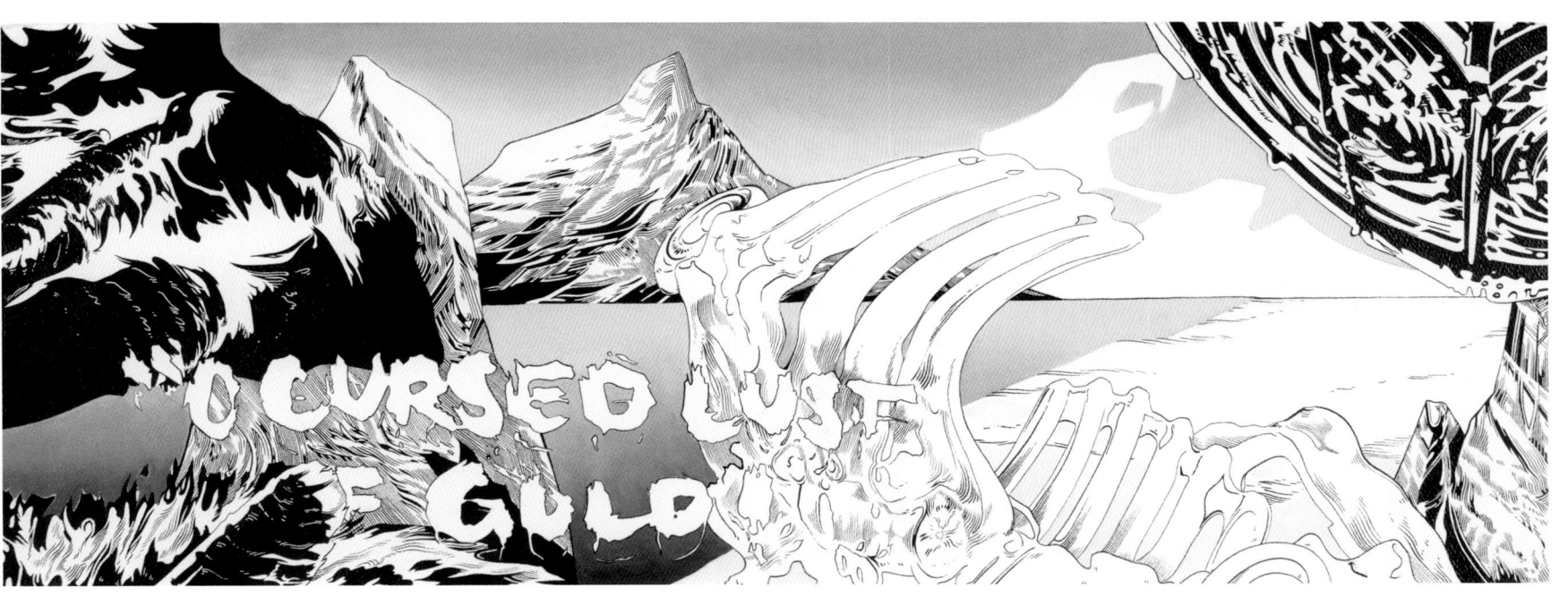

Raven Chacon

Diné

First and foremost, I am a listener. My belief is that sound work cannot always be made in isolation. For me, these are acoustic and conceptual responses to the land and, by extension, to the people who have history in those lands. There are a pedagogy and a generative feedback loop within these land-based practices. This, and the role of improvisation, is the foundation of my work as a teacher and artist.

For Zitkála Šá Series (For Carmina Escobar), 2018, lithograph, 27.9 × 21.6 cm (11 × 8 ½ in.)

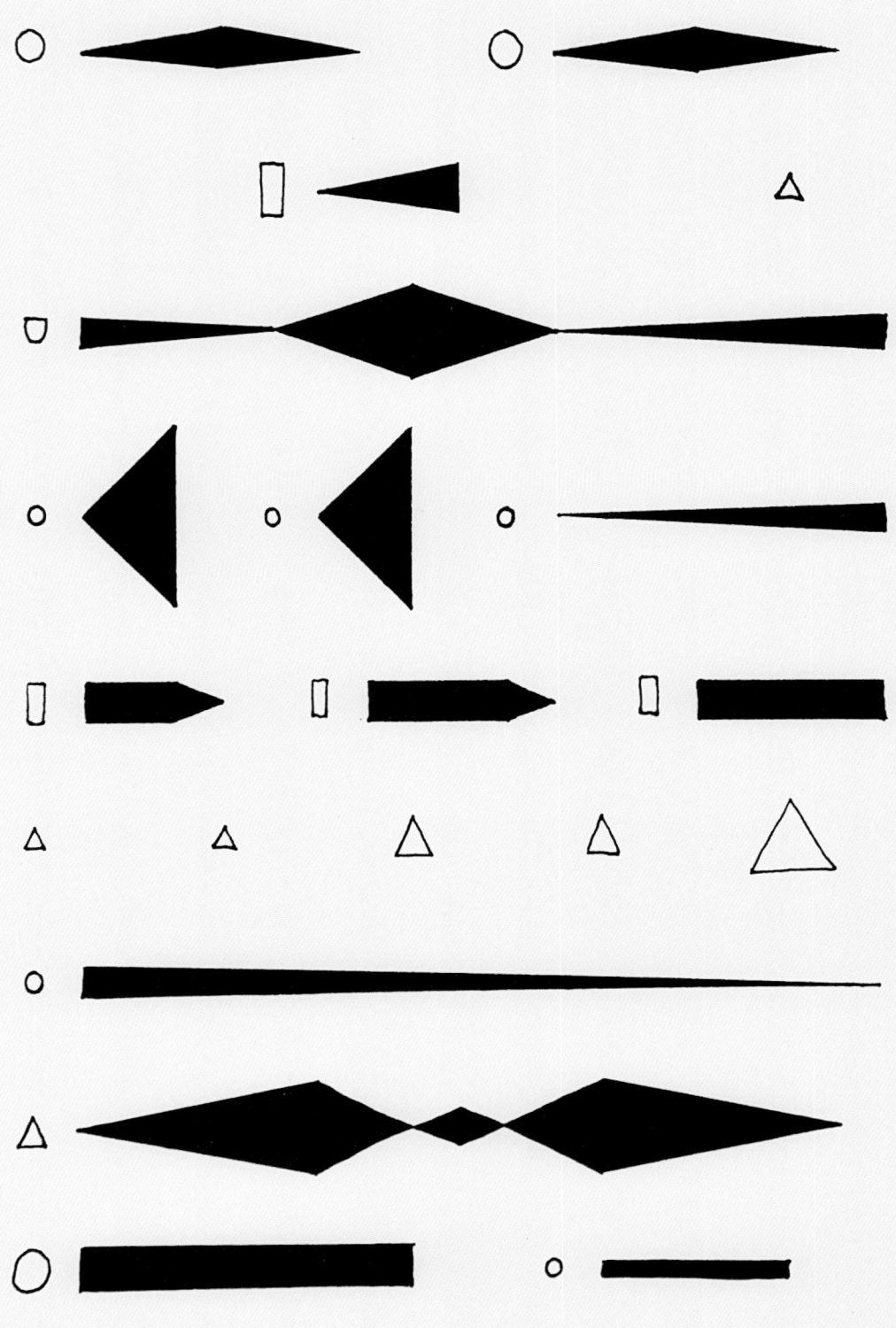

Gerald Clarke Jr.

Cahuilla Band of Indians

I aspire not to romanticize the subjects or content of my work. I strive to "keep it real," and I have found that my best works are inspired by my personal experiences, the land, and my tribal community. Living within the homelands of my people shapes my worldview and inspires me. Beer cans, branding irons, and gourd rattles represent aspects of my reality. These materials reflect who I am and not how the mainstream might understand the contemporary Native American experience. While my work may not appear "traditional," it is part of a continuation of creative responses to the world that the Cahuilla have exercised since ancient times.

Native American Art, 2019, charred watercolor paper, 76.2 × 55.9 cm (30 × 22 in.)

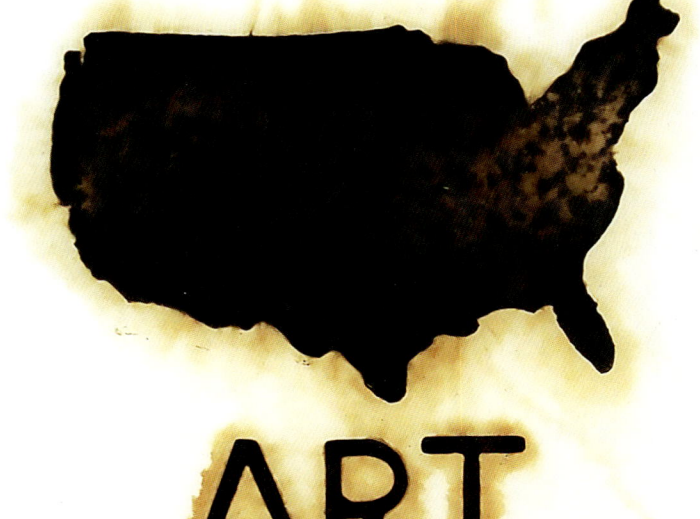

2019

Melissa Cody

Navajo

The foundational material of wool, provided by our reciprocal relationship with the sheep, not only provides us with material but also sustains us by giving shelter and food. The basic materials of the loom come from the earth; the wood that we use comes from the environment around us. All the different facets of my practice are fostered through my family and heritage: the weaving techniques I learned from my mother and the history that was told to me by my grandmother, aunts, and extended relatives. There was an entire community around me from which I gained insight since the age of five. In this sense, weaving has always been a multigenerational experience.

World Traveler is an expression of this multigenerational experience of weaving. This piece forms new traditions and extends the practice of weaving into the contemporary. It is the next new stage of Navajo textiles because it bridges those generational worlds. The composition and movement of the piece guide the viewer through these different worlds, from past to present, through contemporary patterning and motifs.

World Traveler, 2014, three-ply wool, aniline dyes, wool warp, and six-ply selvedge cords, 228.6 × 124.1 cm (90 × 48 ⅞ in.)

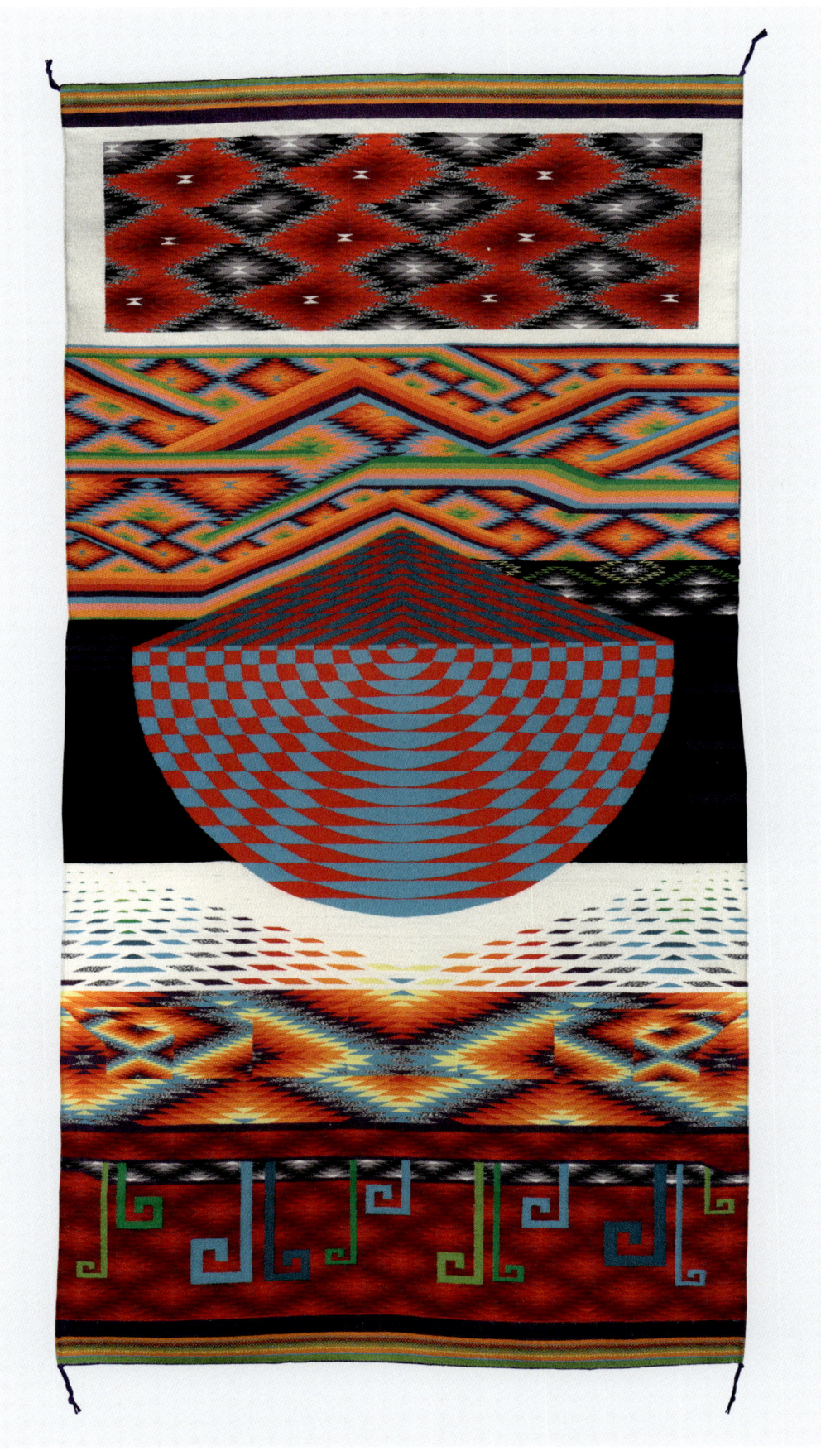

Jim Denomie

Lac Courte Oreilles Ojibwe,
Ajijaak Clan

The late Jim Denomie's practice was shaped by his ancestry and his relations to land in a myriad of conjoined and interwoven ways. In turn, much of his work centered the dimensional and reciprocal relations tethering Indigenous peoples to their lands. Wabooz (the rabbit) was a particularly prominent and recurring relative in his work. A simultaneous relation and reflection of himself, Wabooz emulated and carried the rich and varied histories Denomie labored to capture and depict. His plethora of relations were both subjects and agents of his work, mobilizing his narratives and meticulously offering tandem emotions like humor, rage, and grief.

Edward Curtis, Paparazzi: Chicken Hawks, 2008, oil on canvas, 88.9 × 101.6 cm (35 × 40 in.)

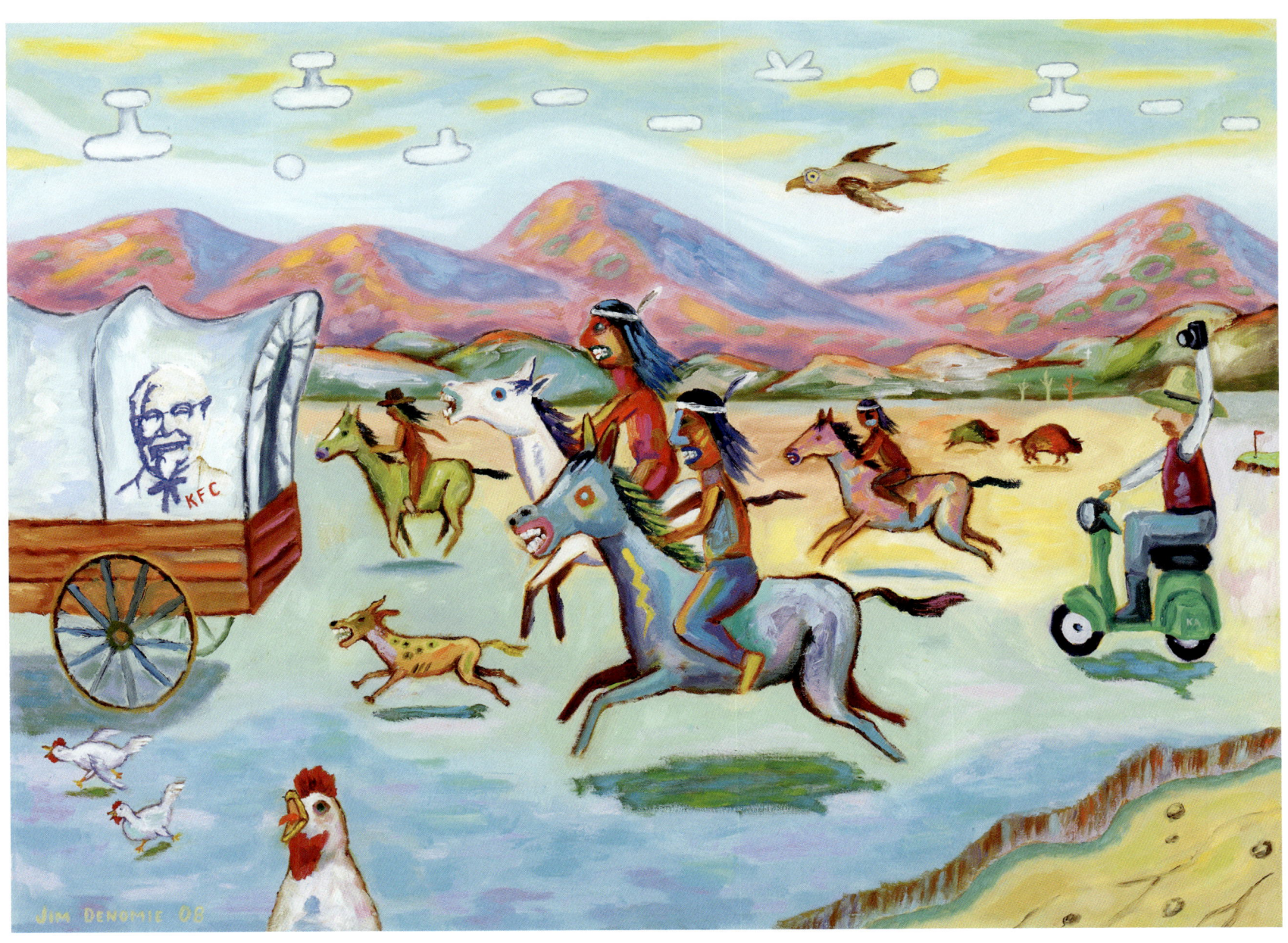

Demian DinéYazhi'

Diné

This work draws from settler-colonial popular culture by way of the 1939 movie *The Wizard of Oz*. L. Frank Baum published the famous fantasy children's book in 1900, 36 years after my ancestors were removed from our traditional lands and forced to migrate over 300 miles to an experimental "internment camp" at Fort Sumner, New Mexico. It also subverts the mantra recited by Dorothy, the main character, as she clicks her heels and repeats, "There's no place like home." In the print, *hózhó* replaces the word "home," thereby pointing to a spiritually and philosophically significant Diné concept. Hooghans (traditional dwellings of the Diné tribe) dance and twirl, as a rez dog appears to scrounge for food.

No Place Like Hózhó contemplates contemporary issues of detachment and longing that many Indigenous people confront while living under the crushing weight and cruel betrayal of the settler-colonizer nation-state. It is also a hopeful and regenerative reminder of the power of Indigenous resilience and the importance of our ancestral lands.

No Place Like Hózhó, 2017, six-color lithograph, 101 × 76.2 cm (39 ¾ × 30 in.)

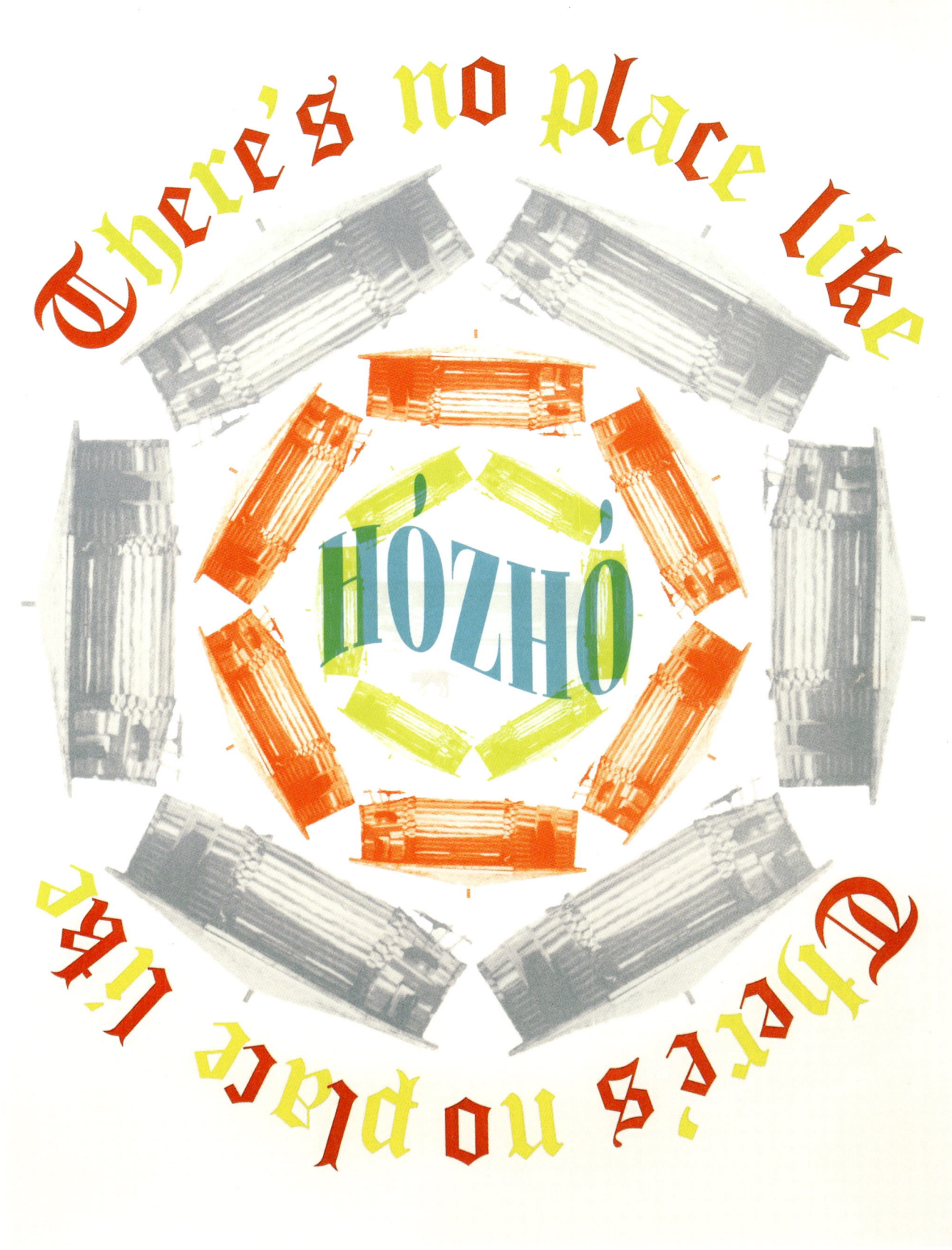

Duwawisioma
(Victor Masayesva Jr.)

Hopi Tribe

My lifelong work in various media (prints, photography, film and video, VR) is a constant engagement with the appropriateness of Western technology to convey our ancestral experiences.

The Tuwapongya narrative series reveals the Hopi belief that Earth is an altar (Tuwapongya), and we should act accordingly. Among Tuwapongya's blessings are that water is Life, with Palolokong (Snake) as its spirit. Water in the Colorado and Little Colorado rivers is an essential visual in the narrative of these lithographs. It is prevalent in our rainmaking rituals and ceremonies, where eagle feathers are offered with regard for the sun's passage across the sky. If successful, our prayers for rain renew Life and refresh the land. Tuwapongya offers another perspective and approach to revitalize our ancestral knowledge.

Tuwapongya (Earth Altar) Part I, 1993, lithograph, image 34.3 × 43.2 cm (13 ½ × 17 in.), sheet 48.9 × 58.4 cm (19 ¼ × 23 in.)
Tuwapongya (Earth Altar) Part II, 1993, lithograph, image 43.2 × 34.3 cm (17 × 13 ½ in.), sheet 58.4 × 48.9 cm (23 × 19 ¼ in.)
Tuwapongya (Earth Altar) Part III, 1993, lithograph, image 43.2 × 34.3 cm (17 × 13 ½ in.), sheet 58.4 × 48.9 cm (23 × 19 ¼ in.)
Tuwapongya (Earth Altar) Part IV, 1993, lithograph, image 43.2 × 34.3 cm (17 × 13 ½ in.), sheet 58.4 × 48.9 cm (23 × 19 ¼ in.)

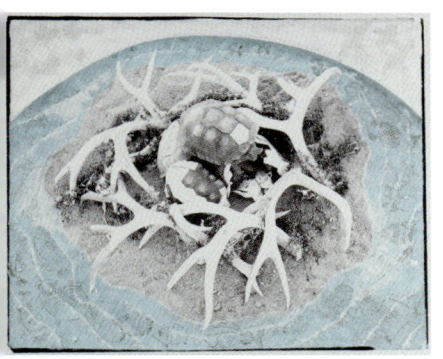
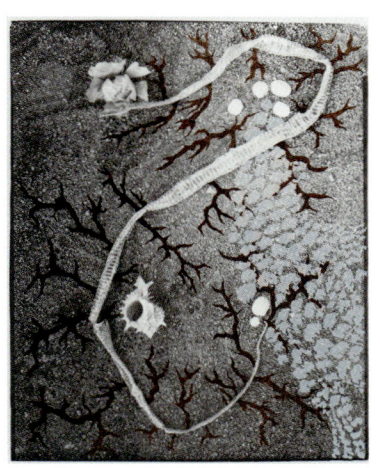
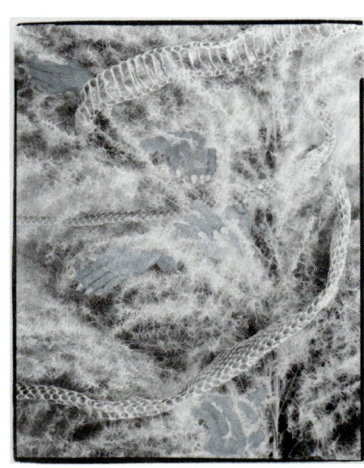
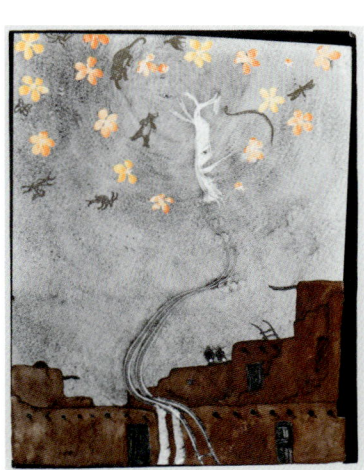

Ka'ila Farrell-Smith

Klamath/Modoc

Created at Crow's Shadow Institute of the Arts in Umatilla, Oregon, this monoprint refers to a large abstract petroglyph located at Hart Mountain in southern Oregon. The glyph predates the massive volcanic eruption that blasted Mount Mazama 7,700 years ago and formed Crater Lake. Hart Mountain is a sacred place of my ancestors, the Klamath, Modoc, and Northern Paiute peoples. They hunted, gathered, and lived off the land and the large lakes that make up this high desert landscape. They also created this image. I've had multiple experiences at Hart Mountain, visiting the glyphs, herds of antelope, and sage grouse families and soaking in the medicine hot springs.

G' EE' LA, 2018, lithograph, 55.9 × 38.1 cm (22 × 15 in.)

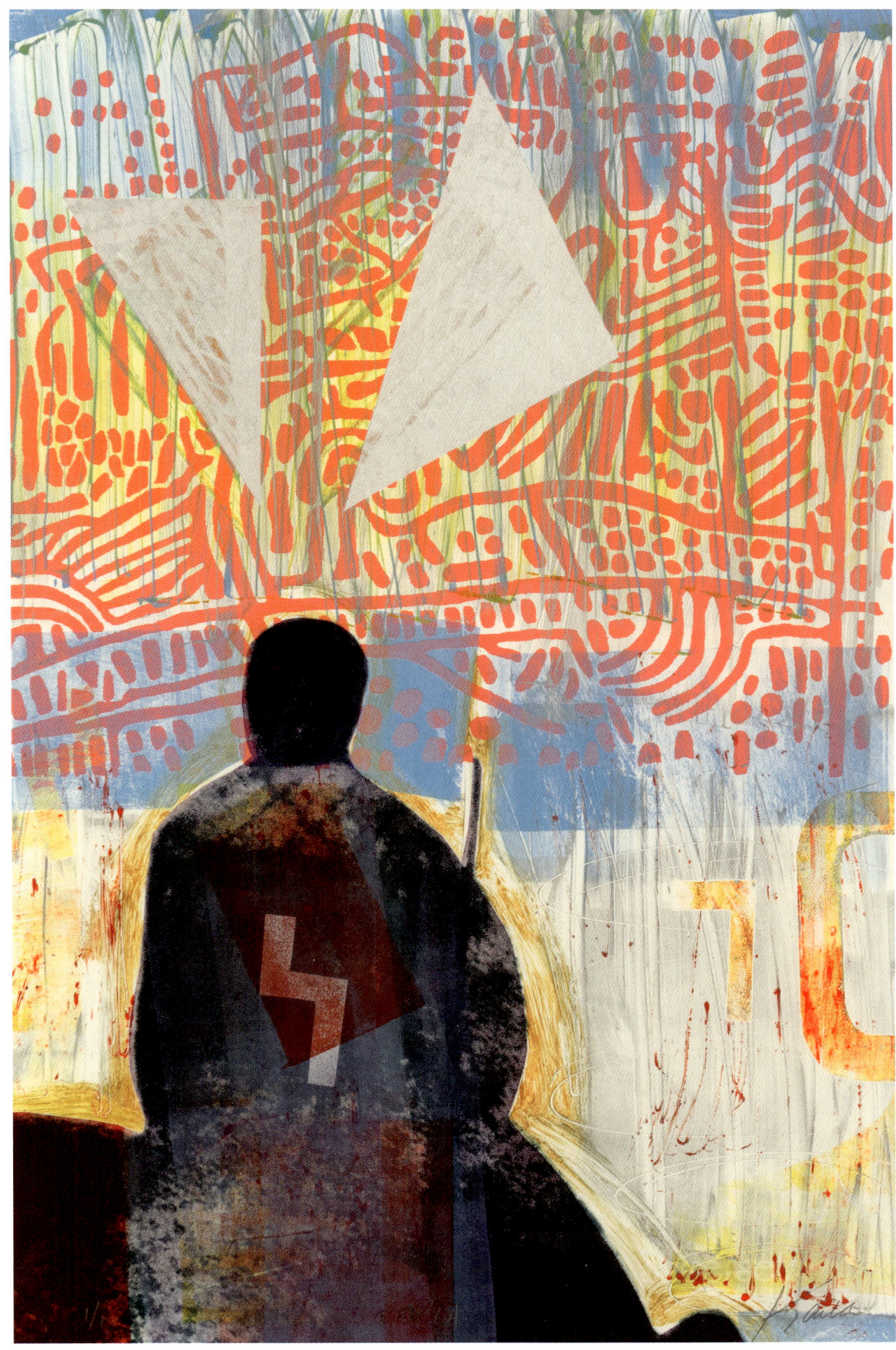

Joe Feddersen

Colville Confederated Tribes

I gather inspiration from the world around me. My artwork exhibits relationships between the world of the Plateau culture and contemporary life. It creates an interplay with the built environment, animate beings, and symbols, building narratives to articulate current issues facing our people today. I live on the traditional lands of the Okanogan peoples. My work draws from my Native worldview as an Okanogan and Arrow Lakes person as well as my relationships with mentors and teachers whose lessons have sharpened my perception and strengthened my connection to my homeland.

Inhabited Landscapes I, 2020, unique print on Rives BFK paper, 66 × 50.8 cm (26 × 20 in.)

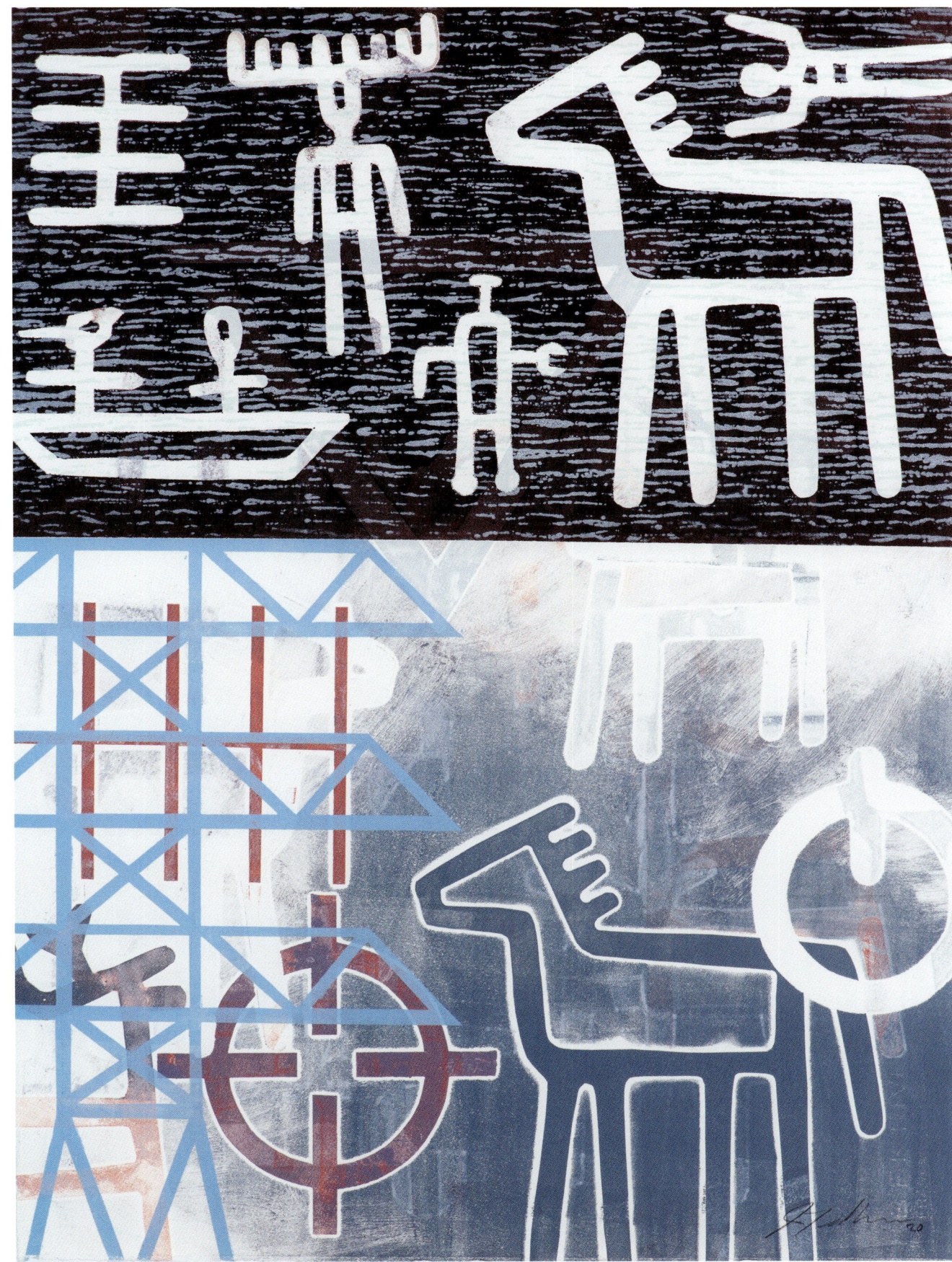

Nicholas Galanin

Lingít/Unangax̂

Culture is rooted in connection to land; like land, culture cannot be contained. I am inspired by generations of Lingít and Unangax̂ creative production and knowledge connected to the land I belong to. From this perspective I engage across cultures with contemporary conditions.

My process of creation is a constant pursuit of freedom and vision for the present and future. Using Indigenous and non-Indigenous technologies and materials, I resist romanticization, categorization, and limitation. I use my work to explore adaptation, resilience, survival, active cultural amnesia, dream, memory, and cultural resurgence, as well as connection to and disconnection from the land.

Merritt Johnson

Unaffiliated

My work is rooted in collective dependence on land and water, creation as necessity, intersection and disconnection. *Creation with her Children* envisions safety as children play at being dangerous without risk. The figure embodies the agency and persistence of creation, cutting away a garment of colonization and carving her face from the land.

Creation with her Children, 2017, carved wood, fabric, dentalium shells, cast plastic and resin, metal leaf, fish skin leather, carving knife, fringe, plastic tarp, cast hydrocal, rabbit fur, jaw set, paint, 157.5 × 213.4 cm (62 × 84 in.)

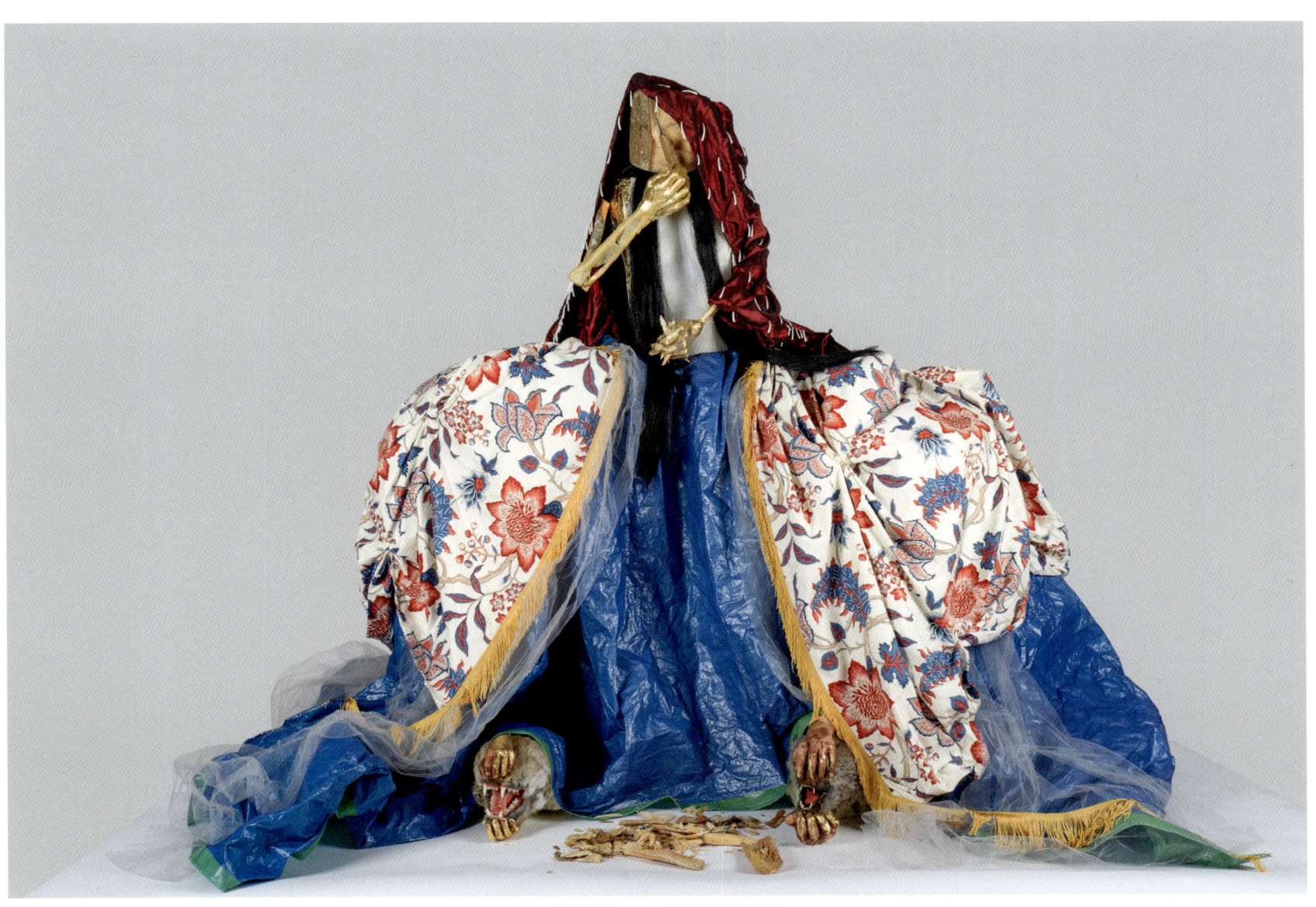

Jeffrey Gibson

Mississippi Band of Choctaw
Indians/Cherokee Nation

Indigenous kinship philosophies have provided
the conceptual and philosophical framework
for my work. These perspectives acknowledge
the elements of our natural environments
as our equal ancestors, living relatives, and
extensions of our own minds and bodies.
When we damage or treat the land without
regard for its own sustainable well-being, we
are in turn hurting and damaging ourselves
and disregarding our own well-being, safety,
and health.

TO FEEL MYSELF BELOVED ON THE EARTH,
2020, found punching bag, expanding foam, acrylic
felt, plastic beads, glass beads, artificial sinew (two
views), 144.8 × 38.1 × 38.1 cm (57 × 15 × 15 in.)

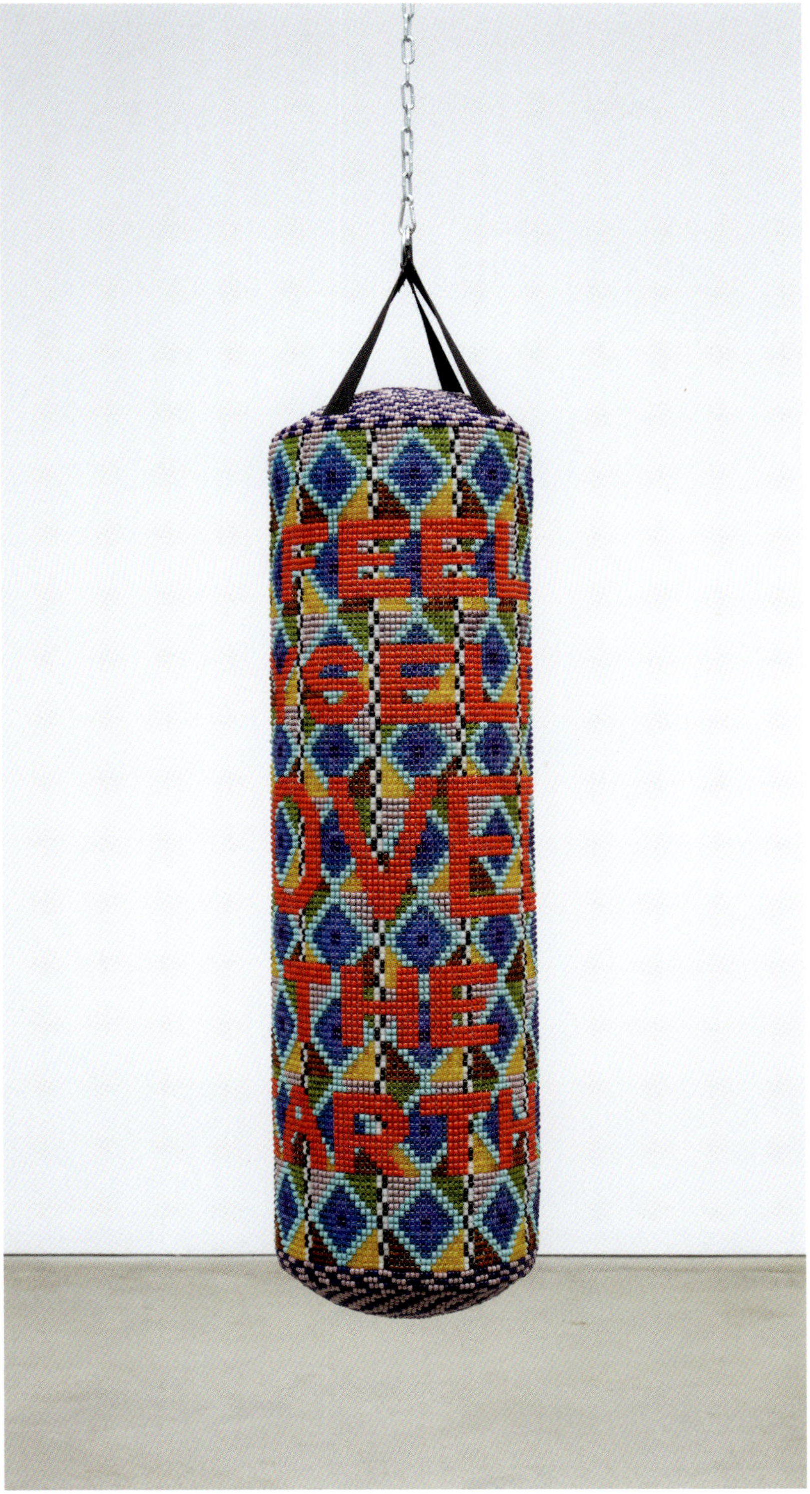
FEEL
SEL
OVE
THE
ARTH

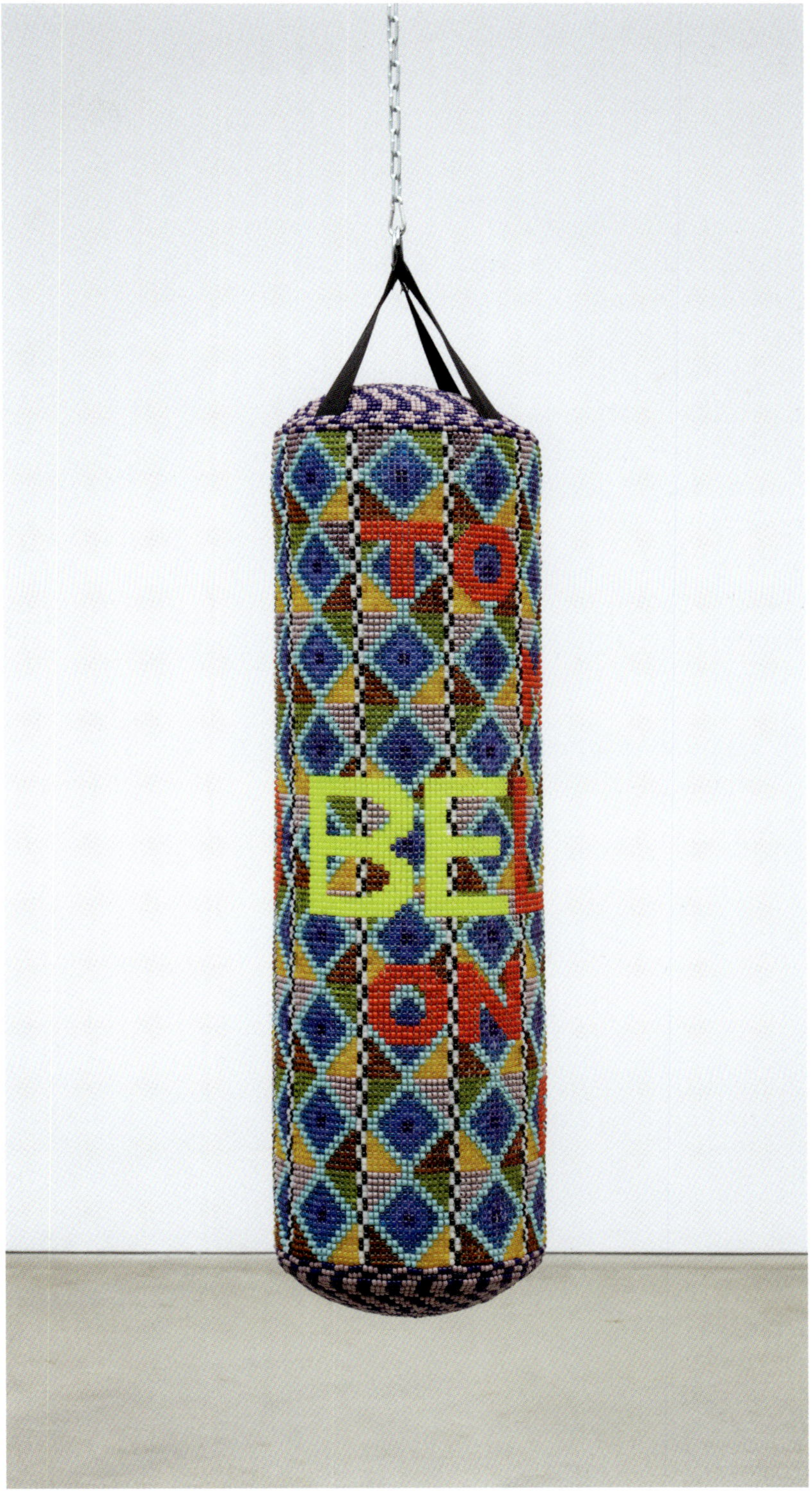
TO
BE
ON

Teri Greeves

Kiowa

Through the ages Kiowa people have almost always adorned their footwear. I understand the immediate appeal of beaded sneakers — they are whimsical, fun, and familiar — yet the illustrations tell a more complex story. Most of my shoe stories deal with our living history, culture, society, and daily life through imagery from a particular dance or custom.

They also tell of our survival from genocide. We, as Kiowas, have a violent, dangerous, awesome, and proud history, and I believe in some way these shoes stand as testament to our lives and values today. These shoes are my hopeful and joyful expression of the continuance of the Kiowa people.

Kiowa Ah-Day, 2004, canvas, glass beads, commercial rubber, each 31 × 11 × 15.5 cm (12 ³⁄₁₆ × 4 ⁵⁄₁₆ × 6 ⅛ in.)

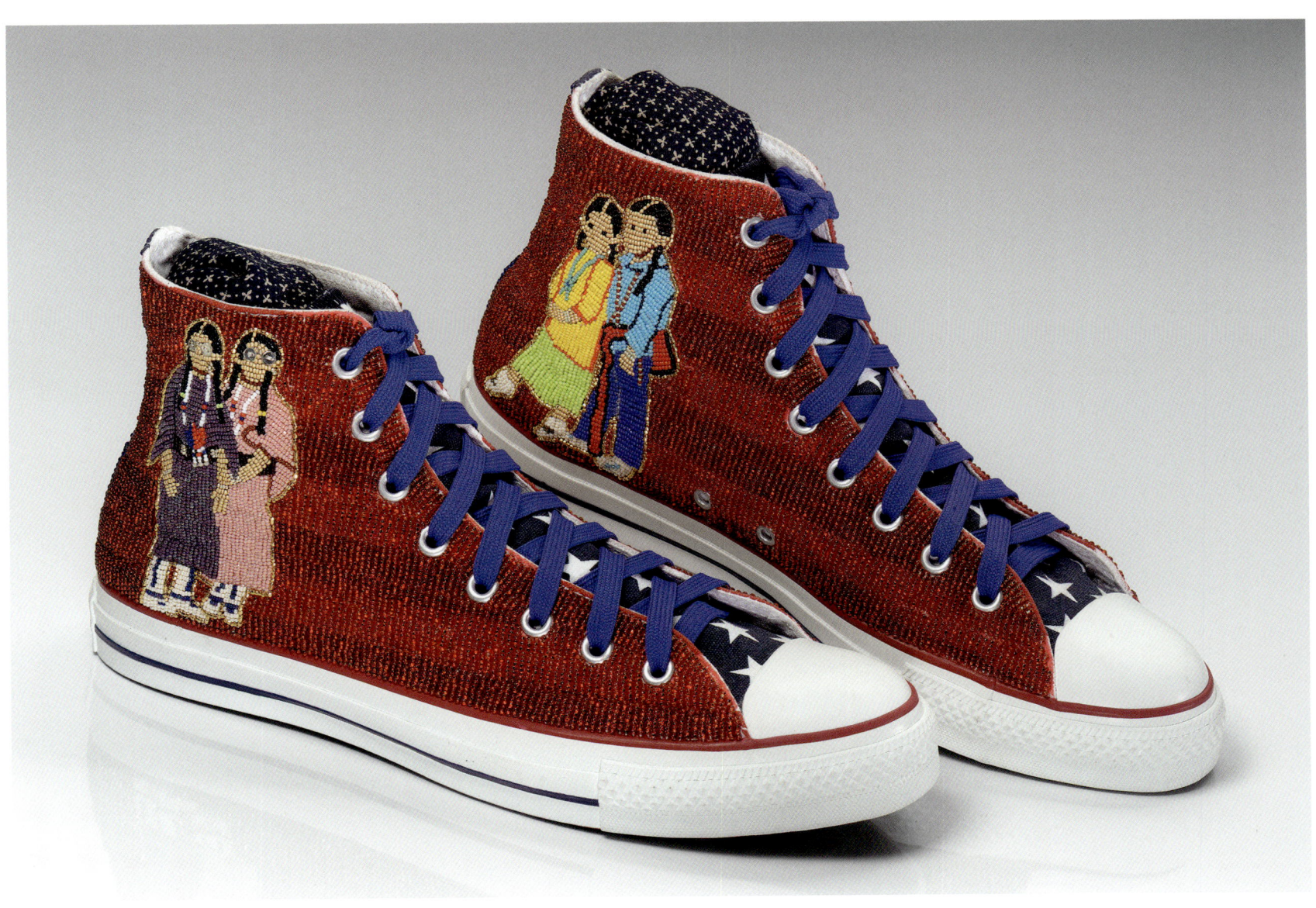

Raven Halfmoon

Caddo Nation

The clay I use is literally from the earth. The
pottery and clay-making traditions employed
by my ancestors go back at least 5,000 years
in the Southern and Southeastern regions of
the United States. Most of my work reflects my
female ancestors and family lineage. They are
the faces of Native people who are indigenous
to this land and from whom I draw my strength
as an artist and a woman.

Iichíile (horse | Crow/Apsáalooke), 2021, stoneware,
glaze, 91.4 × 132.1 × 50.8 cm (36 × 52 × 20 in.)

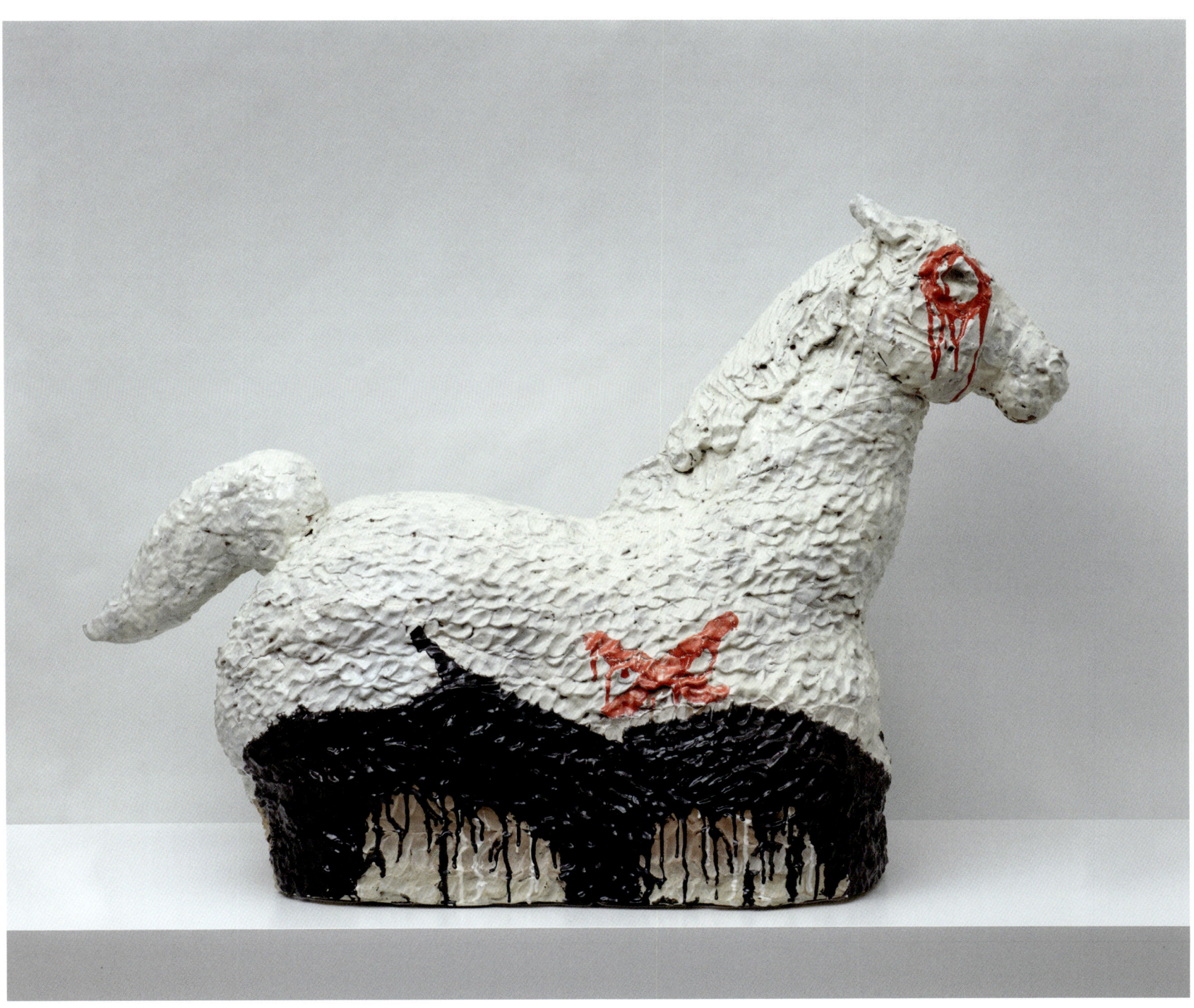

Edgar Heap of Birds

Cheyenne and Arapaho Nations

Following the violent 1868 Washita Massacre at the hands of Lt. Col. George Custer and his troops, the Cheyenne and Arapaho Nations struggled to recover. Tribal leaders were shackled as prisoners of war, and grave poverty, fear, dysfunction, and disruption were brought to the tribes in what later became western Oklahoma.

Nearly 82 years later, Charles and Margaret Heap of Birds, young Cheyenne and Arapaho citizens, respectively, punctured the mainstream American realm by bravely relocating from the reservation to Planeview, a segregated district of south Wichita, Kansas. I see my parents' courageous deeds of leadership as my impetus to extend this puncture via provocative artistic endeavors while I live back on our former reservation lands. My creative methods utilize aggressive public art tactics that present complex political ideas in defense of Native nations.

Native Host for Washington D.C., 2022, mylar text on metal sign panel with metal post and floor base, 45.7 × 91.4 cm (18 × 36 in.)

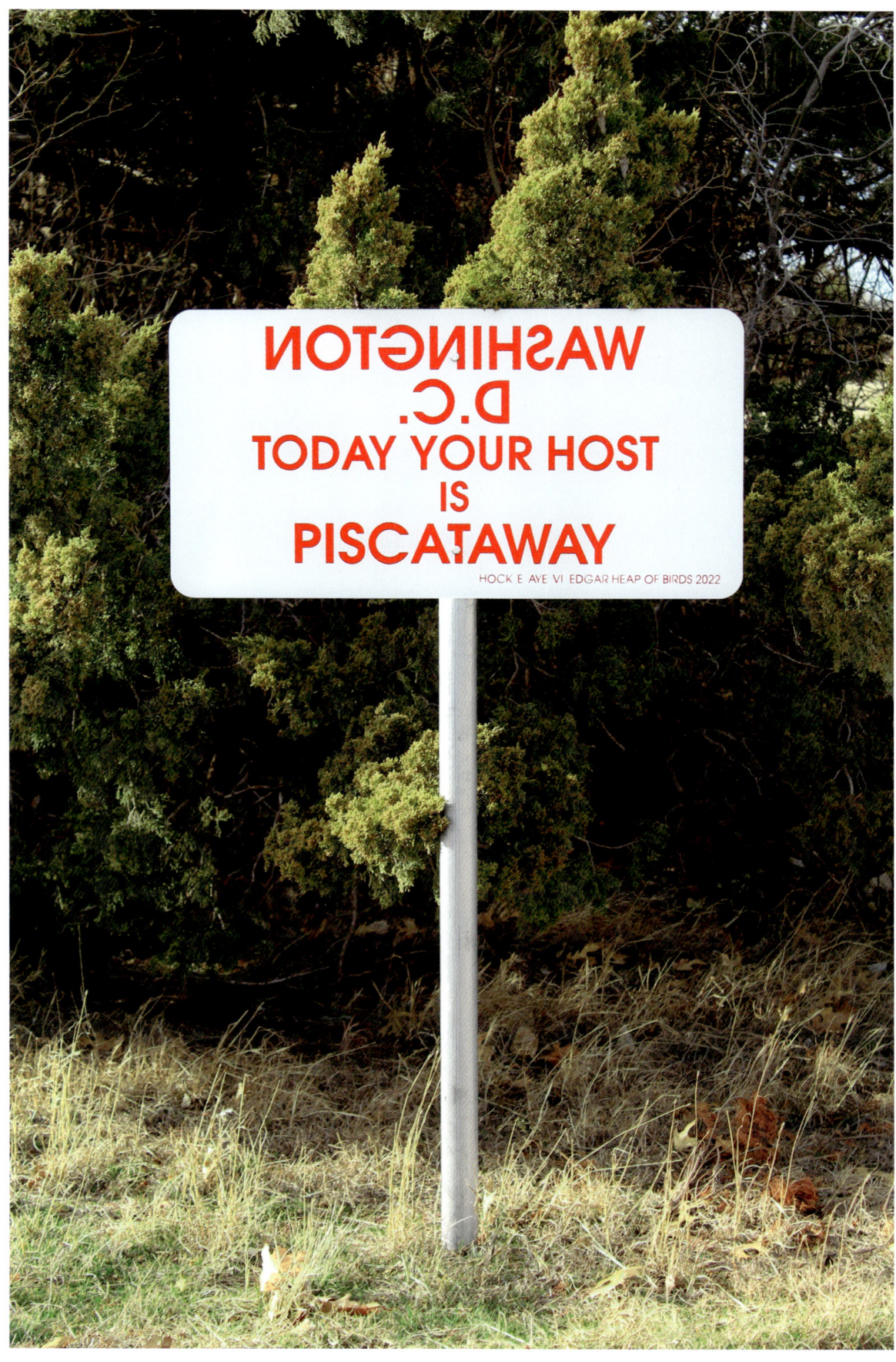

Luzene Hill

Eastern Band of Cherokee Indians

Through work informed by precontact culture of the Americas, I advocate for Indigenous sovereignty: linguistic, cultural, and individual dominion. I employ early autochthonous matrilineal motifs, asserting female power and sexuality, to challenge colonial patriarchy. Research into the past, to know my origins, also gives me direction for the future. Matrilines represent a continuum of our culture, both literally and figuratively. Indigenous societies existed in balance, strength, and harmony with nature and across genders. Focused contemplation of nature and the earth gives me solace and guidance. It encourages a sense of being, a sense of self — then the art comes from within me.

Untitled, 2021, ink, charcoal, tea stain, gouache, and colored pencil on Stonehenge paper, 38.1 × 55.9 cm (15 × 22 in.)

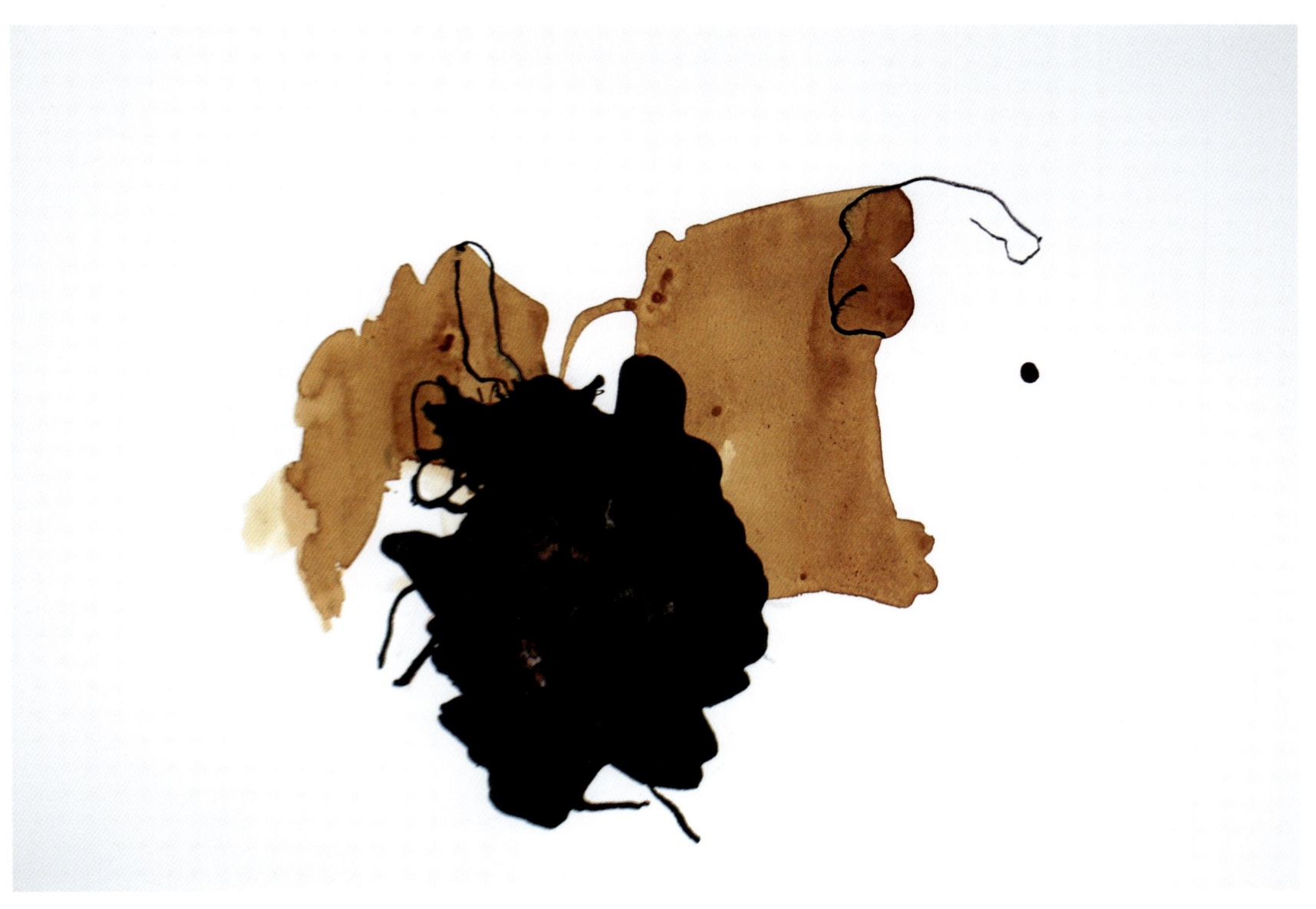

John Hitchcock

Comanche/Kiowa/European descent

I use the print medium, with its long history of social and political commentary, to explore relationships of community, land, and culture. *Impact vs. Influence*, a multimedia installation of printed matter, references the trauma of war and the fragility of life. Familiar images of US military weaponry (tanks and helicopters) are set against unfamiliar mythological and hybrid creatures (buffalo, deer, birds). The Wichita Mountains in western Oklahoma inspired me to explore the notion of assimilation and control. I grew up on Comanche tribal lands located in the Wichita Mountains area next to the military base at Fort Sill near Lawton, Oklahoma. My visual storytelling helps me to understand my relationships to the beauty of the mountains and the complexity of the military base.

Impact vs. Influence, 2023, screen printed felt, paper, and acrylic paint, with contributions by Emily Arthur, dimensions variable

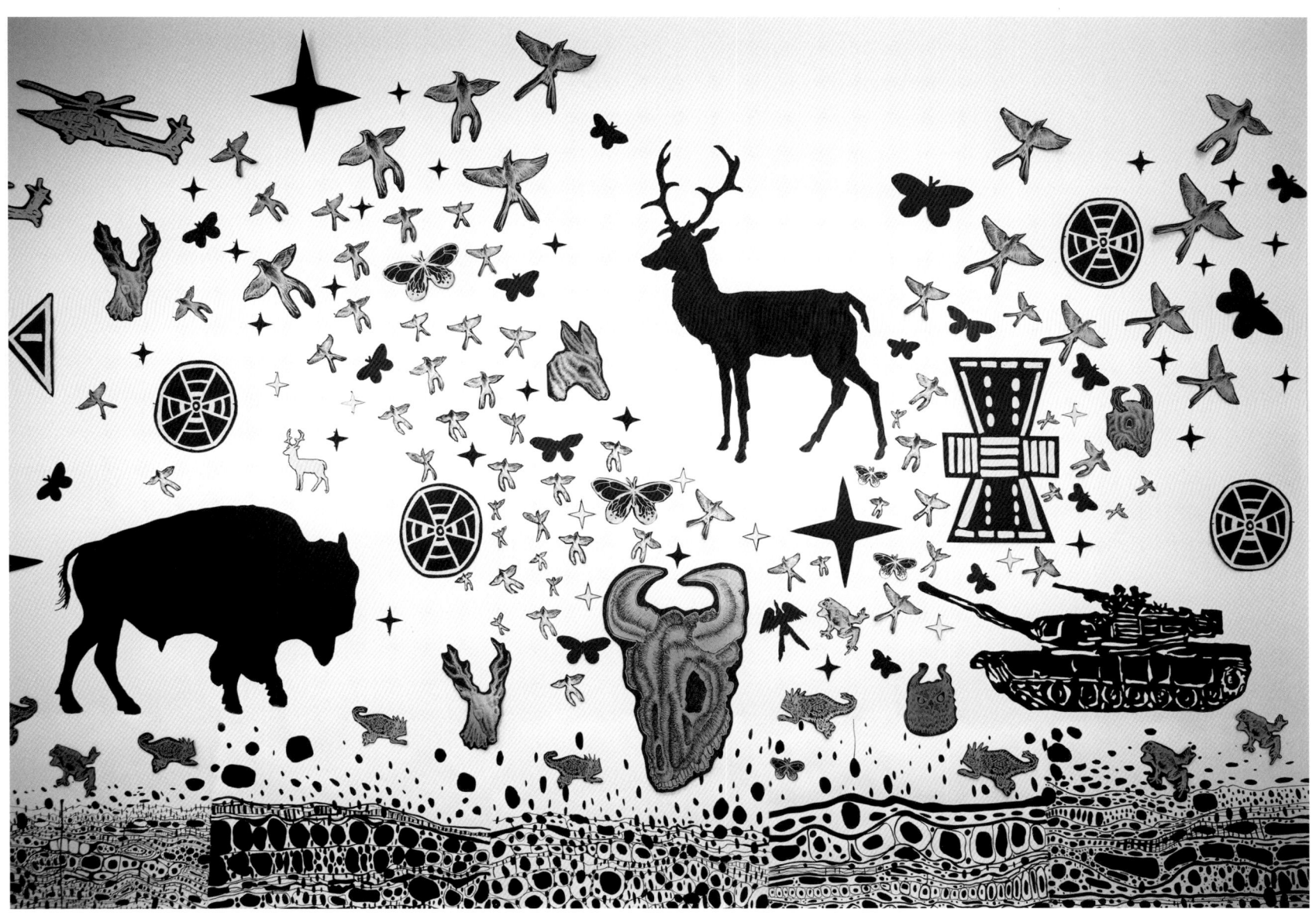

G. Peter Jemison

Seneca Nation of Indians,
Heron Clan

When I was a kid, we had something called
a Bazaar. I can vividly remember the smell of
cooking and the colors of the blankets that
individual craftspeople used on their tables.
After I got my education and began to work in
the "White World," I did not find that sense of
comfort from my childhood until I returned
home to Seneca Nation. There I experienced
that same feeling of peace and comfort that I
felt as a child at the Bazaar. As Onöndowagah,
or People of the Great Hill, we seek peace. We
are about maintaining and keeping traditions
alive and relevant.

The sunflower has a particular prominence
in our Creation Story; it is the first light. This
painting was created at Ganondagan, where
we are taking back our original homeland
and bringing it back to life through growing
traditional medicine and foods. That's what
this painting is about. There is a season for
growing and a season for resting and returning
to the earth.

Sentinels (Large Yellow), 2006, acrylic, oil, and collage
on canvas, 91.4 × 101.6 cm (36 × 40 in.)

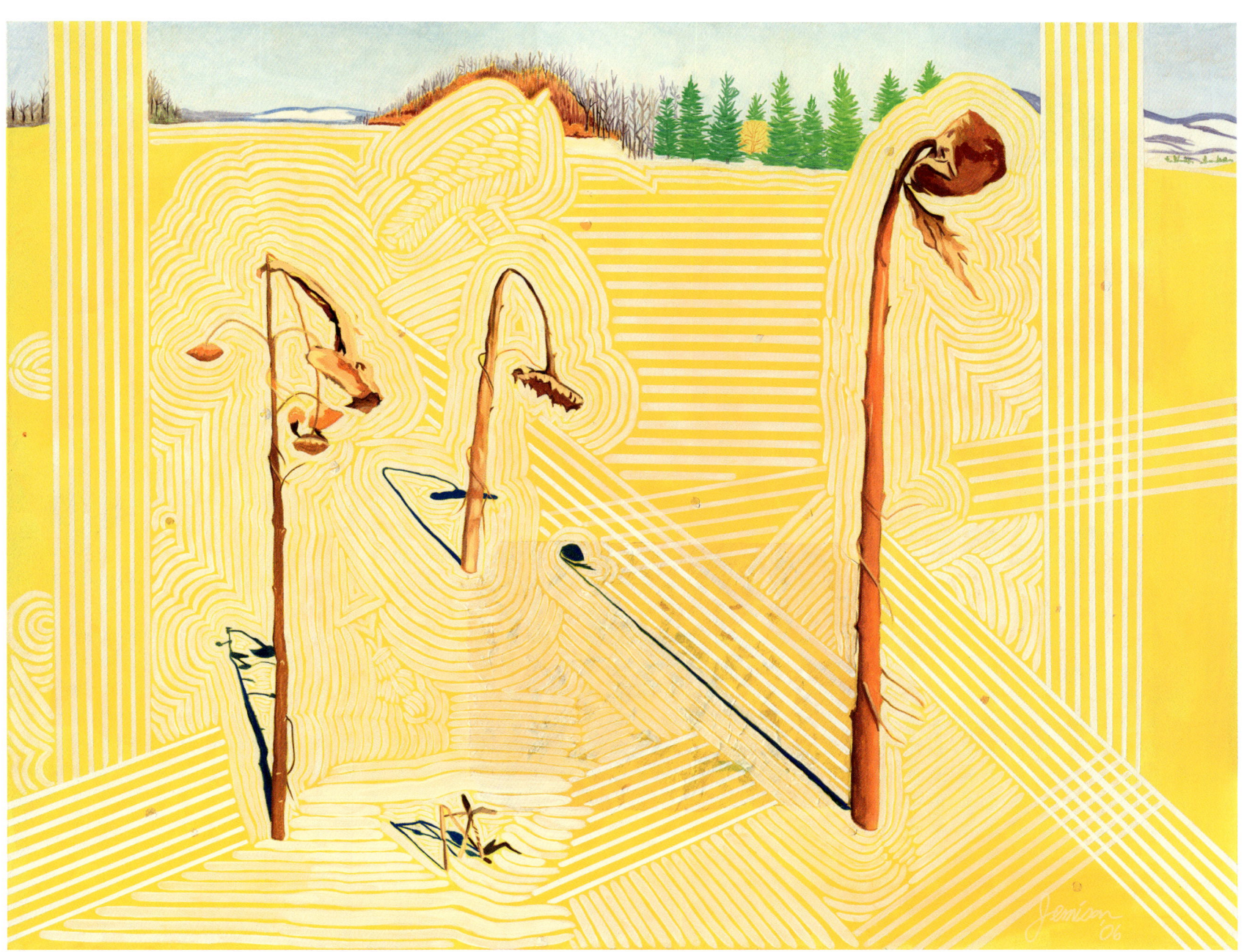

Tom Jones

Ho-Chunk Nation

The small plastic toys I use in my photography series act as stand-ins for the landscape and represent the Native Americans who continue to inhabit this continent. I am questioning how the history of the North American landscape comes to be known and perceived through the education of our children. Toys have the power to teach children about history and the world around them.

Throughout history toys have been essential to children's intellectual growth. They learn about their environment through play and gain new information about cause and effect, communication, manipulation, and problem-solving life skills. Toys depicting Native Americans allow children an imagined power over land and people. This series gives them an understanding of the history of this land and its original people.

A Hopi Landscape, 2013, archival digital print, 63.5 × 50.8 cm (25 × 20 in.)

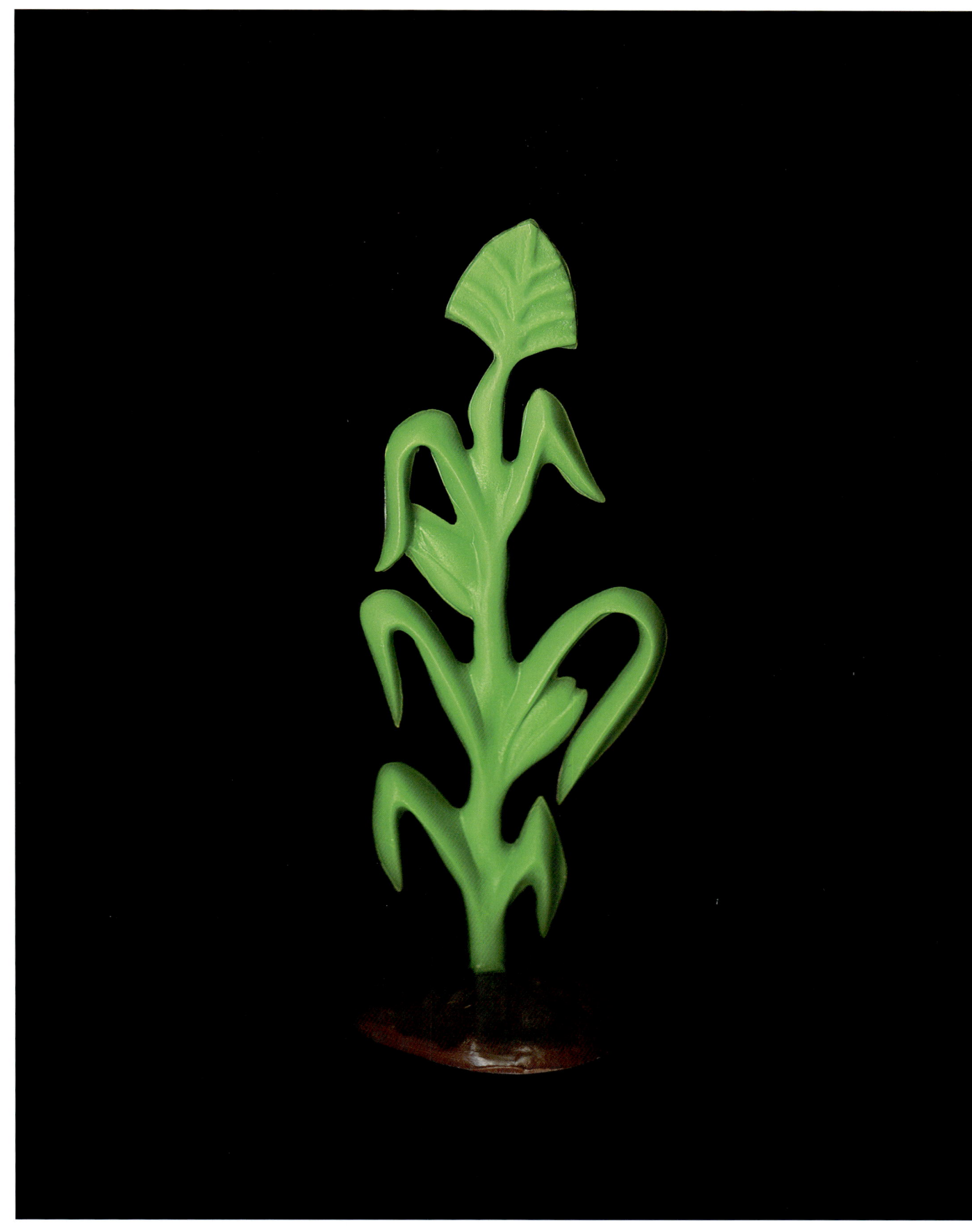

Linda King

Confederated Salish and Kootenai Tribes

I believe that artistic talents are wonderful gifts from the Creator, and these skills and knowledge are meant to be shared and not to be owned. To pass this information on through my teachings of beadwork and woven baskets as well as other cultural arts contributes to keeping cultural knowledge alive for our tribal community. Through the cultural arts, important historical stories are handed down, shared, and maintained from past generations. When we create our own stories today, we provide a path to our future.

Teaching of the Tree People, 2018, waxed cotton, waxed linen, Red Cedar, and buckskin, height 29.2 cm (11 ½ in.), diam. 22.9 cm (9 in.)

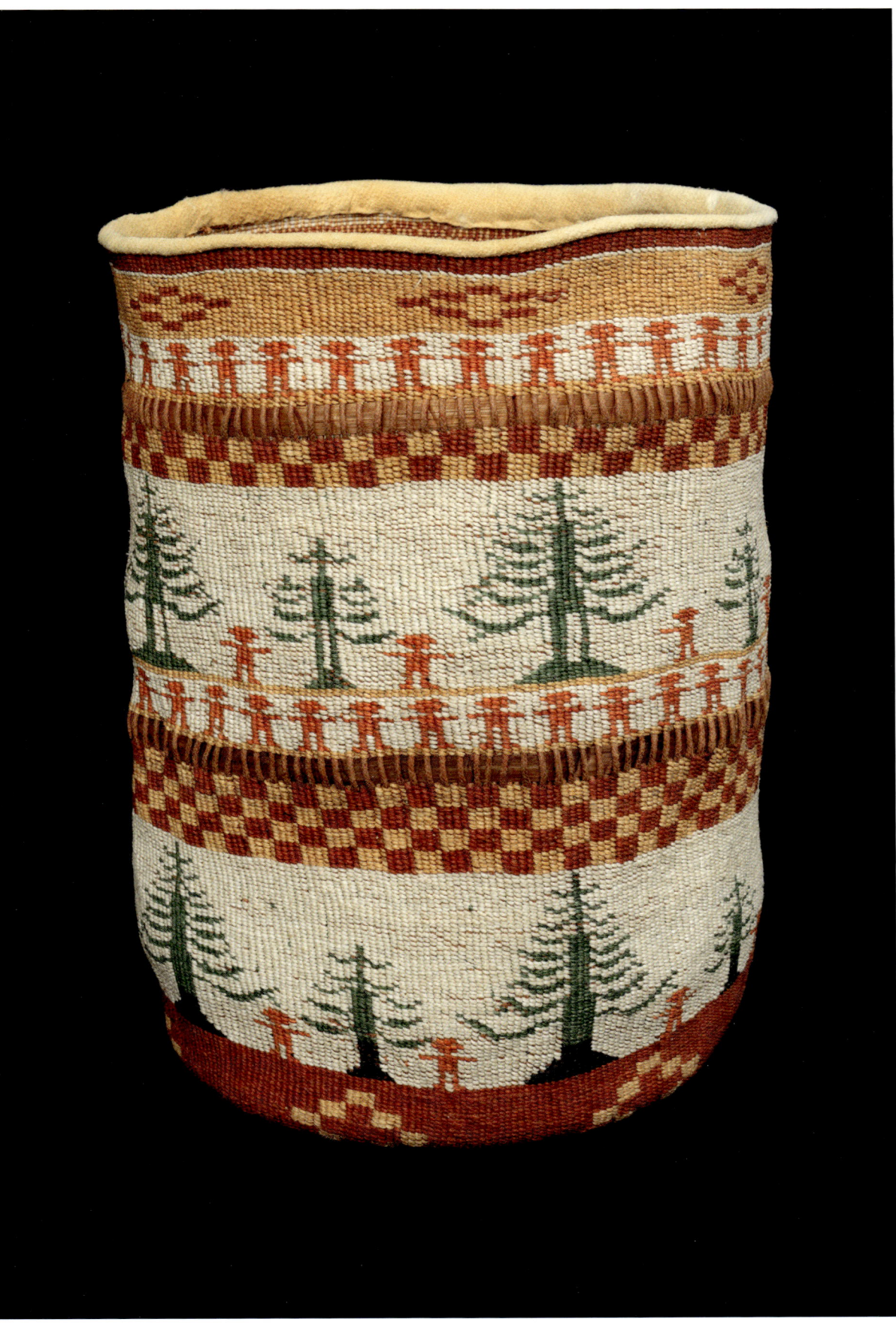

Athena LaTocha

Keweenaw Bay Ojibwe/Standing
Rock Lakota

In the wake of Earthworks artists from the 1960s
and 1970s, my work explores the relationship
between human-made and natural worlds.
Using ink, lead, earth, wood, and other materials
found in urban or natural environments, my work
is influenced by my upbringing in the wilderness
of Alaska. My process is about being immersed
in these environments while responding to the
storied and, at times, traumatic cultural histories
that are rooted in place.

Untitled No. 22, 2015, sumi and walnut ink and shellac
on paper, 43.2 × 85.7 cm (17 × 33 ¾ in.)

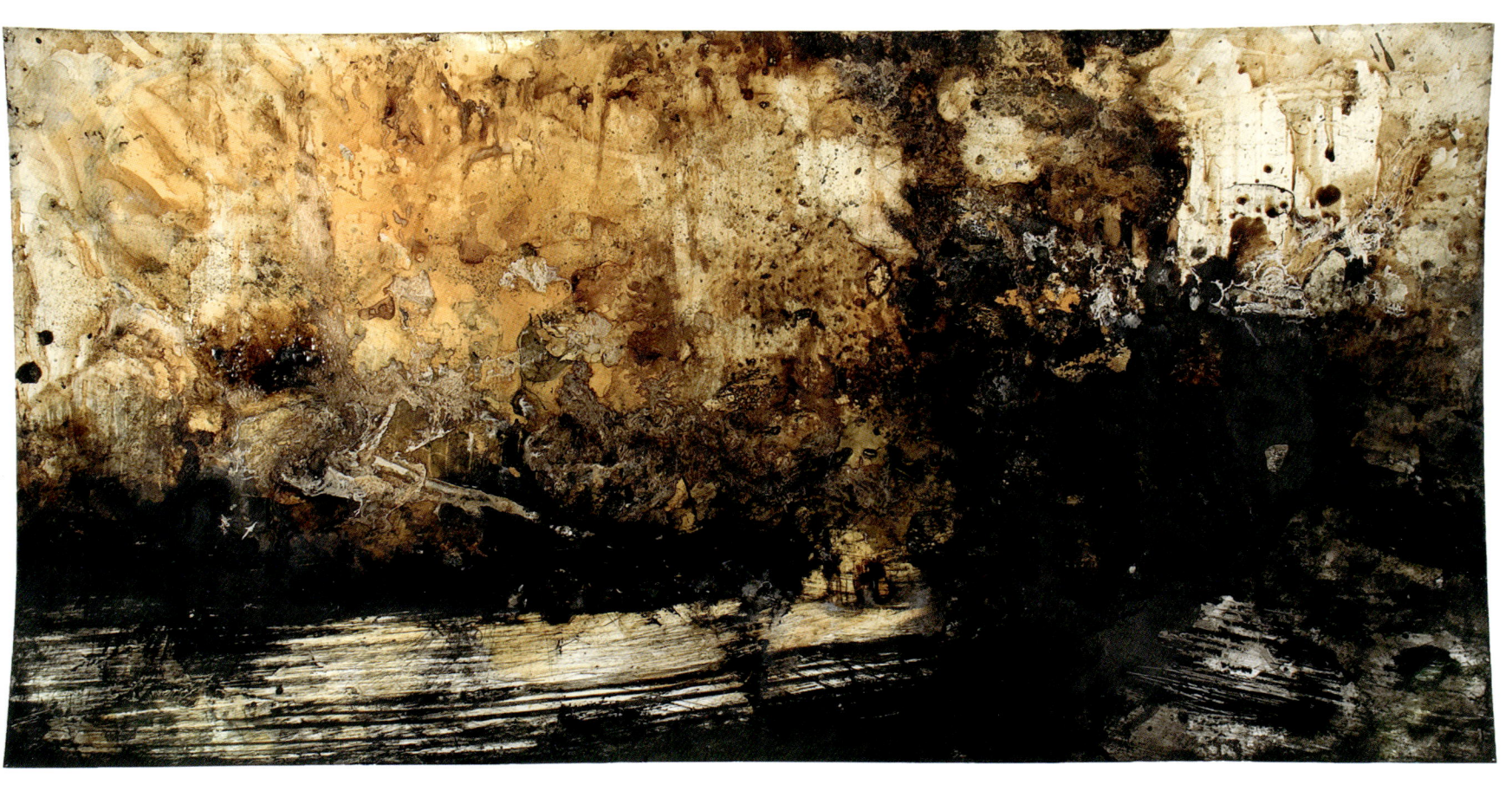

James Lavadour

Confederated Tribes of the Umatilla
Indian Reservation, Walla Walla

I am a painter who occasionally makes prints.
I learn when I paint and become involved in
the printmaking process. Both provide ways
to listen to the land and to practice perception
and discovery. The drips and patterns in wet
paint, much like the lines, colors, and forms in
prints, are identical to the snaking and braiding
of river channels. It's all the same stuff. Every
outcropping of basalt is a portal to the history
of the universe. The way my body moves is the
same as the wind and fire and flowing water.
Painting and making prints are revelatory events
that spark light into the unknown and expand
my understanding of being alive.

Duotone 2, 2011, lithograph, 38.1 × 28.3 cm (15 × 11 ⅛ in.)

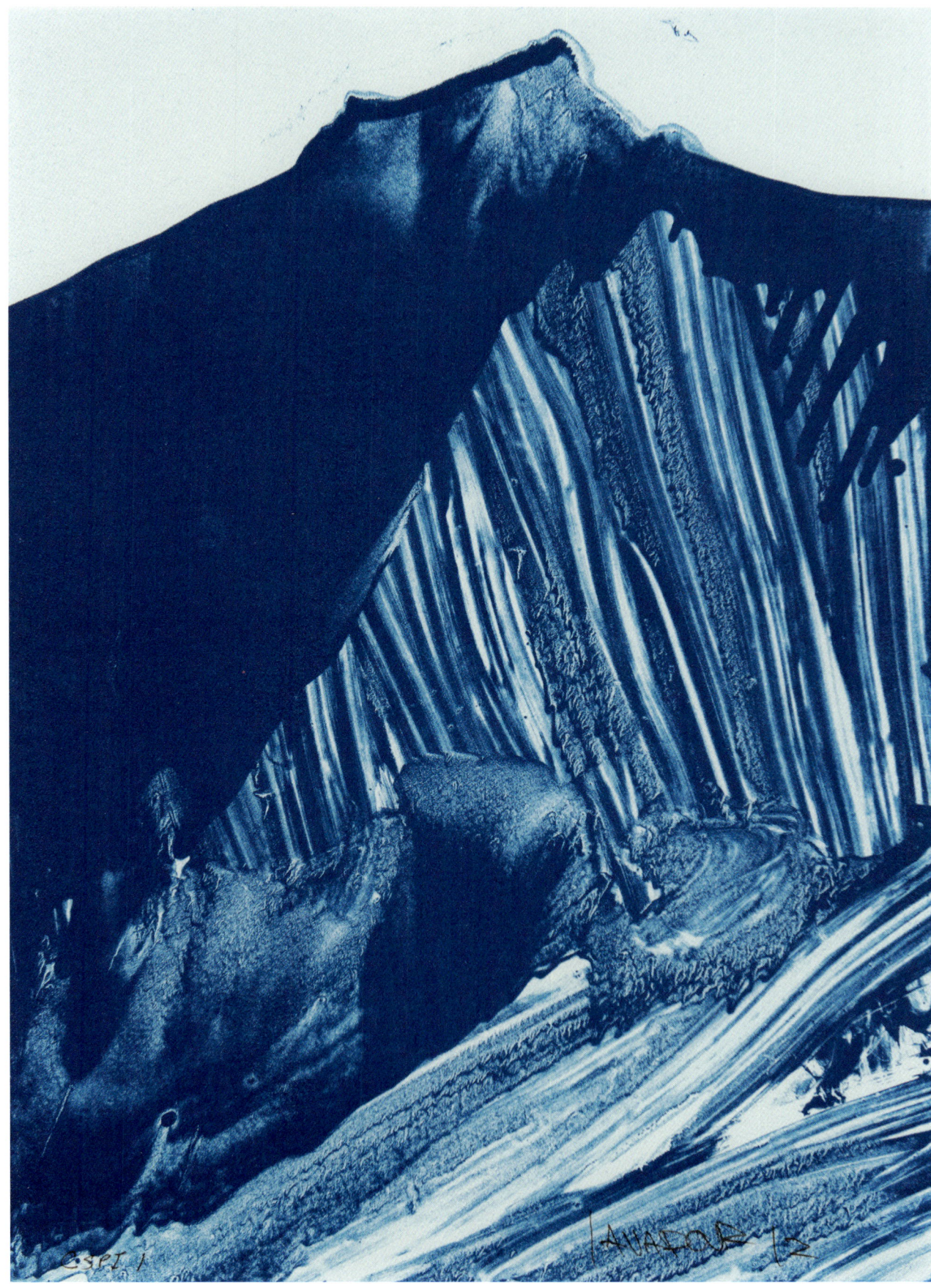

Linda Lomahaftewa

Hopi/Choctaw

Most of my work references land in some way. I do personal land research of the Southeast to make connections with my Hopi and Choctaw heritage. A road trip with my good friend, Cherokee artist America Meredith, set the course for this work. Our route from the Southwest to the Southeast and back was more than 3,500 miles, with the main goal to visit Nanih Waiya (Choctaw Mother Mound) in Mississippi and Kituwah (Cherokee Mother Mound) in North Carolina. Our hope — to better understand our relationship to our people through the land — was enhanced by also studying neighboring tribes, looking for similarities and differences.

Parrots Prayer Song, 1989, lithograph, 76.2 × 55.9 cm (30 × 22 in.)

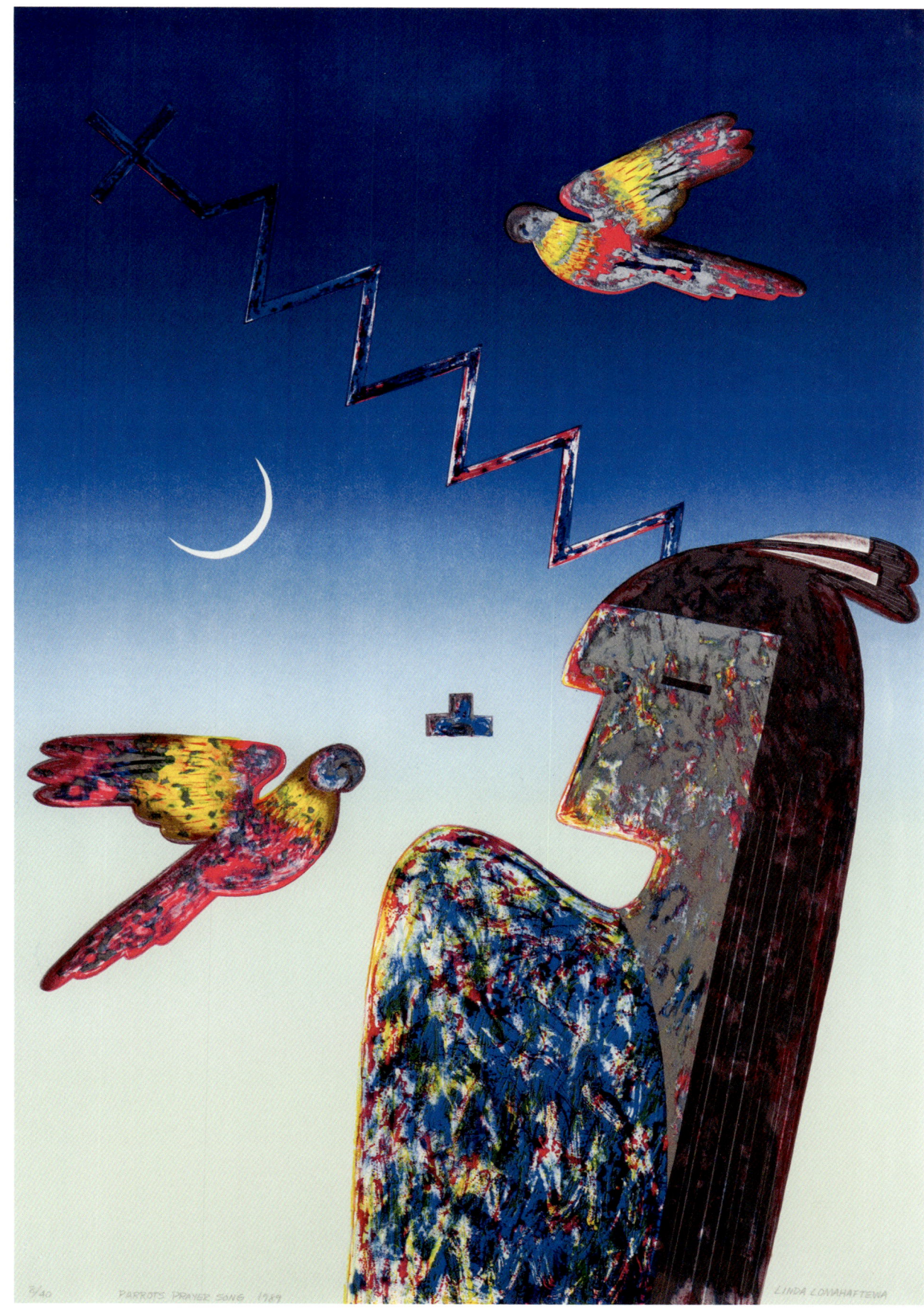

Parrots Prayer Song, 1989   Linda Lomahaftewa

George C. Longfish

Seneca/Tuscarora

When I work, I am often in communication spiritually with my subjects. I ask them to tell me about the direction they would like the work to take. I work to bring to light issues related to Indigenous people that have been largely overlooked by history as it is taught in the United States. I use humor, color, and words in hope that the viewer questions stereotypes and previously held assumptions about Indigenous people. In *As Above So Below*, I endeavor to speak to the significance of how our modern diet differs socially and physically from our traditional one. And how that change has brought about bigger changes to our community.

As Above So Below, 1997, acrylic on canvas, 182.9 × 134.6 cm (72 × 53 in.)

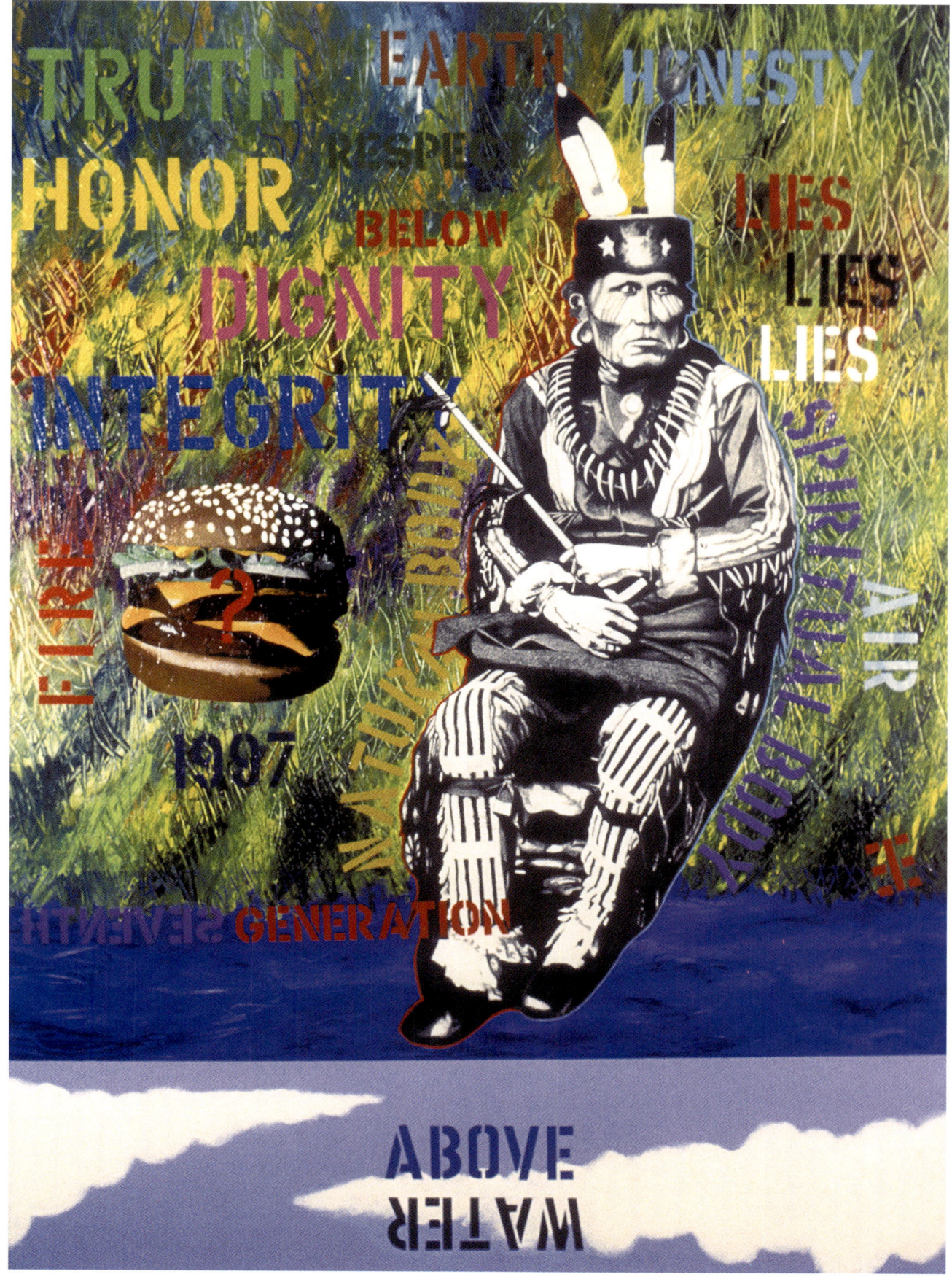

Cannupa Hanska Luger

Mandan/Hidatsa/Arikara/Lakota

I am motivated to reclaim and reframe a more accurate version of 21st-century Native American culture and its powerful global relevance. Given the legacies of cultural appropriation and annihilation brought on by colonization, the endurance of our continuum is characterized by resilience, adaptability, and survivance. In recognition of this legacy, I place myself between the realms of contemporary art and Indigenous culture, moving amidst museums and the front lines, to enact a more complex understanding of contemporary Indigeneity. The materials I use — clay, textiles, steel, and digital media — are emblems of human civilization that I distill into an object, installation, or action. Whether working with institutions, communities, or the land itself, my work is inherently social and requires engagement. I aim to lay groundwork, establish connections, and mobilize action.

Mirror Shield Project — The River (The Water Serpent), Oceti Sakowin, North Dakota, 2016, single channel video

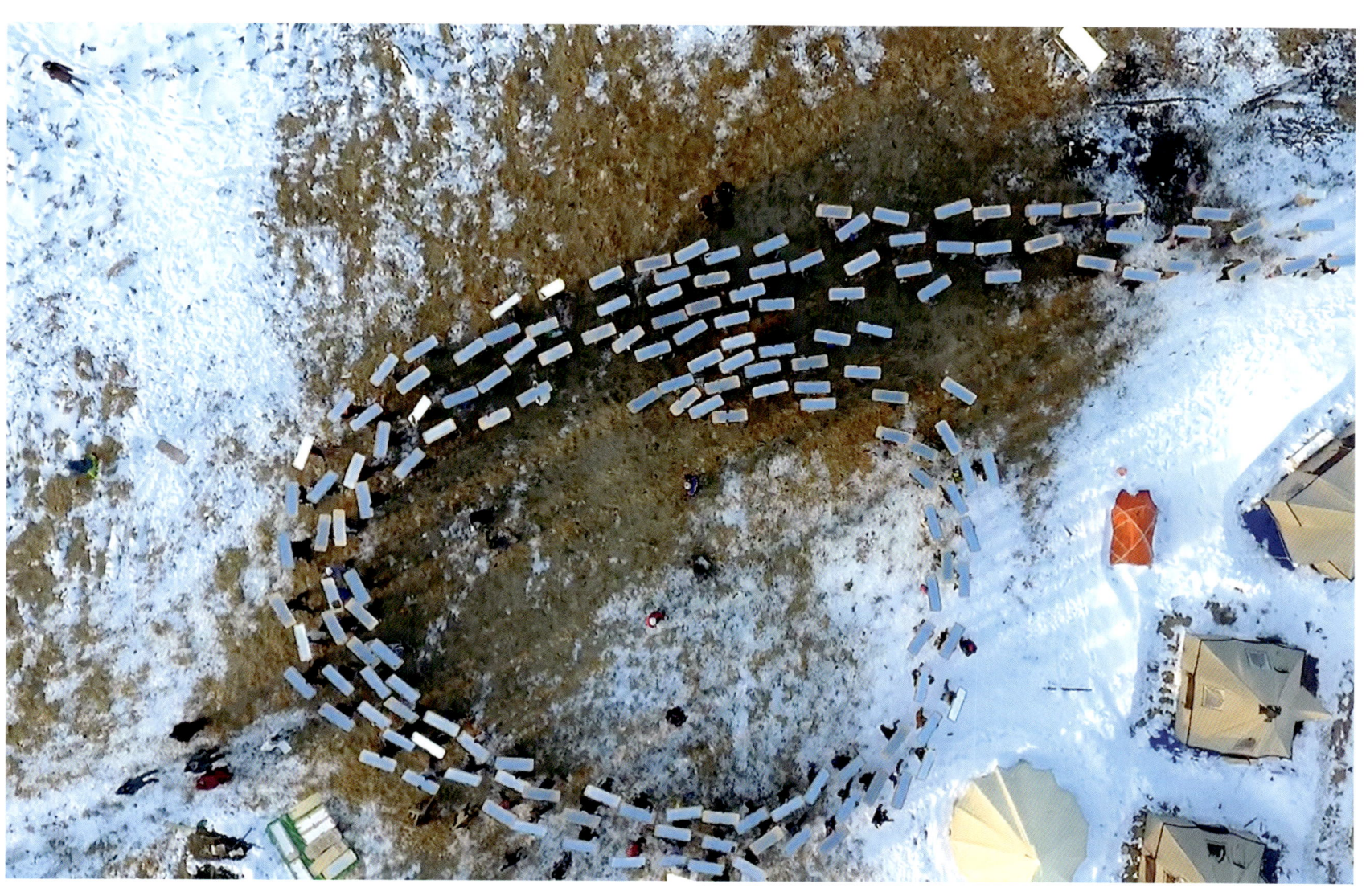

Brenda Mallory

Cherokee Nation

Texture and repeated rhythmic forms are instrumental to my abstract compositions. Using mainly reclaimed materials, I explore ideas of disruption, repair, and interconnections in long-established systems in nature and human cultures. The ideas of disruption and "making-do" with found materials have broad references in the world we live in, but personally I think of my ancestors who had to adapt to new lands and ways after being forcibly and illegally removed to Oklahoma from their homelands in the Southeast.

The Plural of Nexus, 2016, one-color lithograph on Rives BFK white paper, 76.2 × 56.8 cm (30 × 22 ⅜ in.)

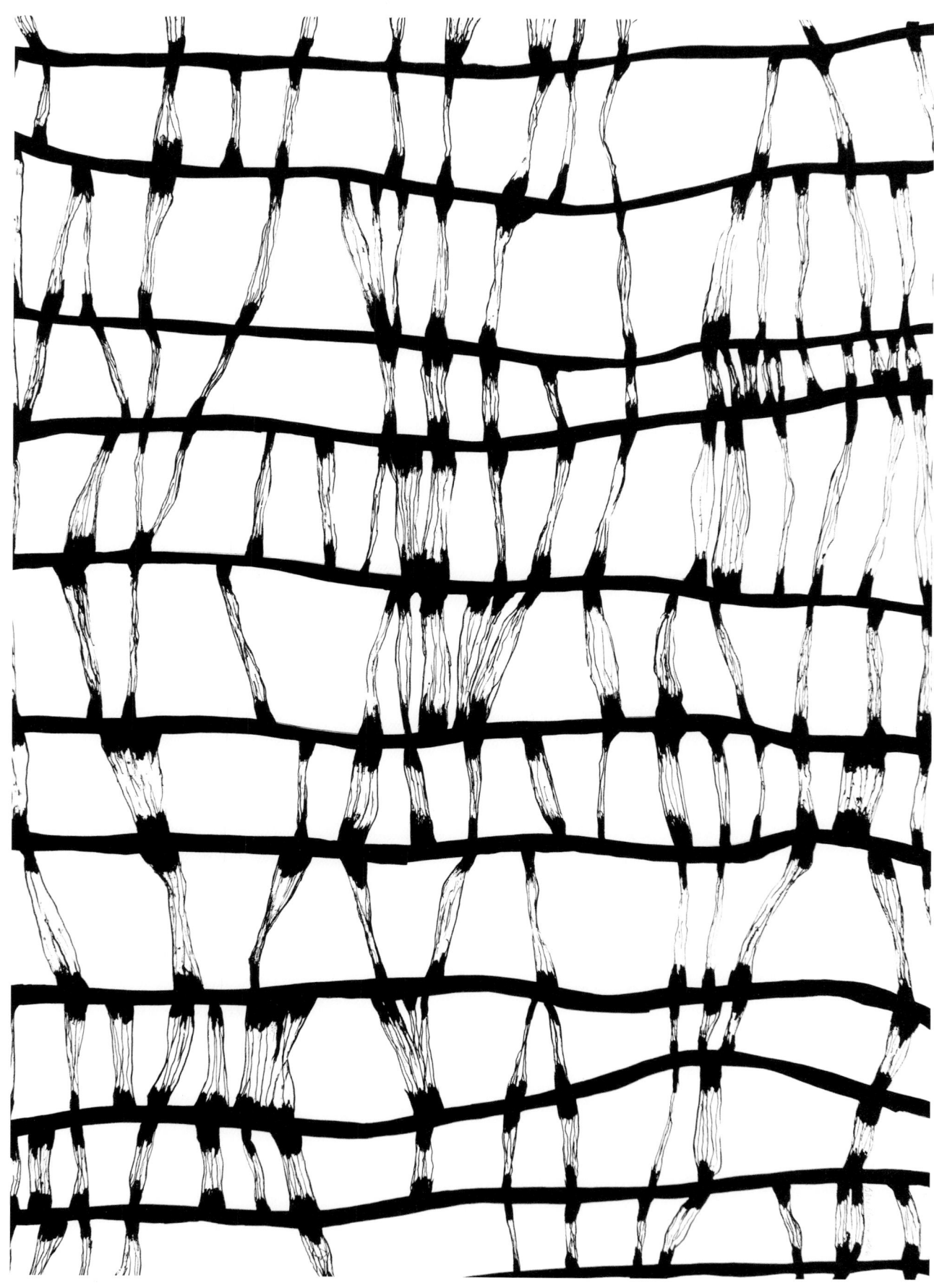

Mario Martinez

Pascua Yaqui Tribe of Arizona

My work derives from the great Western modernist abstract tradition. My Yaqui Indian heritage and spiritual concepts form the inner core of my vision. In my paintings, drawings, prints, and public works, the manipulation of their plastic qualities is primary.

I feel abstraction is the best visual expression of the vast non-physical energy and actual matter of the Universe. It also has the same qualities of/in the earth. In my abstract works I reference the organic and geometric shapes that are related to visual earthly physicality and also to the physical and atomic/subatomic non-physical energetic makeup of the Universe.

Esoteric Vibration Landscape, 2019, colored pencil and oil pastel on paper, 61 × 48.3 cm (24 × 19 in.)

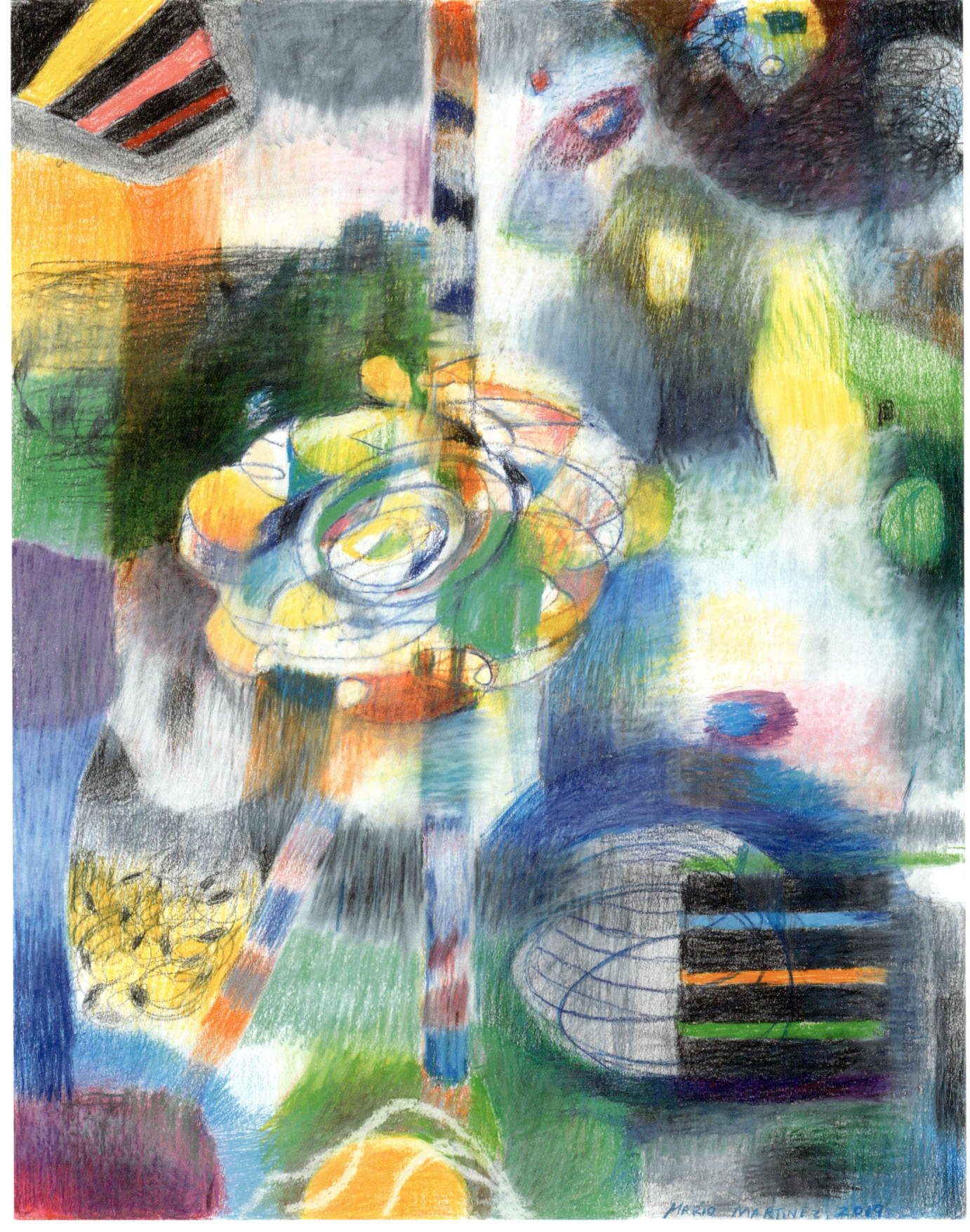

Melissa Melero-Moose

Fallon Paiute-Shoshone Tribe

Drawing from my connection to my homelands, my work abstracts place, identity, and memory. My imagery integrates basketry shapes and textures with willow, pine nuts, and paint washes layered intuitively to create a visual in which Indigenous life is told through my perspective as a Native woman, mother, and American artist. *Access Denied* is about two parallel concerns to Indigenous peoples in the Great Basin: limited access to natural resources, and limited representation within positions of power, specifically as it relates to the visibility of Indigenous artists. The basketry images transform into the barbed wire that separates Indigenous peoples from access to the basket materials, food, and water on our homelands in Nevada, which is the essence of our traditions and our survival.

Access Denied, 2021, acrylic and mixed media with pine nuts on canvas, 91.4 × 122 × 5.1 cm (36 × 48 ¹⁄₁₆ × 2 in.)

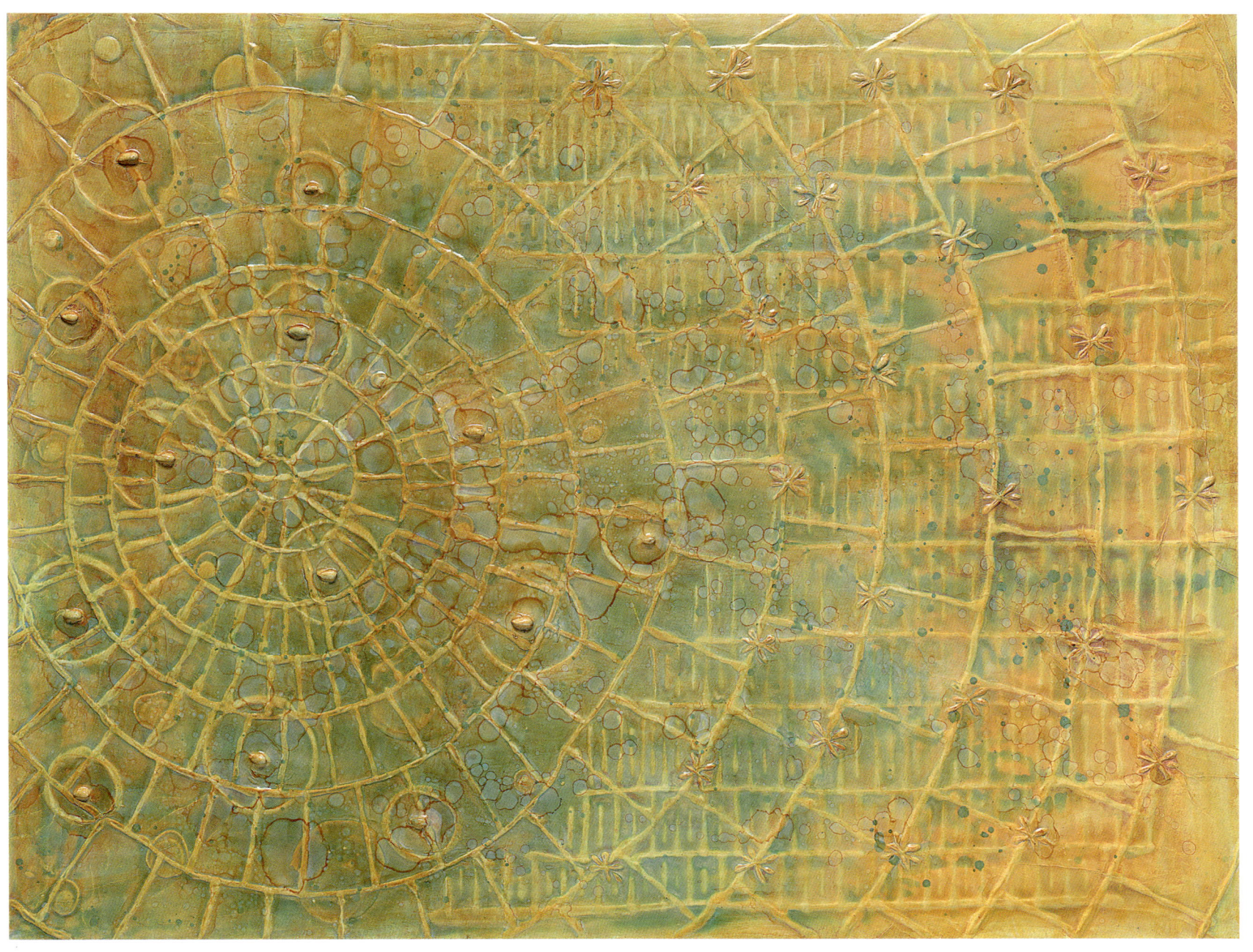

Jamie Okuma

La Jolla Band of Luiseno Indians

These beaded boots honor my childhood companion, a California scrub jay named Peep. Scrub jays are known for their long tail and blue coloring, but they don't often interact with people or become household pets. When I was about seven years old, my cousin found him abandoned in an old stove where he had fallen from his nest. After my mother and I nursed him back to health, Peep stayed a part of my family for the next 26 years.

The beaded floral images of lupines and Indian paintbrushes around Peep remind me of my home territory on the La Jolla Indian Reservation. The black and white patterns around the top of the boots are piano keys. Peep loved to sit on the edge of the piano while I took lessons. Even though I played horribly, he loved it.

Peep, 2021, antique glass beads, brain-tanned deer hide, and vintage basket beads on Casadei boots, each 52 × 21.5 × 12 cm (20 ½ × 8 ⁷⁄₁₆ × 4 ¾ in.), circum. 39.3 cm (15 ½ in.)

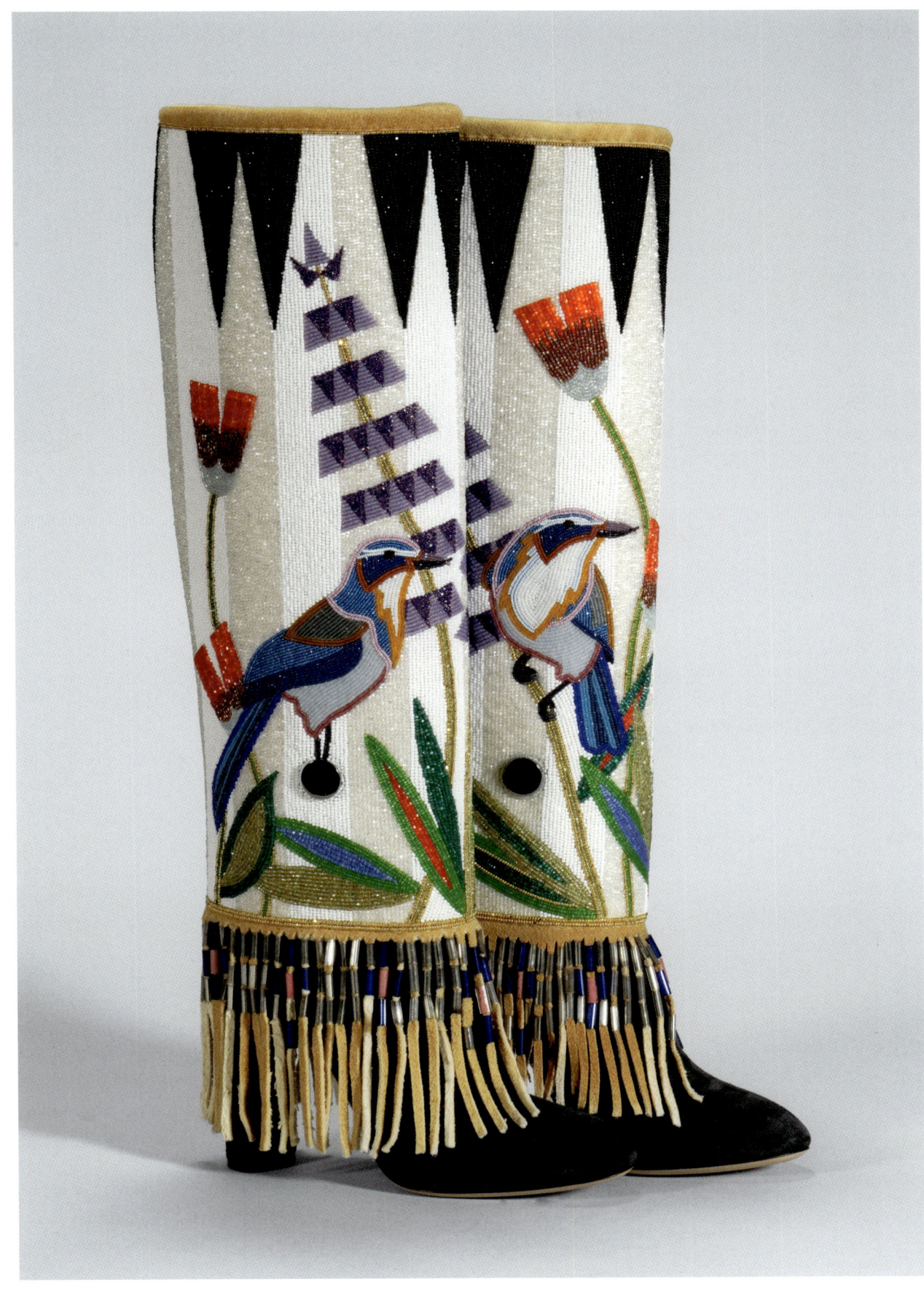

Chris Pappan

Kanza/Lakota

Characterizing images from the past by referencing historical photographs, I transcribe the visages of our ancestors onto historical substrates to honor their sacrifice. Various interpretations of the figures relate a contemporary narrative and require the viewer to think of Native Americans in human terms rather than objectifying them, as we have been taught to do since birth. I will not deny that Native people are historically culpable in perpetuating such objectification, however this complexity reinforces our humanity. One size does not fit all.

Utilizing customary materials, such as graphite, colored pencils, ink, and water-based media, I create my work to suit my personal influences or to convey sociopolitical ideas. Figures or portraits are often mirrored, intentionally creating a new identity that is then open to interpretation. Collaged remnants of maps symbolize our connection to the land and act as a ledger of stolen land.

Atom Heart Mother (Earth), 2016, mixed media on ledger paper, 40.6 × 25.4 cm (16 × 10 in.)

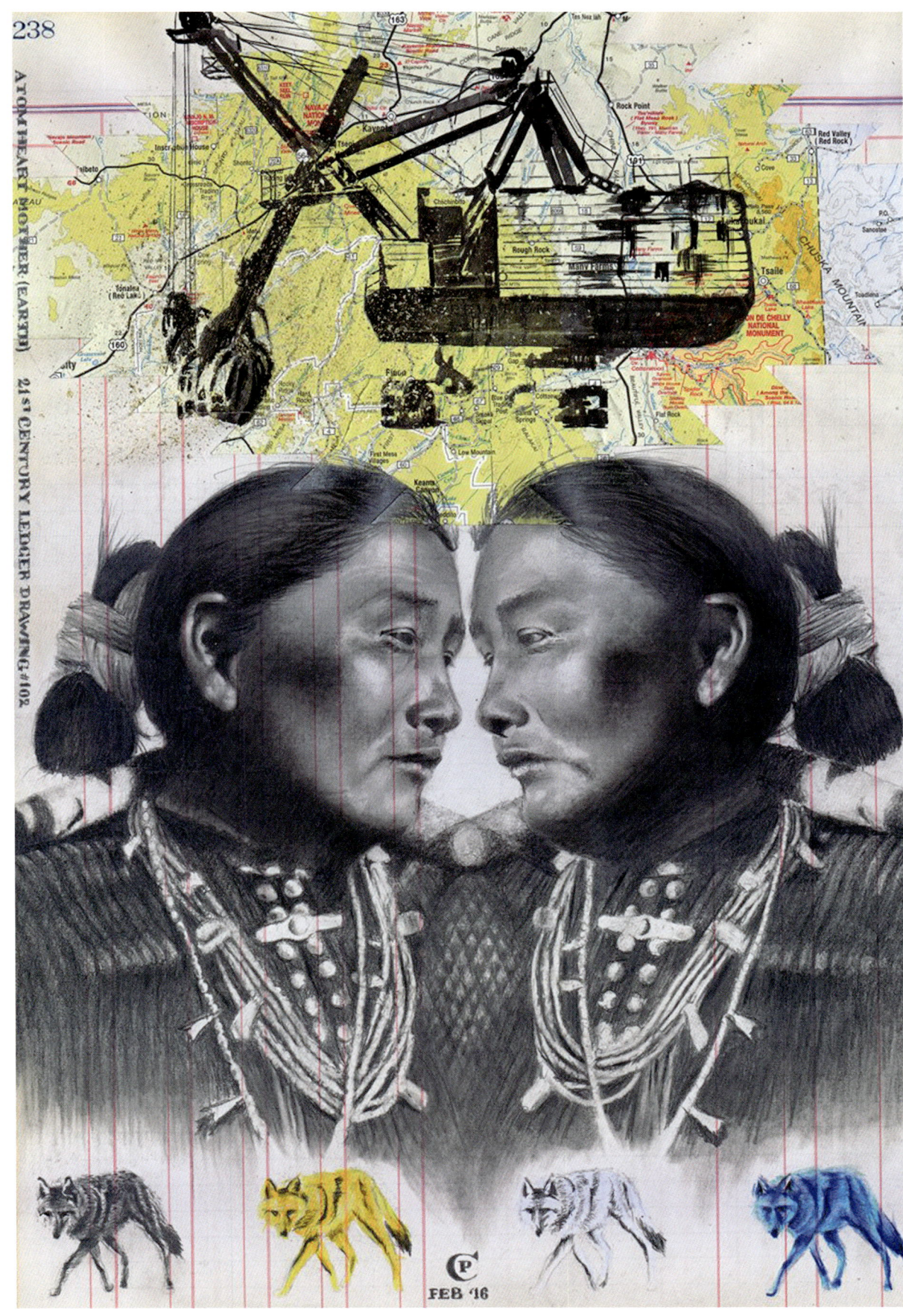

ATOMHEART MOTHER (EARTH)

21ST CENTURY LEDGER DRAWING #102

FEB '16

Rose Powhatan

Pamunkey/Tauxenent descent

Constructed from locally sourced organic materials, *Fire Warrior Woman* pays respect and gratitude to the tenacious Indigenous women who fought for freedom and ownership of their homeland. Early European land encroachment and genocide inflicted upon my ancestors resulted in losses that have never been restored.

My paternal ancestor Keziah Powhatan was *werowansqua* (female chief) of the Tauxenents during colonial times. The first courthouse in Fairfax County, Virginia, built in 1742, was abandoned in 1752 due to "Indian hostilities." Keziah Powhatan led her warriors in the destruction of the courthouse that was built on their unceded tribal land.

Fire Warrior Woman, c. 2007, wood, vine, clay, feathers, height 182.9 cm (72 in.), width variable, base diam. 45.7 cm (18 in.)

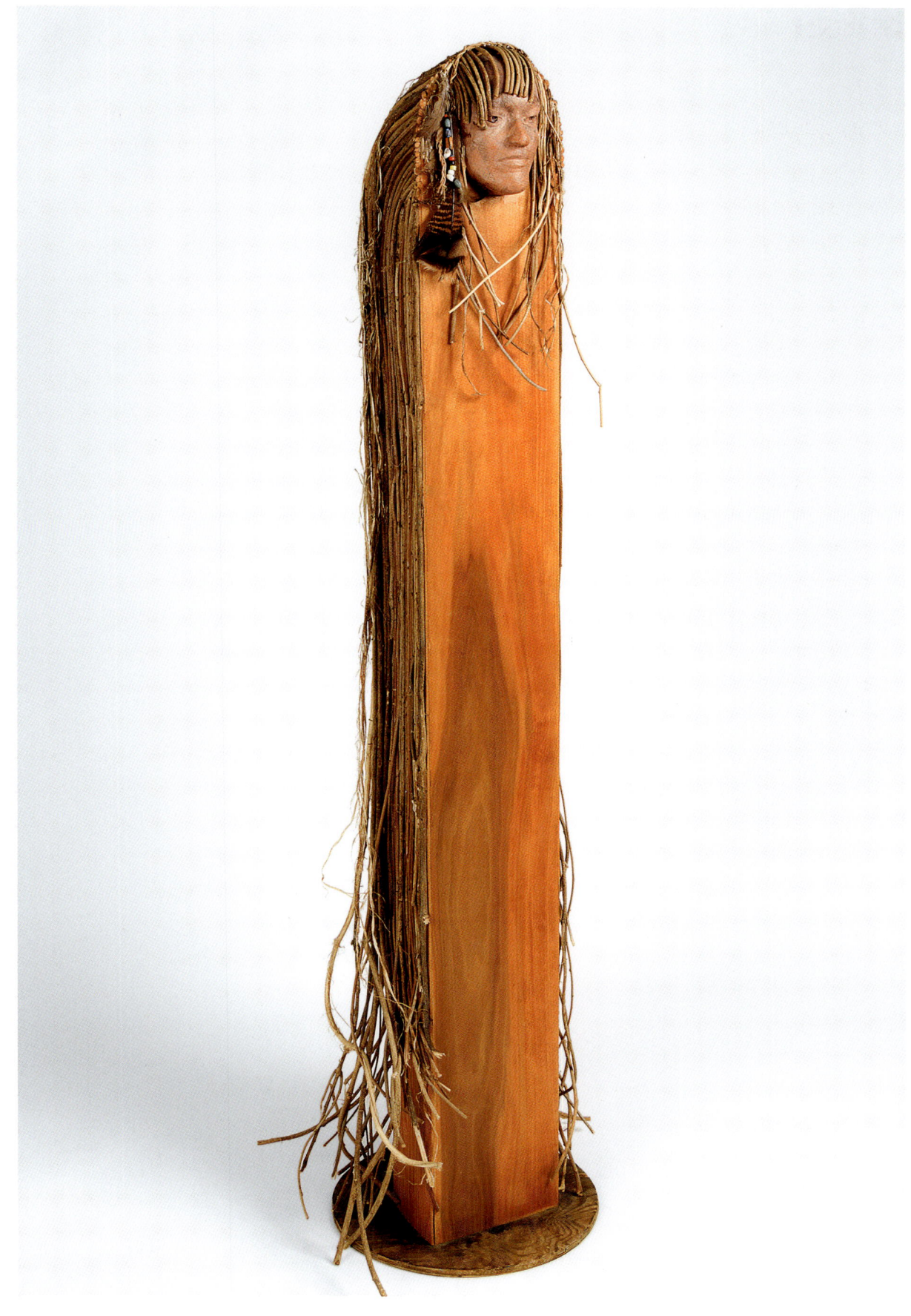

Wendy Red Star

Apsáalooke

I have a deep connection with the land of my ancestors on the Crow Indian reservation, the homeland of my people, Apsáalooke. Located in south central Montana and encompassing almost two-and-a-half-million acres, the Crow reservation includes three mountain ranges, two rivers, numerous creeks, grazing, and farm lands. . . . This is my childhood home, the backdrop of my inspiration, where, of necessity, I spent hours on its roads driving to school or work or social visits. I still smell the smoke of the sweat lodges in the evenings, hear the drums of a sun dance half a mile away, see rows of jeans hanging out to dry on a wire fence, and recall slowing my horse through town to check out who was playing basketball along the curb. . . .

My childhood memories spent growing up on the Crow reservation are a constant source of creative inspiration and what draw me back during the summer months. I doubt I would be an artist without this deep and ongoing connection to my people.

The (HUD), 2010, two-color lithograph with archival pigment ink photographs on Rives BFK white paper, 76.2 × 56.8 cm (30 × 22 ⅜ in.)

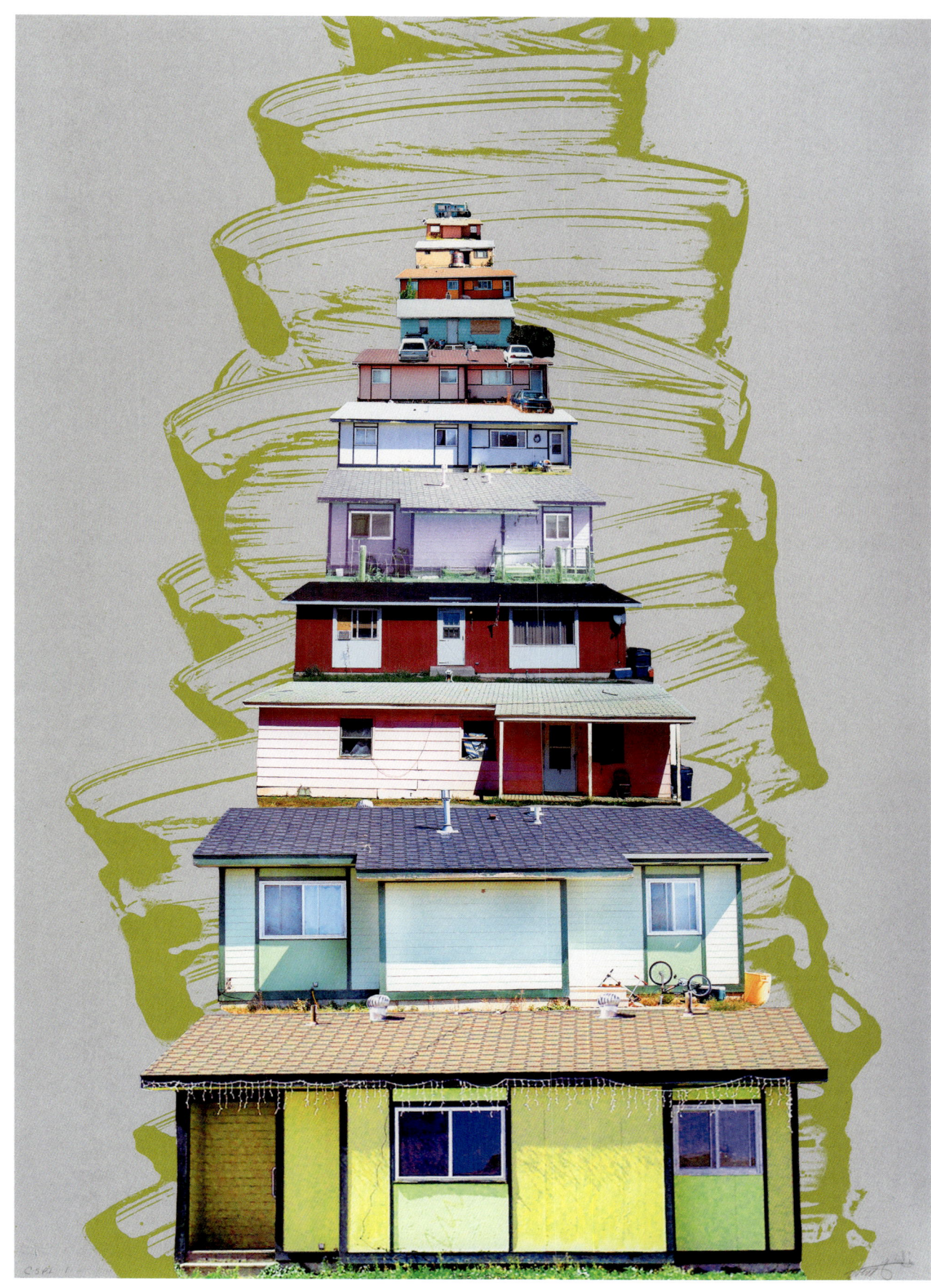

Eric-Paul Riege

Diné

For me, *hózhó* lives in the continuation of the Indigenous weaving and jewelry-making traditions that I inherited within my own family history, particularly from my maternal ancestors. Often displaying these intricate objects as suspended looms and activating them through video and performance, I use space, sound, and gravity like any other material that I manipulate by hand. What results are sensorial installations built in homage to cosmology, craft, and inherited knowledge, where the spiritual and physical realms of memory are bridged as one.

jaatłoh4Ye'iitsoh [3–4], 2020, mixed fiber installation, each 335.3 × 45.7 × 15.2 cm (132 × 18 × 6 in.)

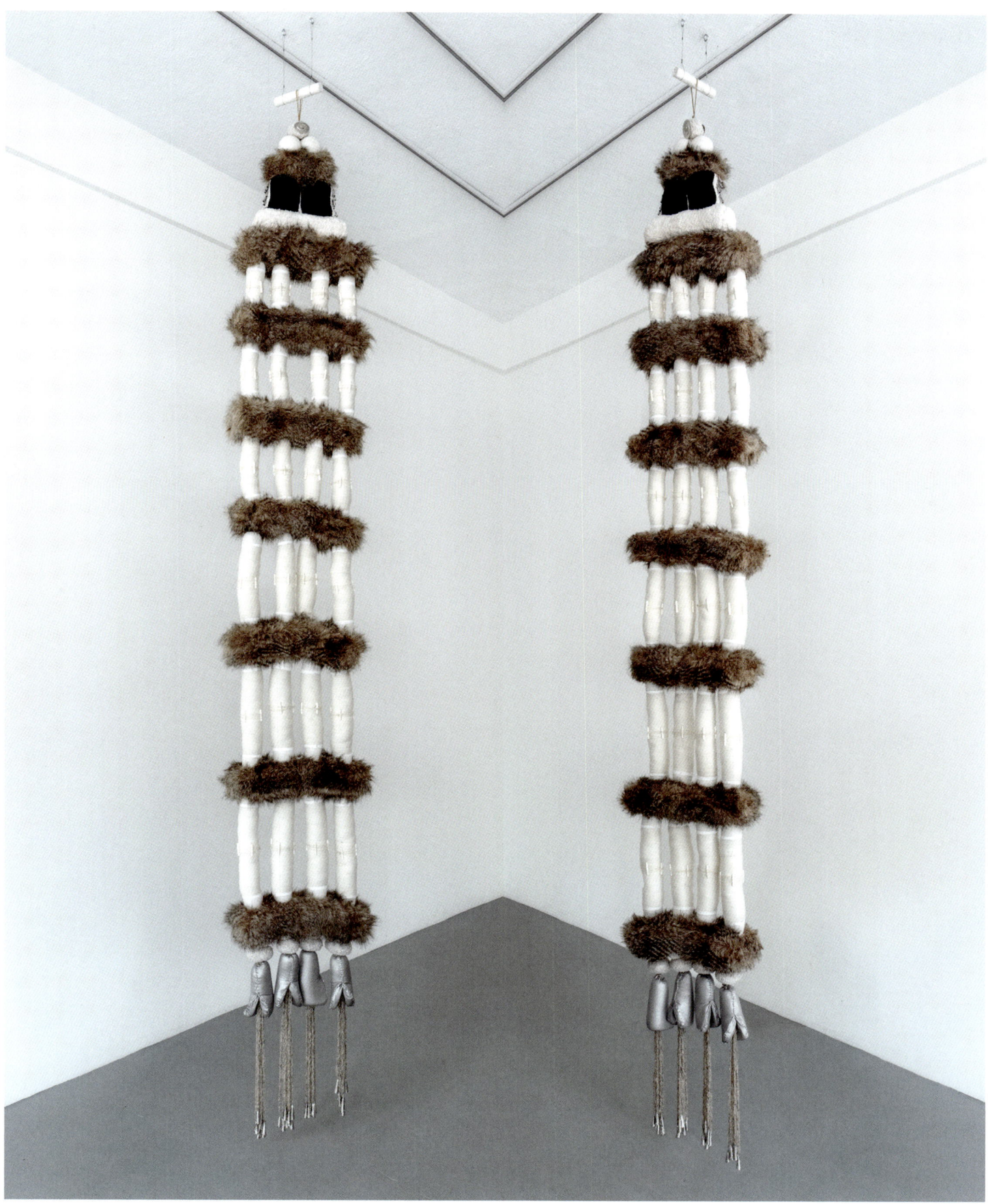

Cara Romero

Chemehuevi

As an Indigenous person, it is essential that I evoke how our relationship to Native American lands differs from that of settler-colonial peoples. We do not see ourselves as socially separate from our ancestral regions. Instead, our creation emerges from these landscapes, and we are bound and committed to each other. We are inseparable from the landscape, and our ancestors are in the landscapes with us. *Indian Canyon* shows a young Chemehuevi as a time-traveling apparition in a sacred landscape of Southern California. The image visualizes how our spirit beings are in the landscape protecting, experiencing, and existing all around us.

Indian Canyon, 2019, archival pigment print, 38.1 × 121.9 cm (15 × 48 in.)

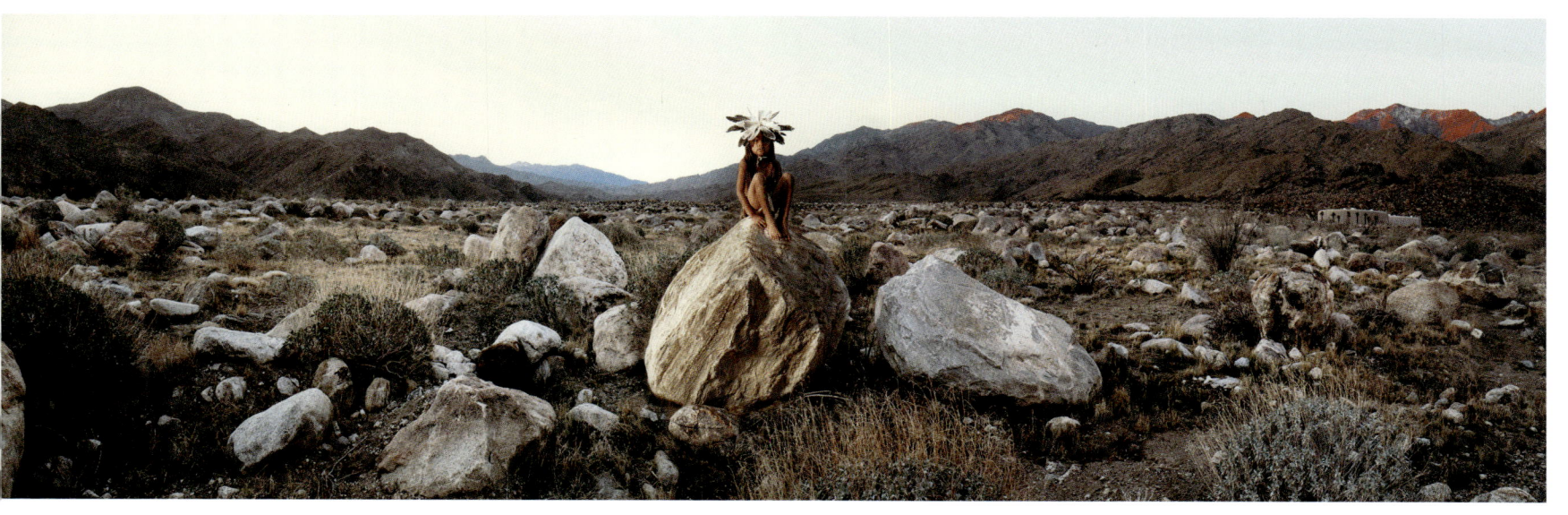

Diego Romero

Pueblo of Cochiti

From early childhood, I can remember being enamored by the books, stories, and illustrations of *The Iliad* and *The Odyssey*, Greek and Roman mythology, Hector and Achilles engaged in battle beneath the gates of Troy. My father told me elaborate stories of battles from ancient cultures, Greek to Cochiti, from Hector to Coyote, and more from his own lived experiences in the Marine Corps in Korea. These moments instilled a lifelong love of storytelling. I can see the cross-cultural similarities in epic storytelling between the oral traditions of our Pueblo culture and those of the epic poems of Homer.

As an artist, I have always viewed the landscape as a mile marker in time. In this print, the mother and daughter engage in the daily affairs of their lives but in the shadows of big industries. Those industries affect both mother and child through environmental racism and their dominance over the land.

Girl in the Anthropocene, 2017, lithograph (printer's proof), 48.3 × 62.2 cm (19 × 24 ½ in.)

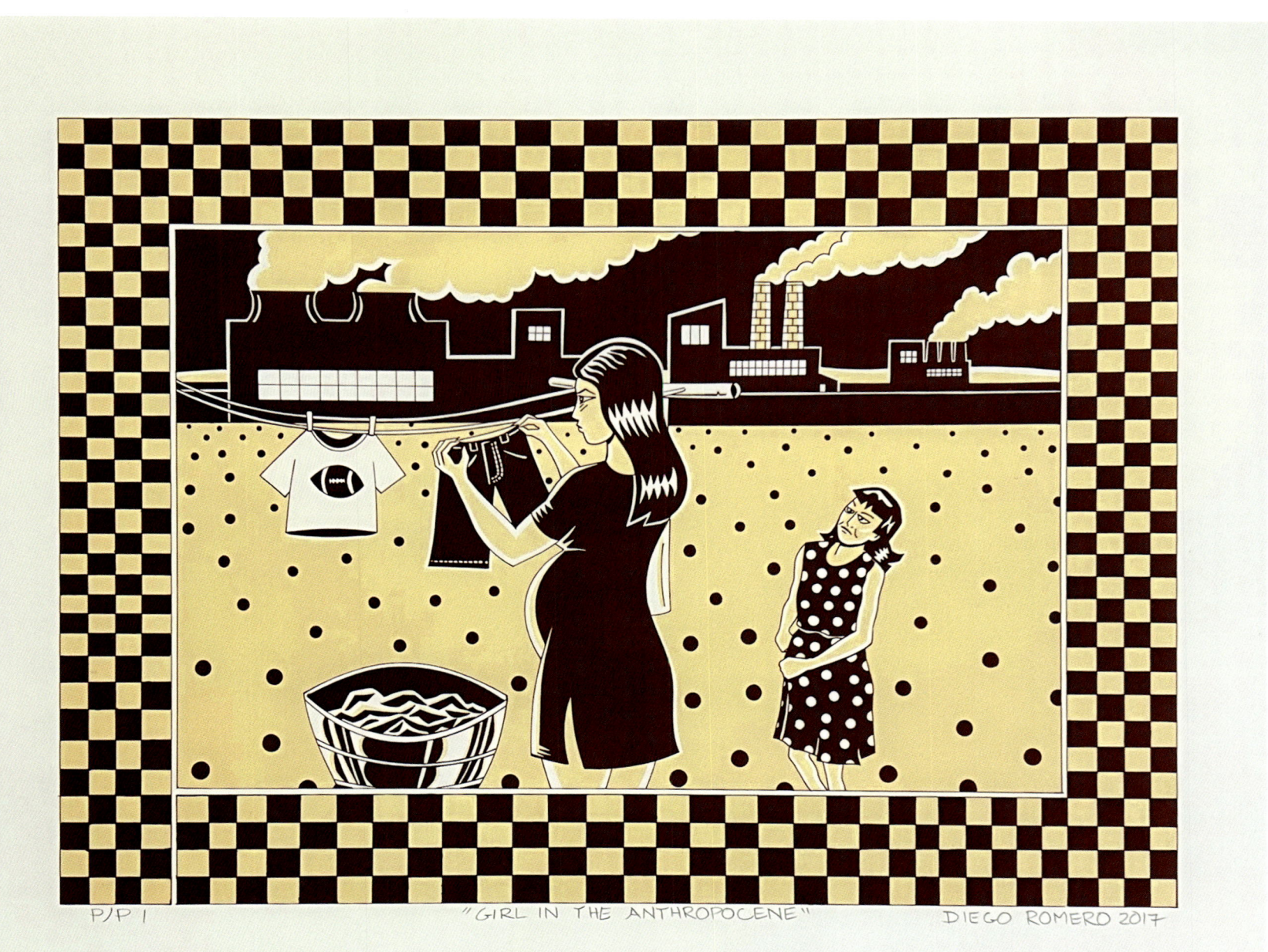

P/P 1   "GIRL IN THE ANTHROPOCENE"   DIEGO ROMERO 2017

Rose B. Simpson

Pueblo of Santa Clara, New Mexico

My life-work is an investigation into what aesthetic tools I can create to heal the damages I have experienced as a human being of our postcolonial (postapocalyptic) era — objectification, stereotyping, and the disempowering detachment of our creative selves through the ease of modern technology. These tools are figurative and interactive sculptures that function in the psychological, emotional, social, cultural, spiritual, intellectual, and physical realms. They exist to witness, and they erode our objectifications. They remind us of the animate truth in all things — from our family of natural world beings to the consciousness in material. They reflect the movement of generations, the very verb of existence itself. The intention of these tools is to cure, therefore, my hope is that they become hard-working utilitarian concepts.

Tonantzin, 2021, ceramic and steel, leather, brass (two views), 119.4 × 45.7 × 34.3 cm (47 × 18 × 13 ½ in.)

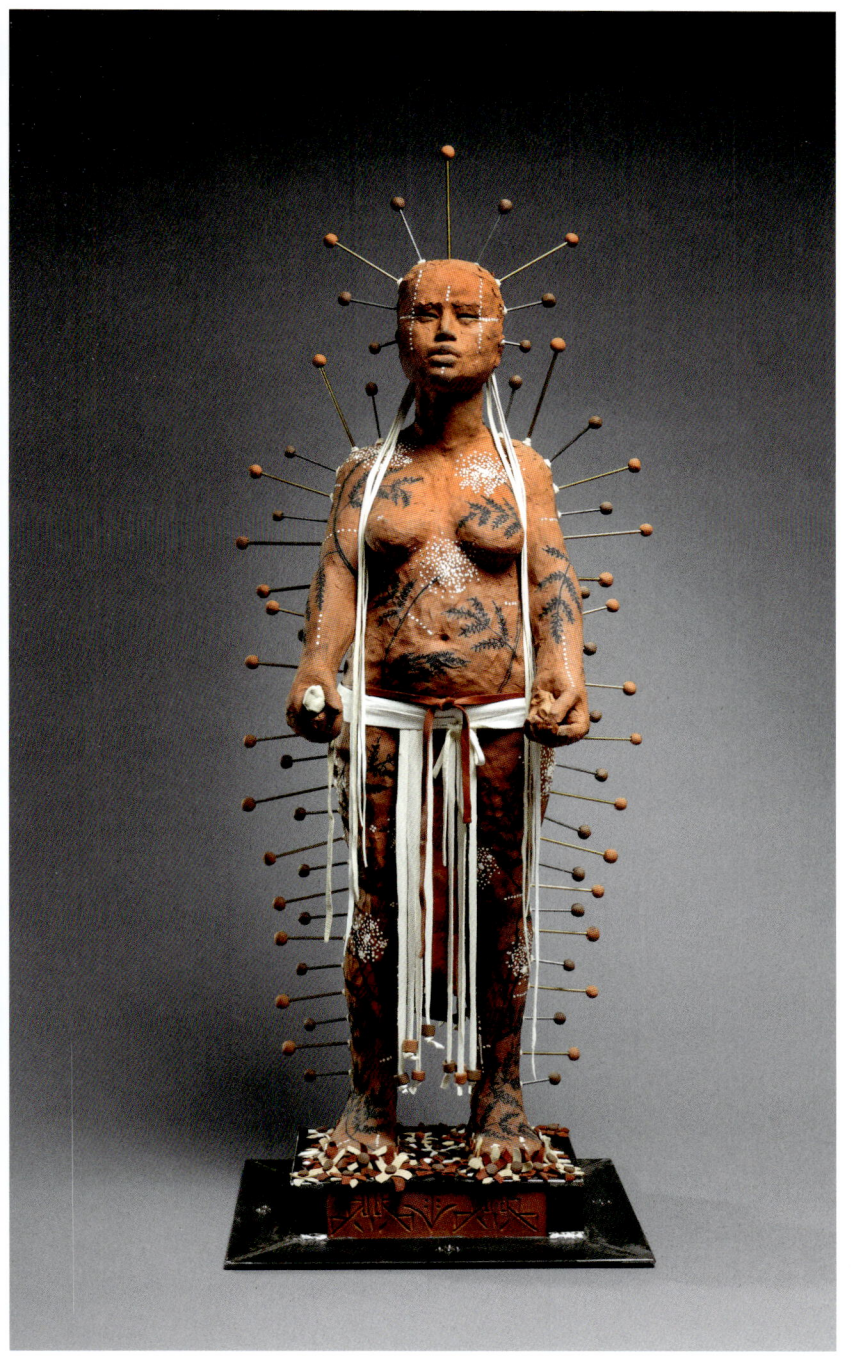
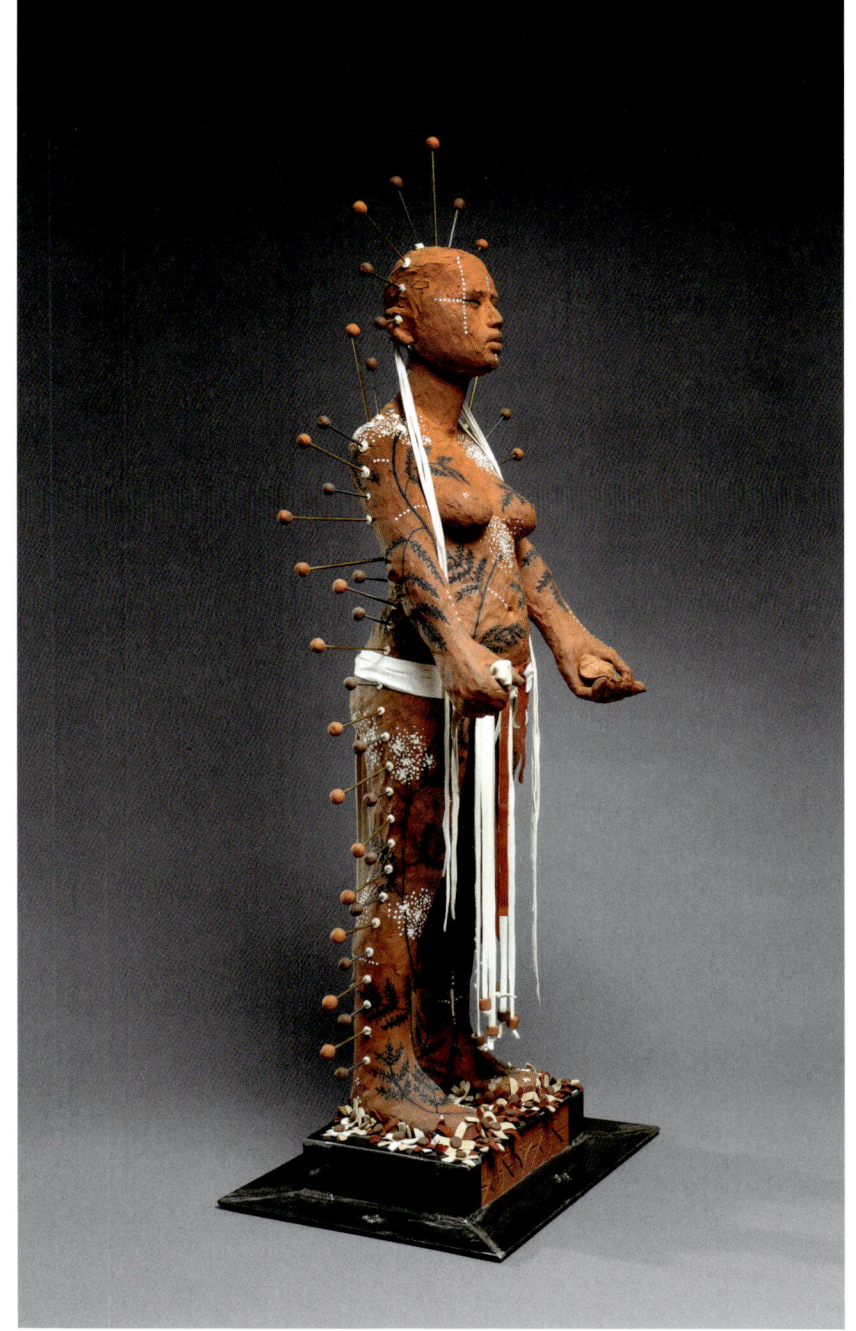

Preston Singletary

Tlingit

I began working with glass in 1982. It was only when I began to experiment with using designs from my Tlingit cultural heritage that my work began to take on a new purpose and direction.

I've come to see that glass brings another dimension to Indigenous art. The artistic perspective of Indigenous people reflects a unique and vital visual language that has connections to the ancient codes and symbols of the land.

My work with glass transforms the notion that Native artists are only best when traditional materials are used. It has helped advocate on behalf of all Indigenous people, affirming that we are still here. We are declaring who we are through our art in connection to our culture.

Raven Steals the Sun, 2017, blown and sand-carved glass, 51.4 × 22.9 × 17.8 cm (20 ¼ × 9 × 7 in.)

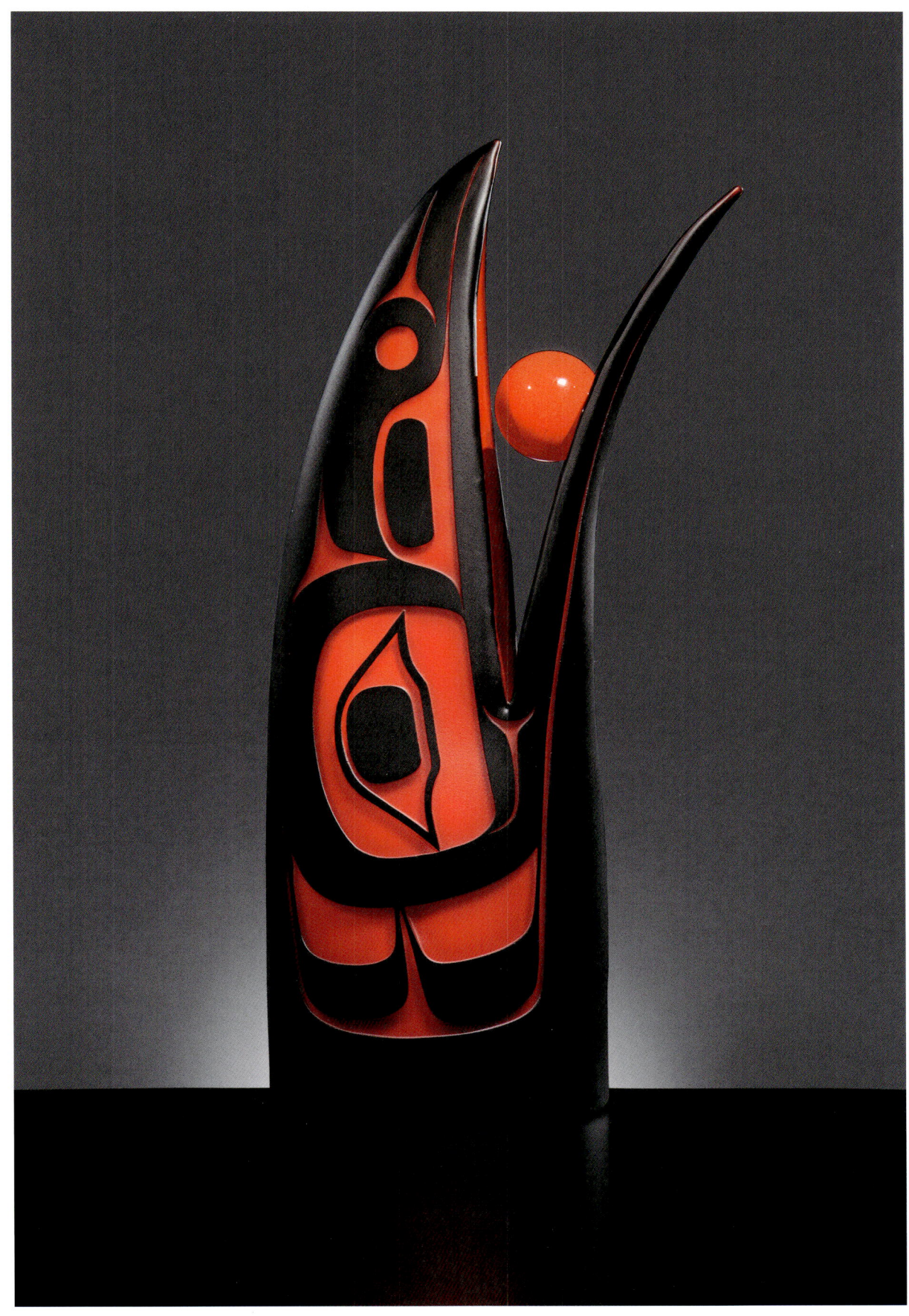

Gail Tremblay

Onondaga/Mi'kmaq descent

This basket is made from sections cut from the 1967 ethnographic film *At the Autumn River Camp, Part 2*. The late Gail Tremblay wove the 16mm footage, white-and-blue film leader, mylar braid, and yarn to create a basket in the form of the ash splint and sweetgrass baskets that her people make.

The film, made by Euro-American settlers who took Indigenous lands, did not give viewers an accurate picture of Netsilik Inuit life in the late 1960s. The filmmakers devised images that give the impression Indigenous people don't change.

Most people today do not understand how Indigenous people protect the circle of things that make life on this planet possible. Instead, many settlers create technologies that endanger plants, animals, and human cultures. We all need to work together to stop poisoning the earth. We must reinvent ways to live in harmony with the land.

After Global Warming, How Long Will it Take to Re-Invent a World Where Everything People Invented Depended on Snow, Frozen Food, Ice, and Digging Through it for Cold Water, 2018, 16mm film and film leader (blue and white), silver metallic braid, silver yarn, 26 × 16.5 × 16.5 cm (10 ¼ × 6 ½ × 6 ½ in.)

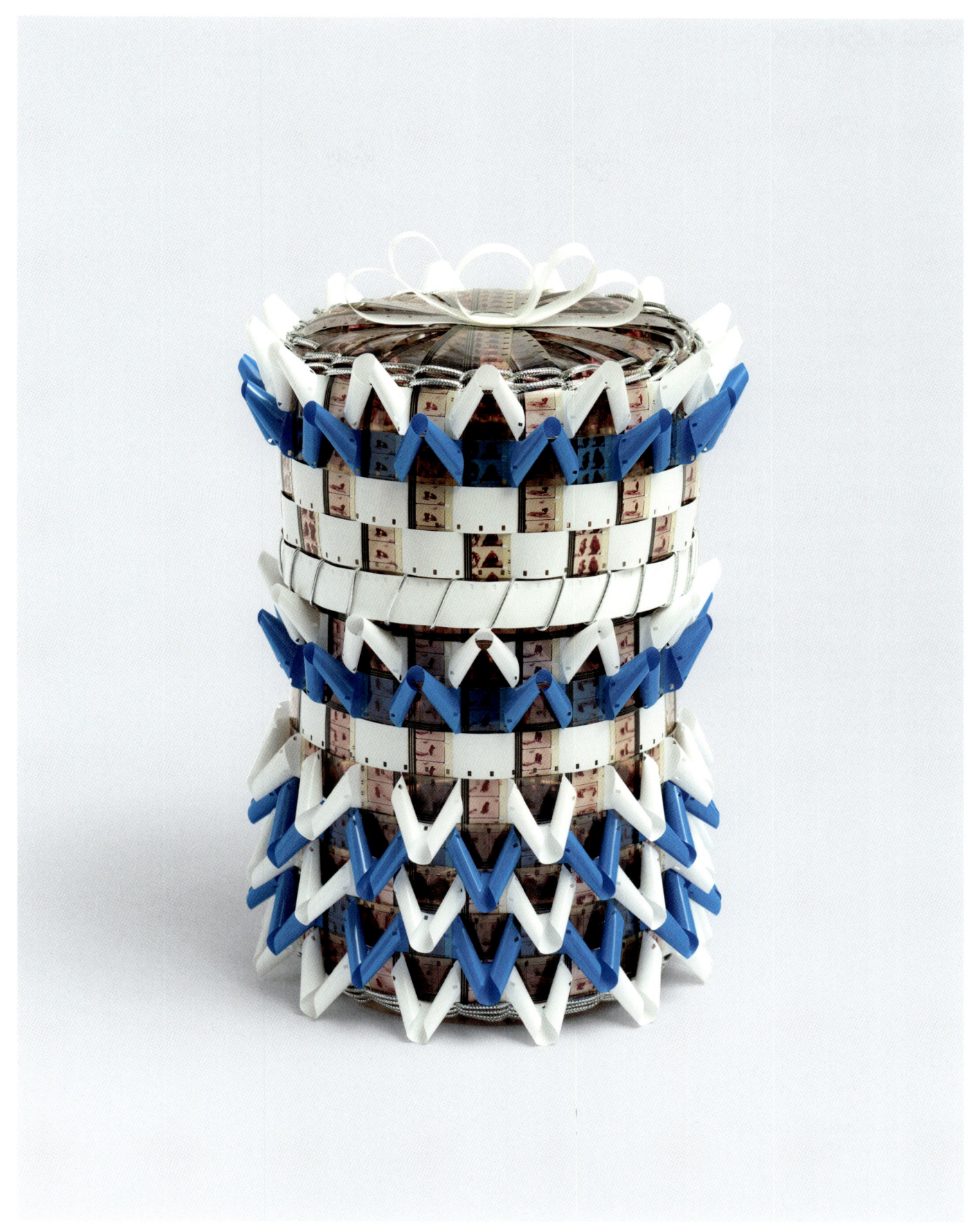

Kay WalkingStick

Cherokee Nation of Oklahoma/
European descent

For decades landscape has been a compelling
subject to me. Some of my paintings prior
to graduate school were about the Hudson
River. Later my abstractions of the 1970s and
early 1980s were seen by many viewers as
geological depictions of our land. The diptychs
of the late 1980s and 1990s were landscape
images combined with psychological-related
abstractions. Today I make large depictions of
the grand American landscape overlaid with
Native American patterns that represent the
heart-owners, the original inhabitants of the
land. I only paint places I have actually seen
and drawn. These paintings are meant to honor
those original inhabitants, many of whom are
still in residence, and to remind us that we all
live in Indian Territory. We all live on ecologically
endangered land. Our beautiful America, our
beloved land, requires our care.

Ute's Homelands, 2022, oil on panel in two parts,
76.2 × 152.4 × 5.1 cm (30 × 60 × 2 in.)

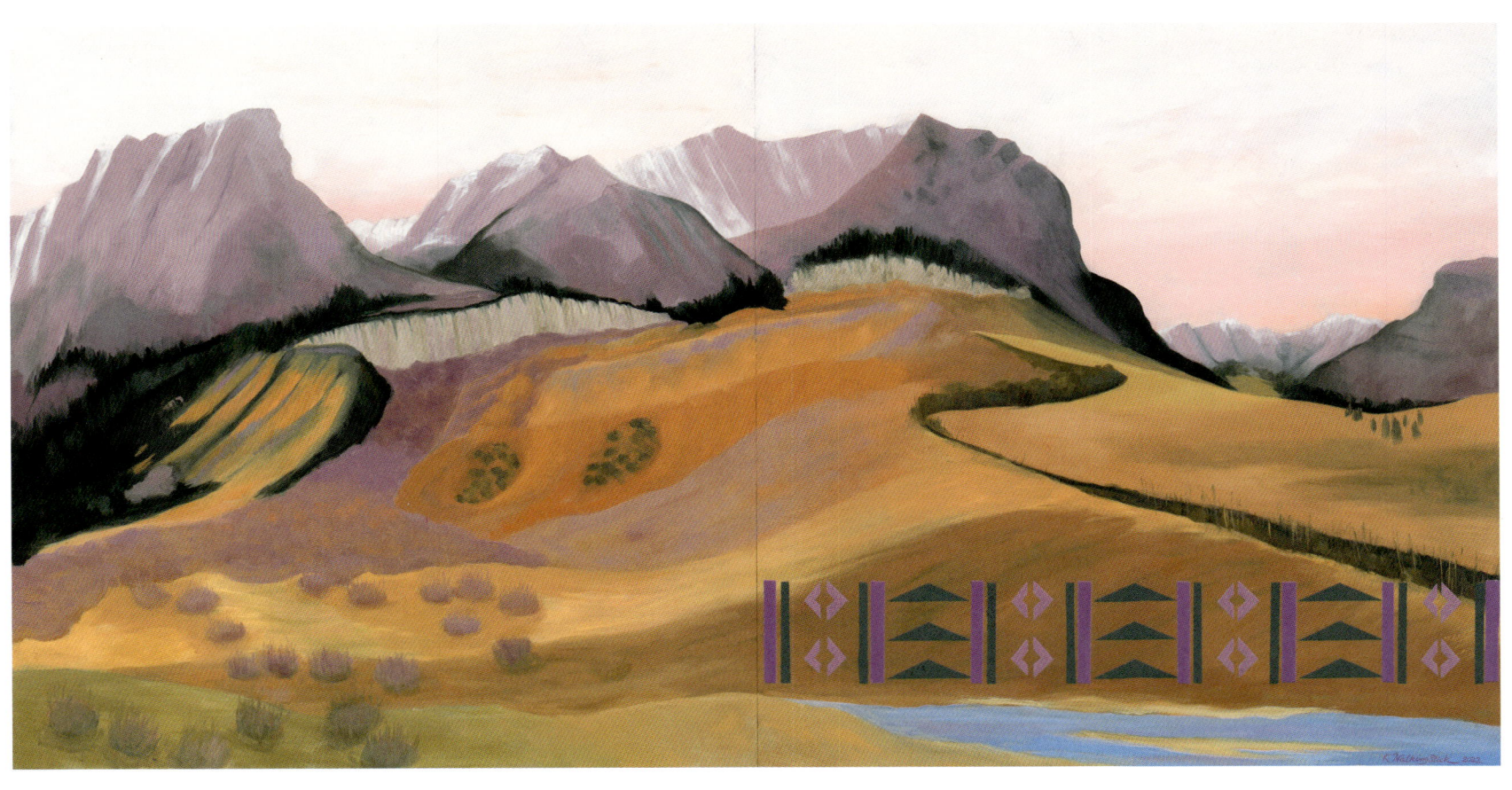

Star WallowingBull

Ojibwe/Arapaho

While I have been fascinated by the geometry and appendages of machines and robots since I was a child, two indelible influences on my art are my family and the earth. I turn to nature in all seasons to get inspired and to find peace and a positive perspective on life. Nature in turn connects me to my family and my history. I often walk along the Red River on both the Minnesota and North Dakota sides. My mother, who is Arapaho and Lakota, lived on the Wind River Reservation near the Grand Tetons in Wyoming. With *Modern Day Indian*, I was thinking about the pollution of our earth and the federal government's practice of dumping nuclear waste on tribal lands, or what I think of as "radioactive reservations."

Modern Day Indian, 2004, lithograph crayon and colored pencil on paper, 56.5 × 76.2 cm (22 ¼ × 30 in.)

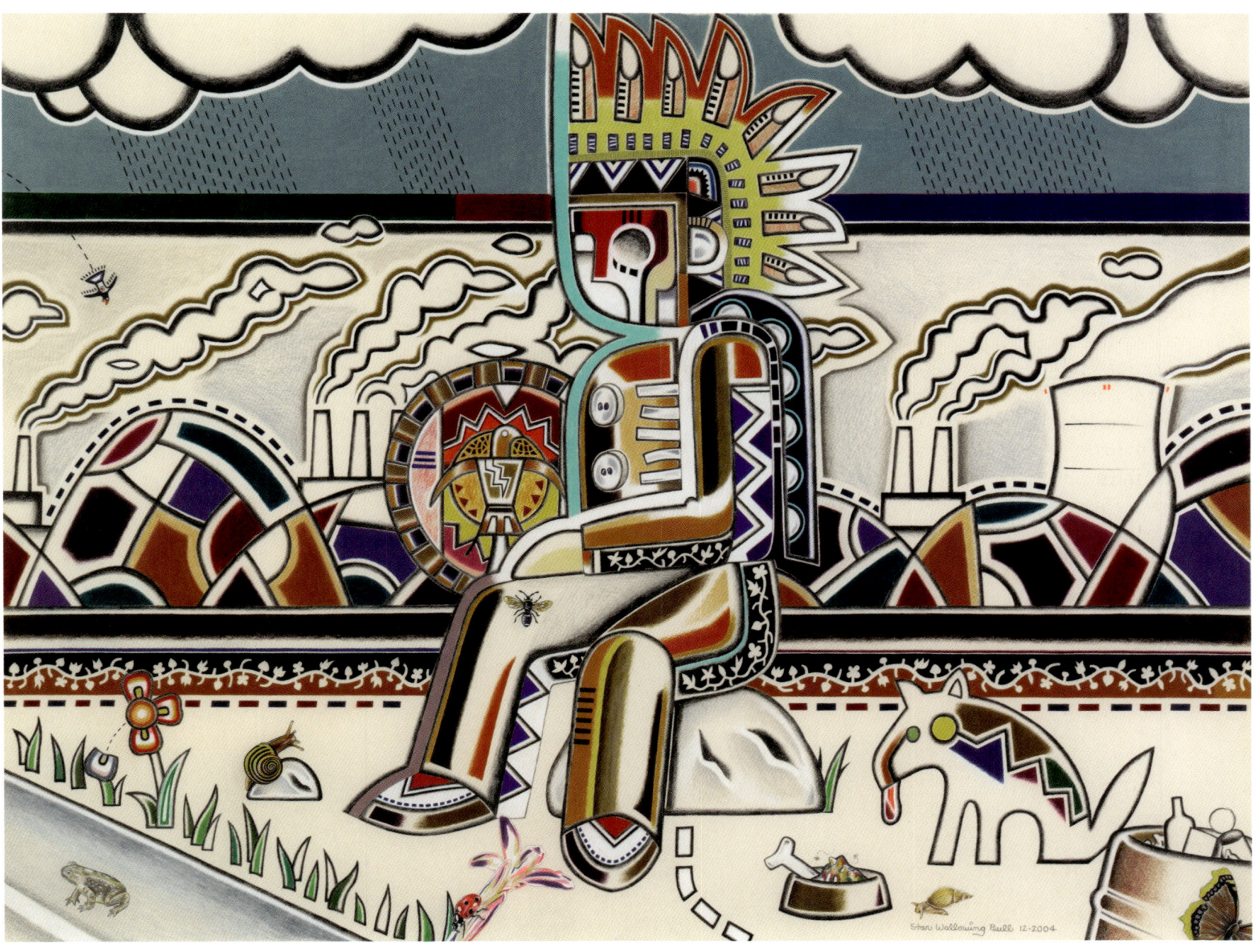

Marie Watt

Seneca Nation of Indians/
European descent

In the cosmology of my Seneca and Hodinöhsö:ni'
ancestors, animals are our relatives and first
teachers, and our relatedness to the natural
world extends to land, water, and sky. I explore
the ongoing question, What would the world
look like if we considered ourselves companion
species? This way of thinking informs all my
work, including *Antipodes*, which recognizes our
relationship to the sky.

The word *skywalker* acknowledges the
Hodinöhsö:ni' ironworkers, known as "skywalkers,"
who helped to build New York City's skyscrapers
in the early to mid-20th century. *Antipodes* is
defined as "the exact opposite or contrary,"
yet it is a mistake to think of opposites as merely
being oppositional. In this work, I explore the
possibilities that arise in the dynamic spaces
between opposites, on both a physical and a
metaphysical level.

Antipodes, 2020, vintage Italian beads, industrial felt,
and thread, top piece (Skywalker) 137.2 × 160.7 cm
(54 × 63 ¼ in.), bottom piece (Skyscraper) 135.9 ×
151.1 cm (53 ½ × 59 ½ in.)

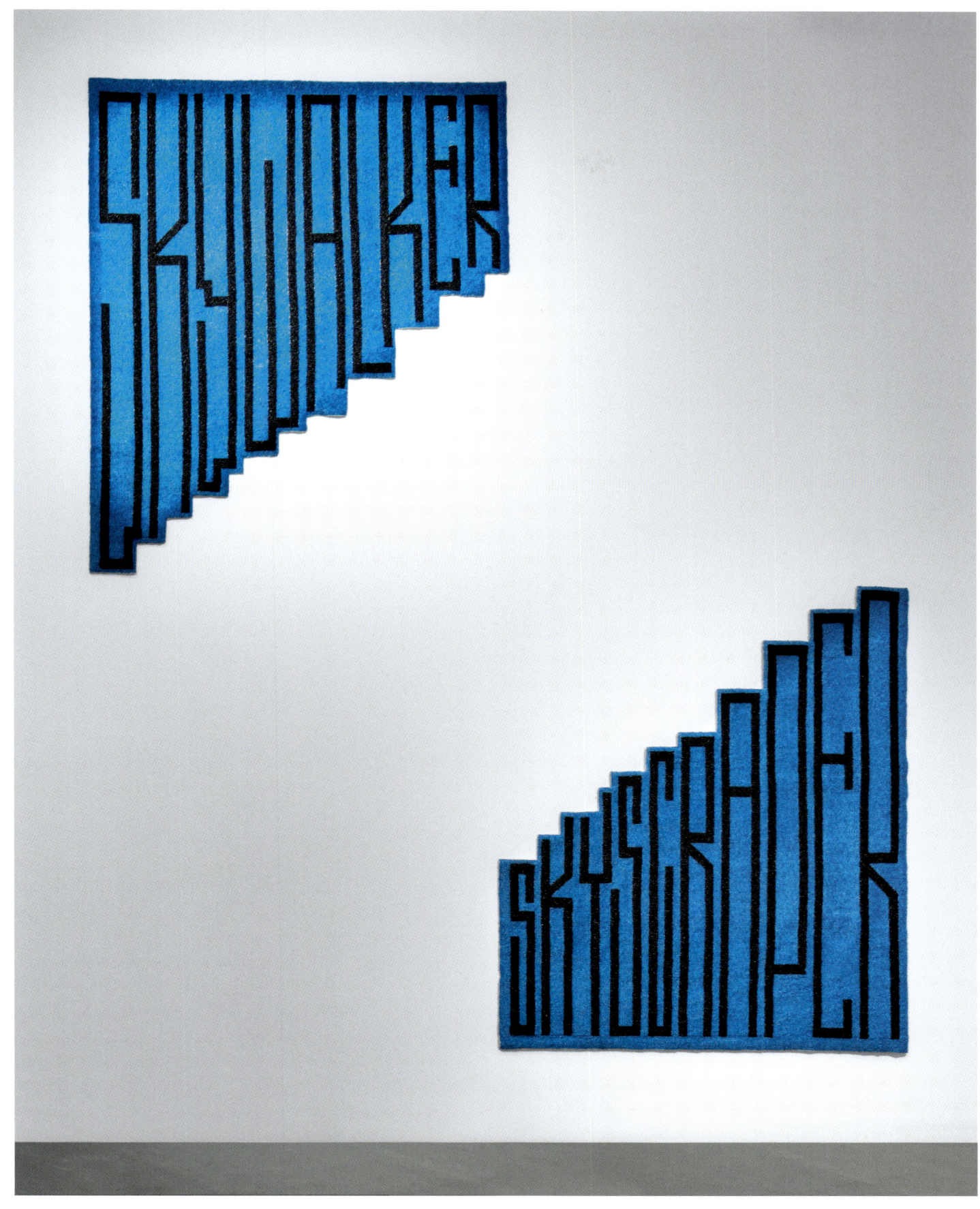

Emmi Whitehorse

Diné

When I began making art, I saw a lot of works by men artists who made large paintings of Indians in full regalia and on horseback. I knew I didn't look like that, and I thought that was already a well-used image to cover all Natives everywhere.

I looked to myself and thought, What is it that I know best?

Landscape was what I knew best. My backyard. I've observed it, painted it, and it provides an endless source of material for me.

Fog Bank, 2020, mixed media on paper on canvas, 129.5 × 198.1 cm (51 × 78 in.)

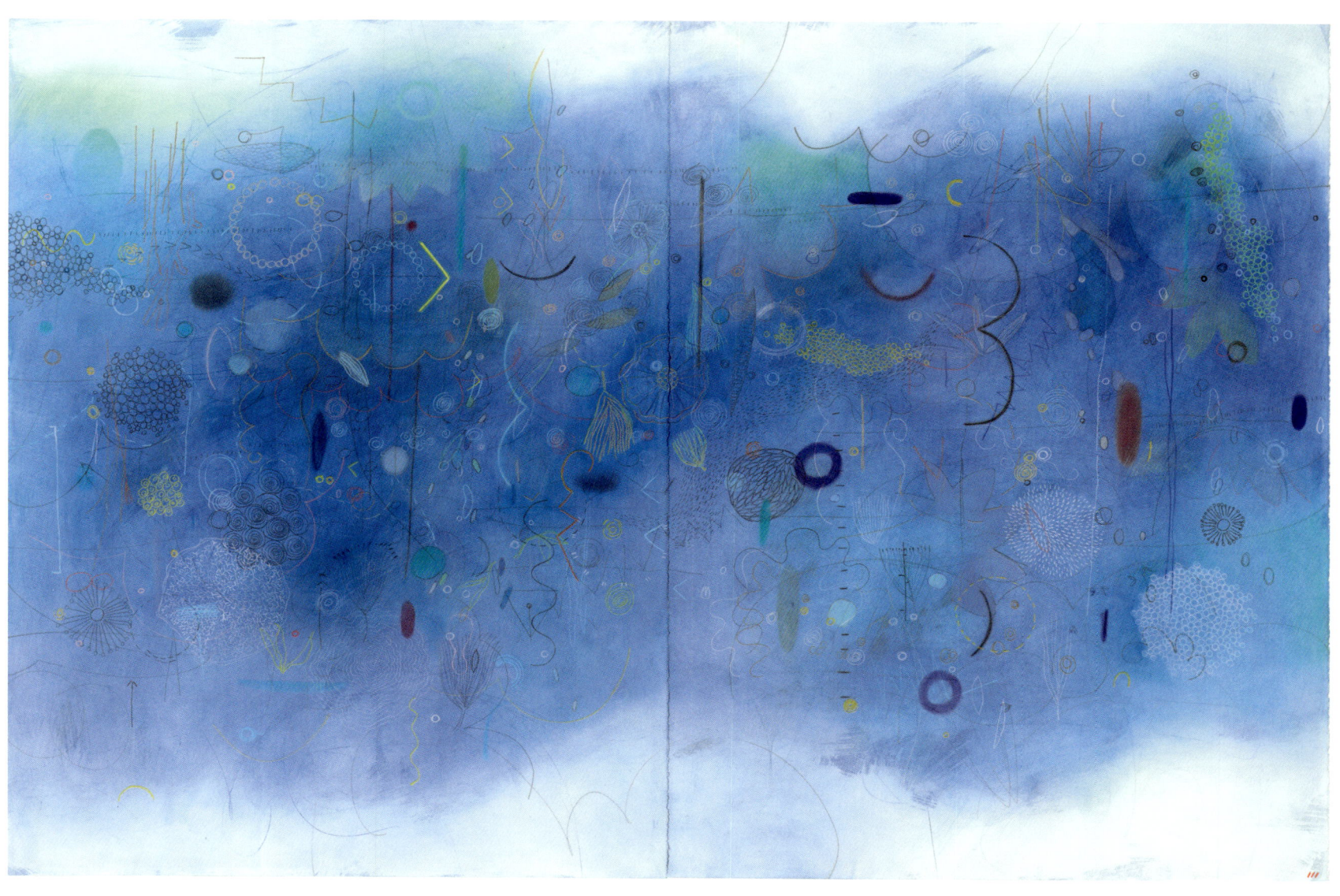

Will Wilson

Diné

Since 2004, I have been creating a series of artworks titled *Auto-Immune Response*, which takes as its subject the quixotic relationship between a postapocalyptic Diné (Navajo) man and the devastatingly beautiful but toxic environment he inhabits. The series is an allegorical investigation of the extraordinarily rapid transformation of Indigenous lifeways, the dis-ease it has caused, and strategies of response that enable cultural survival.

Auto-Immune Response no. 2, 2004, archival pigment print (digital carbon) on archival paper, image 43.8 × 68.6 cm (17 ¼ × 27 in.), sheet 55.9 × 76.2 cm (22 × 30 in.)

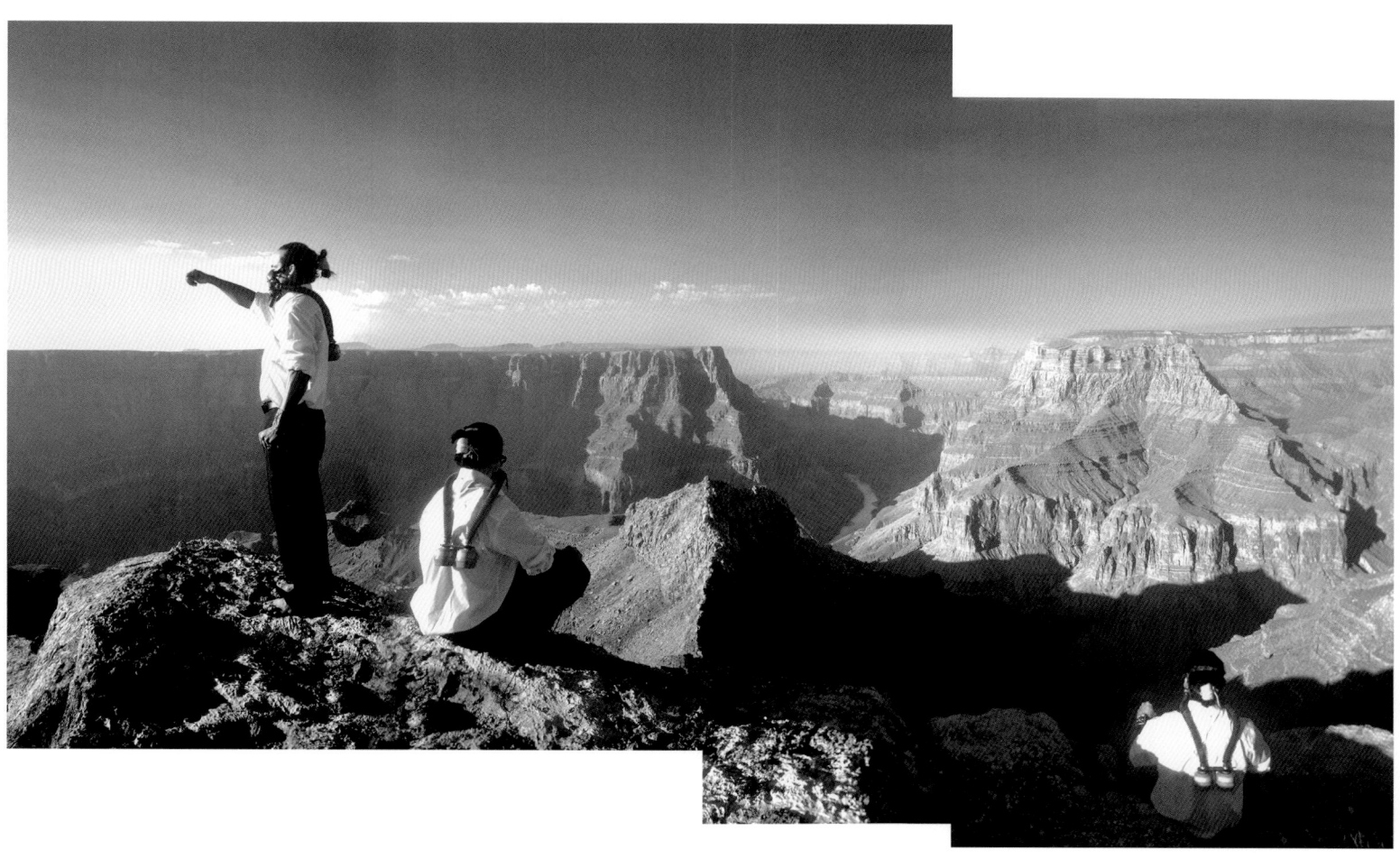

Steven Yazzie

Diné/Pueblo of Laguna, New
Mexico/European descent

As a multidisciplinary artist, I work in painting,
installation, video/film, and community
collaborations. My work explores the
complexities of the post-settler colonial
Indigenous experience as it relates to personal
identity and community relationships. Our
essential connection to the land is the source
of life, stories, conflict, and healing.

Orchestrating a Blooming Desert, 2003, oil on
canvas, 121.9 × 152.4 cm (48 × 60 in.)

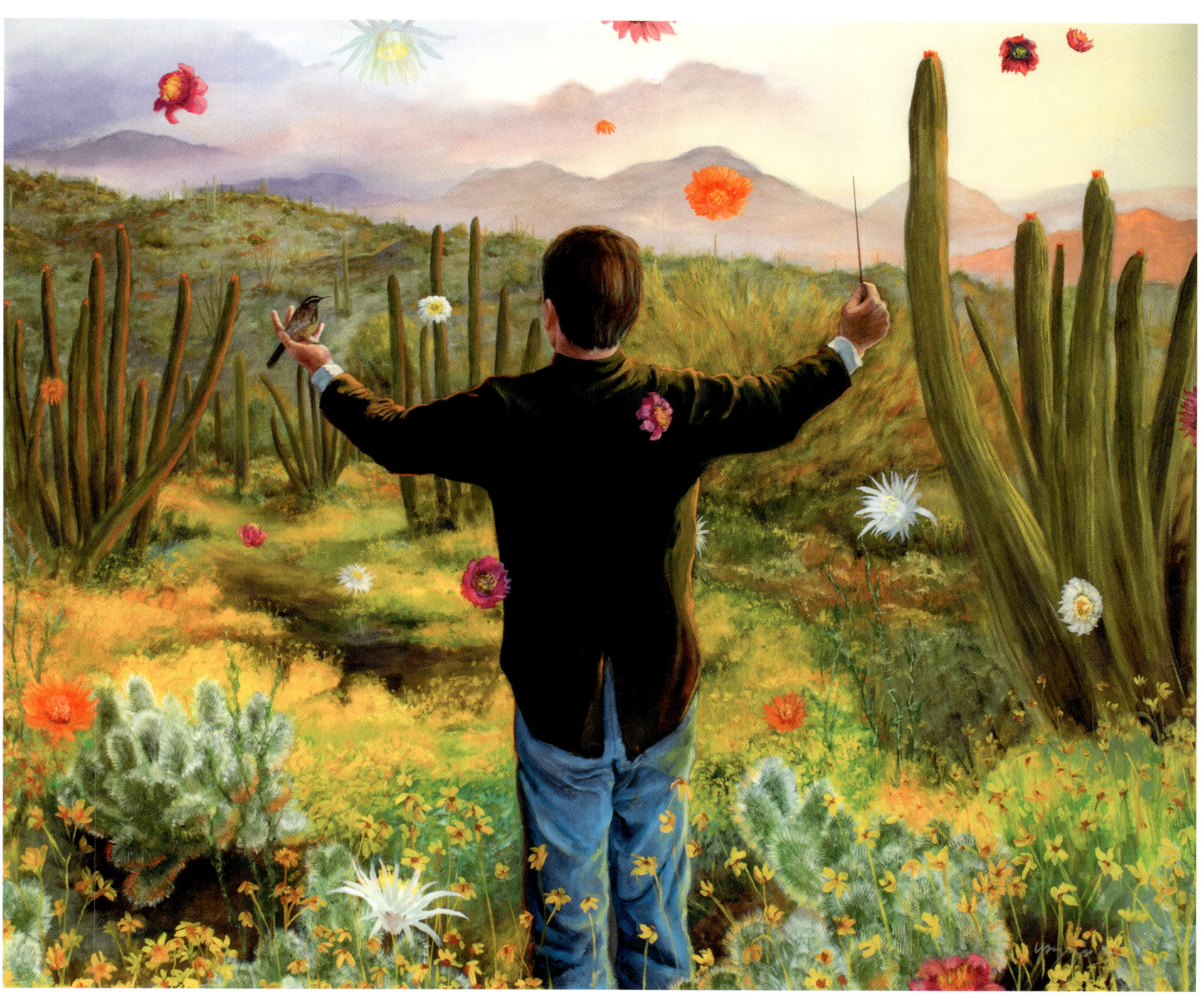

ARTIST BIOGRAPHIES

Each artist generously provided a photograph of a landscape with personal significance. Sites range from ancestral homelands in North Dakota, Oregon, and Arizona to towering mountains in Alaska and windswept lands in Oklahoma, and on to green valleys and lush forests in New York and North Carolina. Together, these photos signify how the land remains a vital part of Native American life and art today.

George Alexander
Muscogee

BORN 1990 IN MASON, OK
LIVES AND WORKS IN SANTA FE, NM

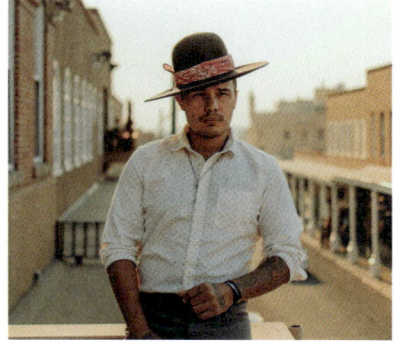

George Alexander's first venture out West was to attend the Institute of American Indian Arts in Santa Fe. There, he met his mentor, Tony Abeyta (Diné), who gave him the name Ofuskie. Alexander's artwork explores themes of global identity and cultural evolution. Through metaphor and surrealist figures, he creates a vision for humanity that is not constricted by social complexes.

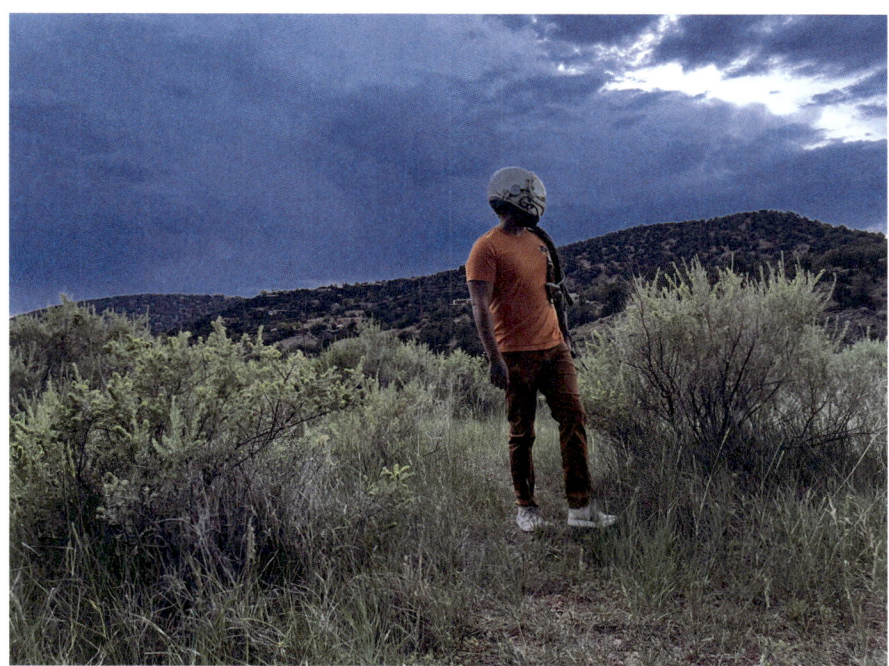

Keri Ataumbi
Kiowa

BORN 1971 IN LANDER, WY
LIVES AND WORKS NEAR SANTA FE, NM

Raised on the Wind River Reservation in Wyoming, Keri Ataumbi was exposed to both traditional Native American aesthetics and contemporary art theory and practice from an early age. She attended the Rhode Island School of Design before moving to Santa Fe in 1990. There, she attended the Institute of American Indian Arts and eventually received a BFA in painting with a minor in art history from the College of Santa Fe.

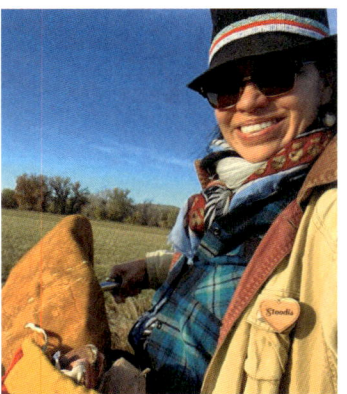

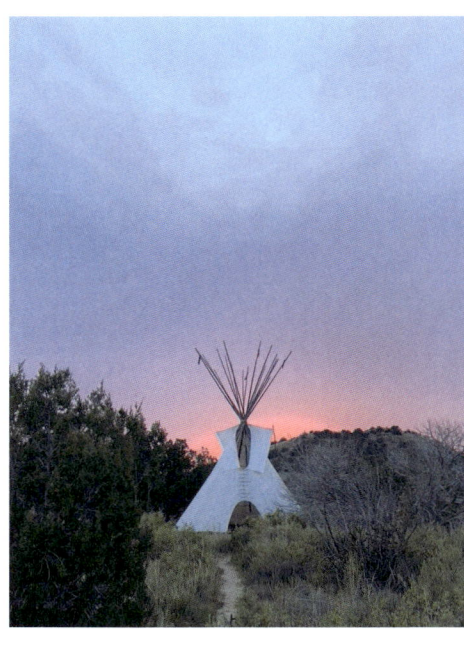

Natalie Ball
Modoc/Klamath

BORN 1980 IN PORTLAND, OR
LIVES AND WORKS IN CHILOQUIN, OR

Natalie Ball has earned three degrees, including an MFA in painting and printmaking at the Yale School of Art. She is the recipient of the United States Artists Fellowship (2023), Eiteljorg Contemporary Art Fellowship (2023), a Joan Mitchell Painters and Sculptors Grant (2020), and a Pollock-Krasner Foundation Grant (2019). Ball returned to her ancestral homelands in southern Oregon to raise her children and is now an elected official serving on the Tribal Council of the Klamath Tribes.

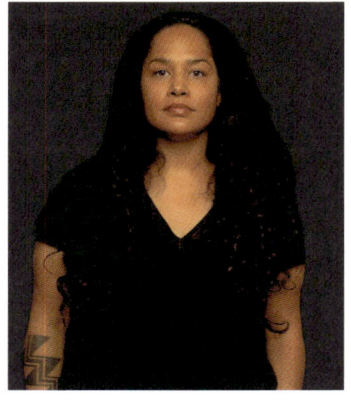

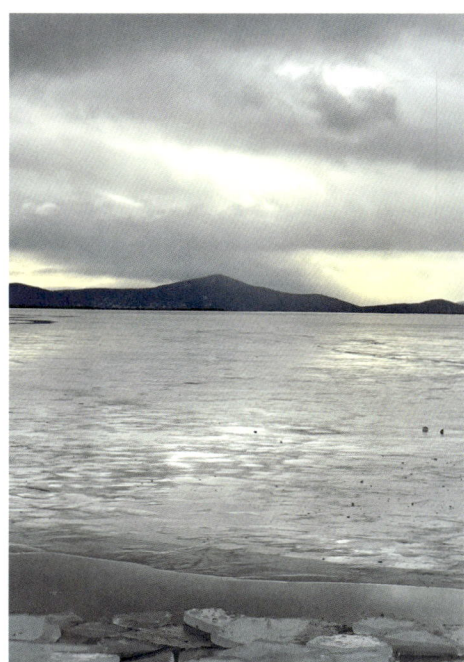

Marwin Begaye
Diné

BORN 1970 IN GANADO, AZ
LIVES AND WORKS IN NORMAN, OK

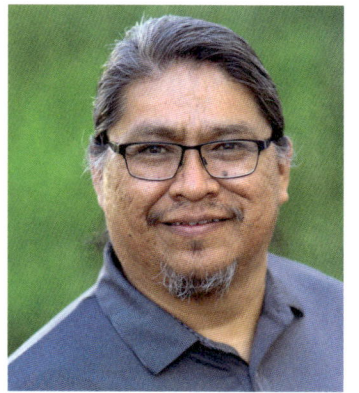

Marwin Begaye was educated at the Art Institute of Pittsburgh, the Institute of American Indian Arts in Santa Fe, and the University of Oklahoma in Norman. He is currently professor at the University of Oklahoma, where his research examines issues of cultural identity through the intersection of Indigenous American and popular cultures. He has received numerous awards for his work, which has been exhibited on five continents and is held in several national collections.

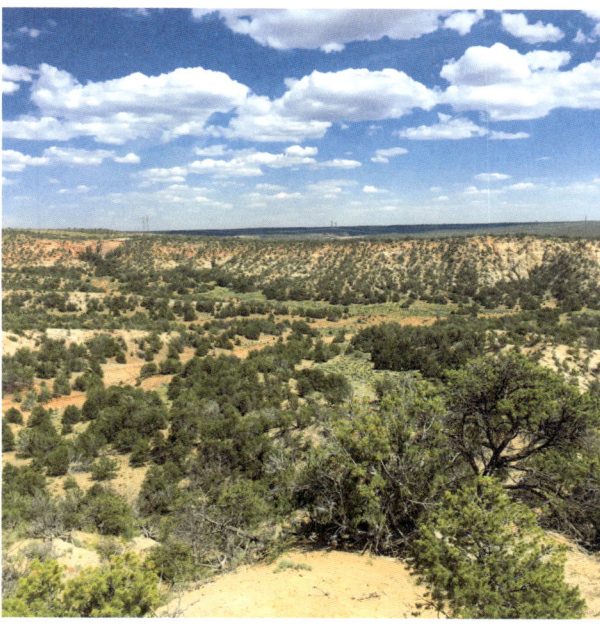

Frank Big Bear
Ojibwe, White Earth Nation

BORN 1953 IN DETROIT LAKES, MN
LIVES AND WORKS IN MINNEAPOLIS, MN

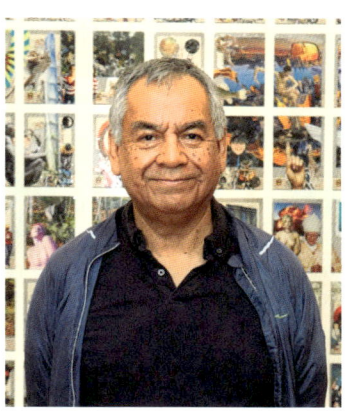

Drawing from a broad constellation of inspirations — from family and dreams to art history and Anishinaabe culture — Frank Big Bear is best known for his vibrant drawings and paintings. Support for his work includes the USA Knight Fellowship from United States Artists (2015), a National Artist Fellowship through the Native Arts and Cultures Foundation (2015), and the Bush Foundation's Enduring Vision Award (2008). His work is in the collections of the British Museum, the Denver Art Museum, the Minneapolis Institute of Art, and the Walker Art Center, among others.

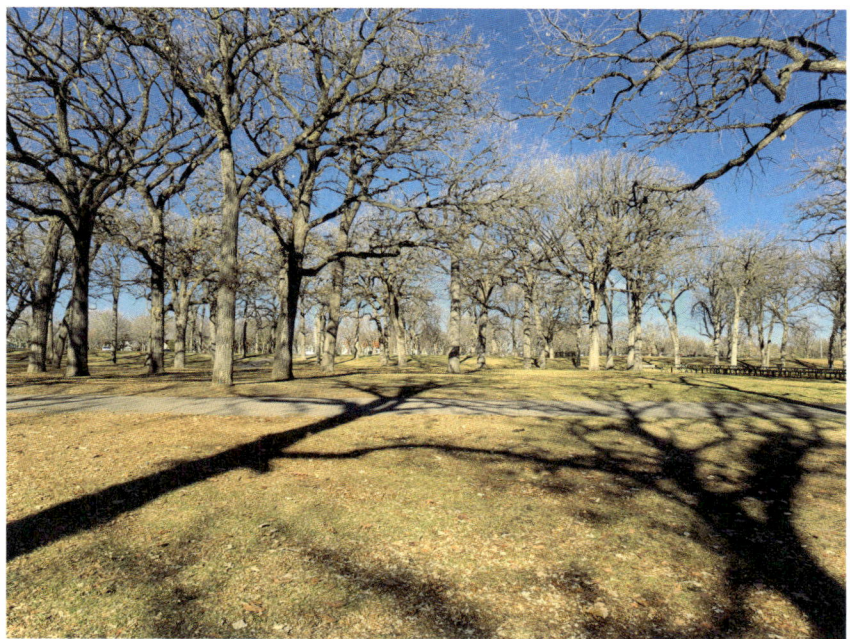

Julie Buffalohead
Ponca Tribe of Oklahoma

BORN 1972 IN MINNEAPOLIS, MN
LIVES AND WORKS IN ST. PAUL, MN

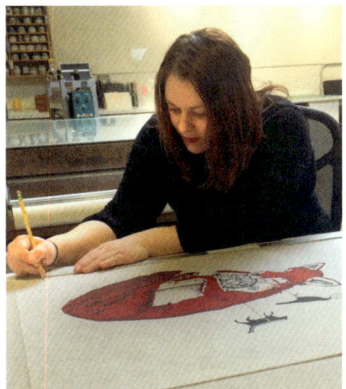

Julie Buffalohead received her BFA from the Minneapolis College of Art and Design in 1995 and her MFA from Cornell University in 2001. She has also received the John Simon Guggenheim Fellowship (2018) and held notable solo exhibitions at the Denver Art Museum (2018–2019), the Museum of Contemporary Native Arts in Santa Fe (2015), and the Smithsonian's National Museum of the American Indian (2012–2013). Buffalohead creates visual narratives told by animal characters that have personhood, agency, and individuality.

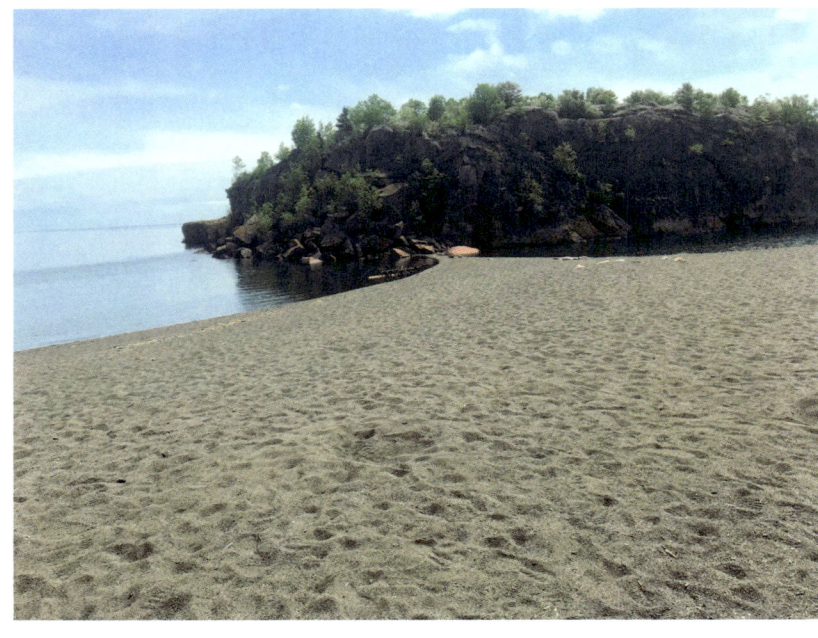

Andrea Carlson
Grand Portage Ojibwe/ European descent

BORN 1979 IN NEBRASKA
LIVES AND WORKS IN CHICAGO, IL

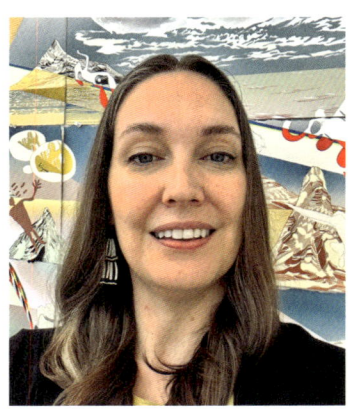

Andrea Carlson maintains a studio practice in northern Minnesota. She received a BA in art and American Indian studies from the University of Minnesota in 2003 and an MFA from the Minneapolis College of Art and Design in 2005. Carlson has also received numerous fellowships for her work, including a 2017 Joan Mitchell Painters and Sculptors Fellowship and a 2022 United States Artists Fellowship.

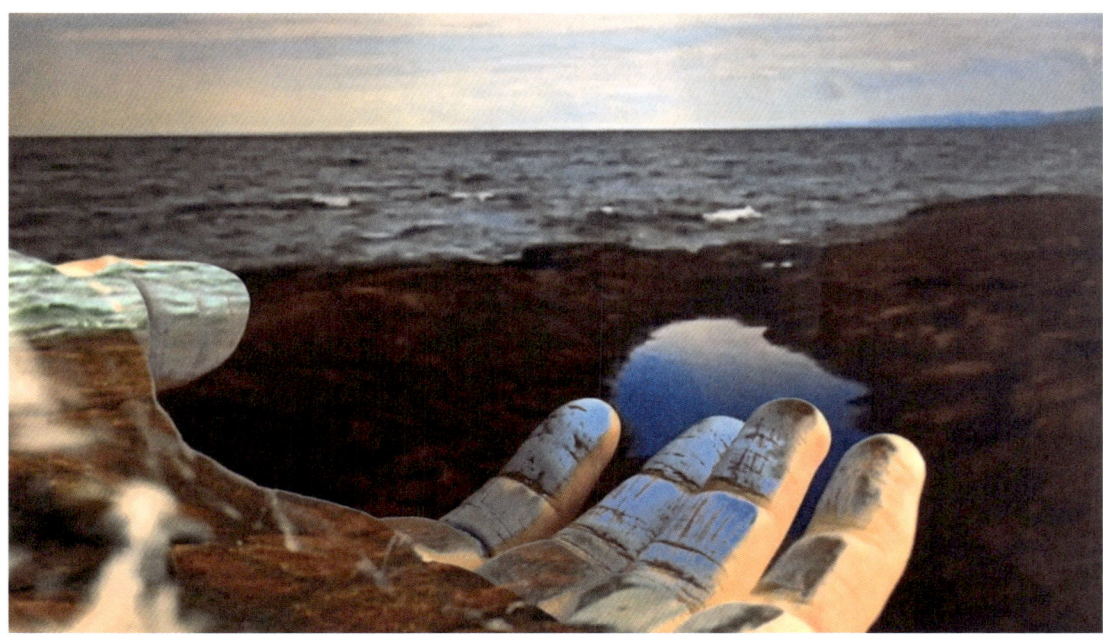

Raven Chacon
Diné

BORN 1977 IN FORT DEFIANCE,
NAVAJO NATION, AZ
LIVES AND WORKS IN RED HOOK, NY

From 2002 to 2004, Raven Chacon studied with James Tenney, Morton Subotnick, and Wadada Leo Smith at the California Institute of the Arts in Valencia. He received a master of fine arts in music with a concentration in composition from there in 2004. Prior to that, he studied with Christopher Shultis at the University of New Mexico and received a bachelor of arts in music in 2001.

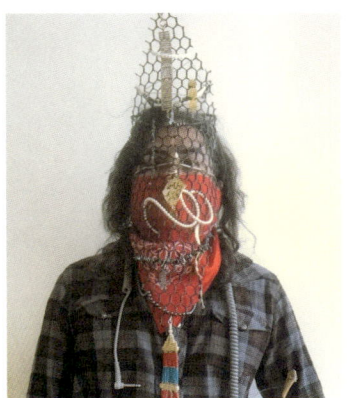

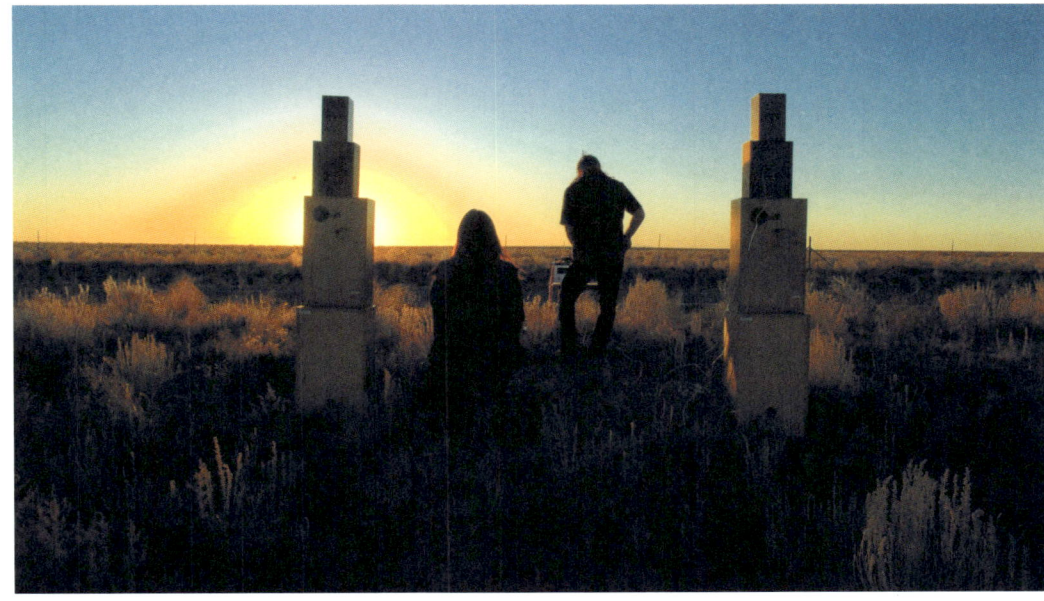

Gerald Clarke Jr.
Cahuilla Band of Indians

BORN 1967 IN HEMET, CA
LIVES AND WORKS IN SOUTHERN
CALIFORNIA

Gerald Clarke lives in the home his grandfather built around 1940 on the Cahuilla Indian Reservation and currently oversees the Clarke family cattle ranch. He holds a BA in art from the University of Central Arkansas and MA/MFA degrees in painting and sculpture from Stephen F. Austin State University located in Nacogdoches, Texas. A professor of ethnic studies at the University of California, Riverside, Clarke teaches classes in Native American studies and is a frequent lecturer, speaking about Native art, culture, and social issues.

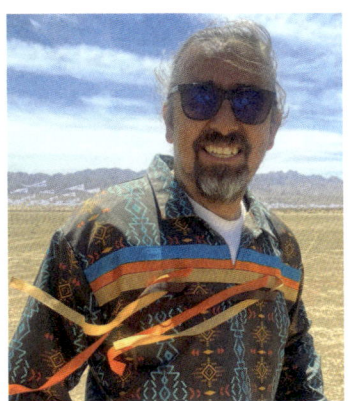

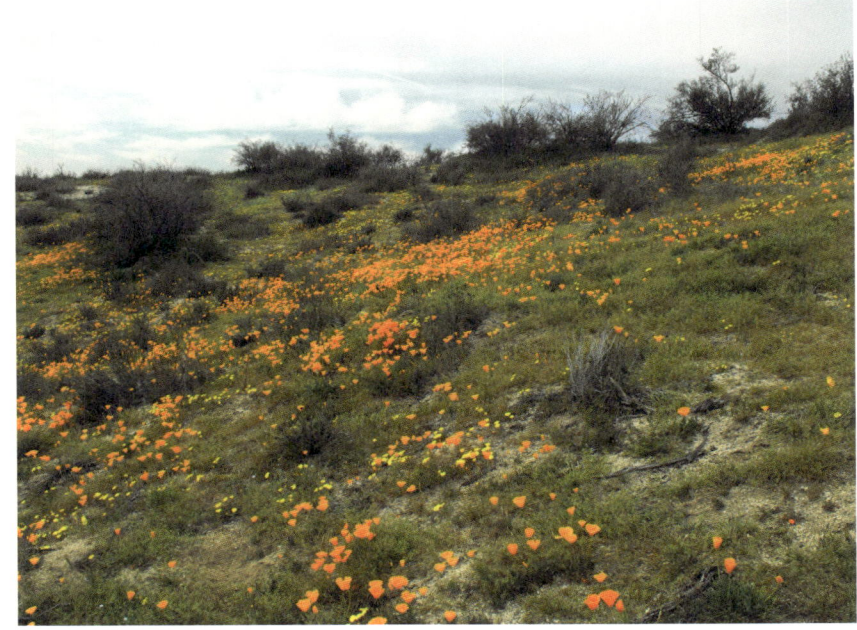

Melissa Cody
Navajo

BORN 1983 IN NO WATER MESA, AZ
LIVES AND WORKS IN LONG BEACH, CA

A fourth-generation Navajo weaver, Melissa Cody balances tradition, history, and contemporaneity in her work. Weaving on a traditional Navajo loom, she recombines traditional patterns into sophisticated geometric overlays and haptic color schemes. She holds a BA in museum studies from the College of Contemporary Native Arts in Santa Fe.

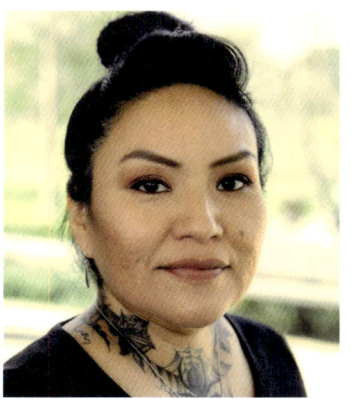

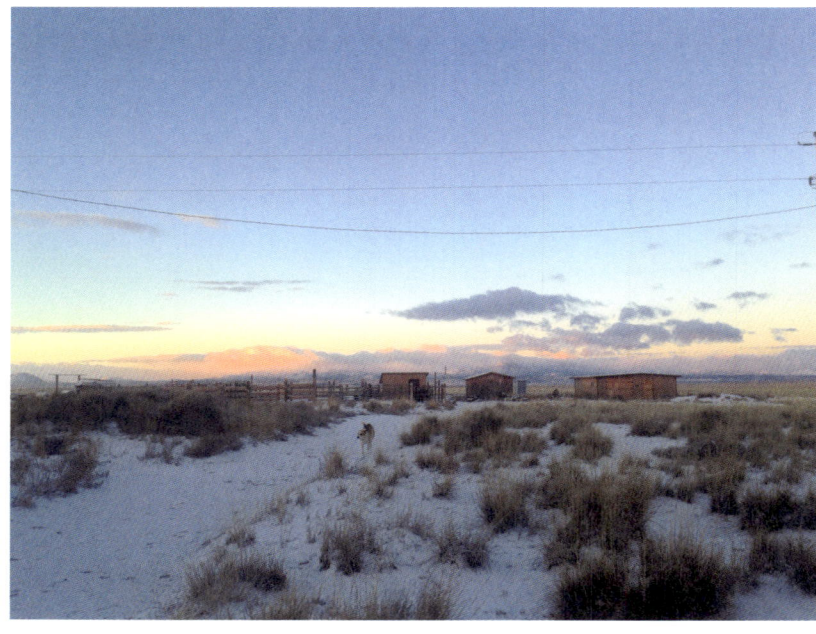

Jim Denomie
Lac Courte Oreilles Ojibwe, Ajijaak Clan

BORN 1955 ON THE LAC COURTE OREILLES RESERVATION, WI
DIED 2022 IN SHAFER, MN

For Jim Denomie, art was simultaneously a form of storytelling, self-expression, and critical analysis. Dissatisfied with standardized compulsory education, Denomie dropped out of high school and subsequently worked in construction trades before formally studying art. At the University of Minnesota he encountered a community of peers and a dynamic blend of cultural and political movements that catalyzed the lasting sociopolitical undercurrent in his work. For the last two decades of his life, Denomie's home and studio in rural Minnesota were enriching spaces that served his solitary practice and the vast community he both nurtured and was nurtured by.

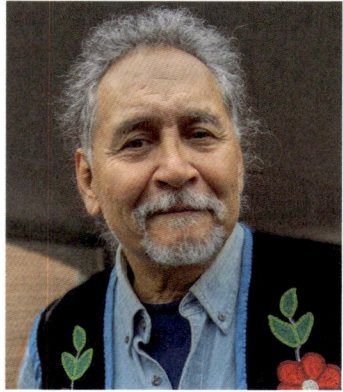

PHOTO BY LARRY MCNEIL

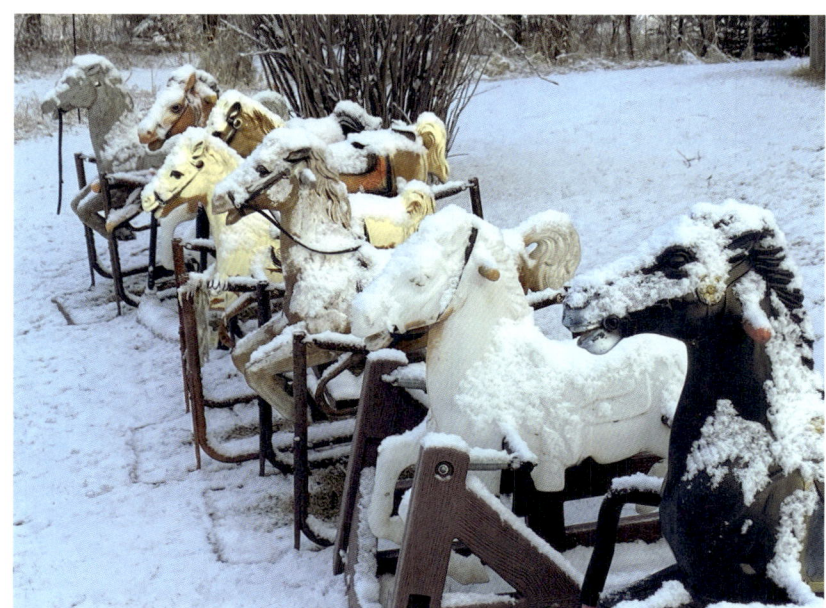

146

Demian DinéYazhi'
Diné

BORN 1983 IN GALLUP, NM
LIVES AND WORKS IN PORTLAND, OR

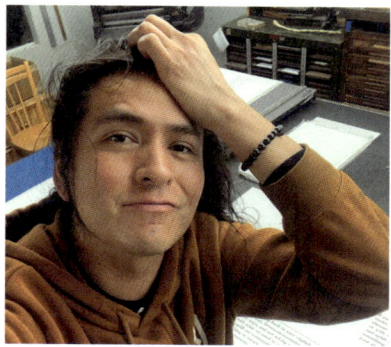

Demian DinéYazhi' is born to the clans Naasht'ézhí Tábąąhá (Zuni Clan Water's Edge) and Tódích'íi'nii (Bitter Water). Their practice is a regurgitation of purported Decolonial praxis informed by the overaccumulative and exploitative supremacist nature of hetero cisgender communities. They are a survivor of attempted european genocide, forced assimilation, manipulation, sexual and gender violence, capitalist sabotage, and hypermarginalization in a colonized country that refuses to center its politics and philosophies around the Indigenous peoples whose land it occupies and refuses to give back. @heterogeneoushomosexual

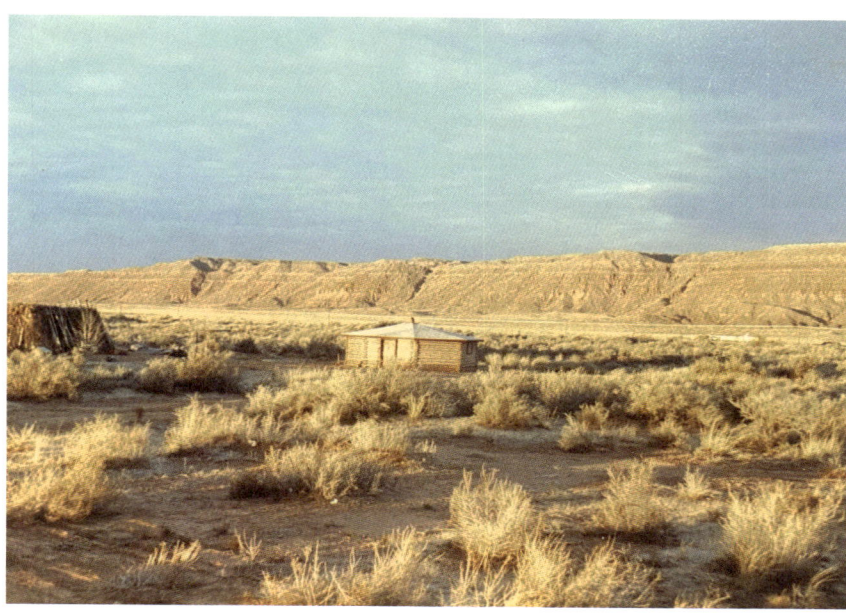

Duwawisioma
(Victor Masayesva Jr.)
Hopi Tribe

BORN 1951 ON HOPI LAND
LIVES AND WORKS IN HOTEVILLA, AZ

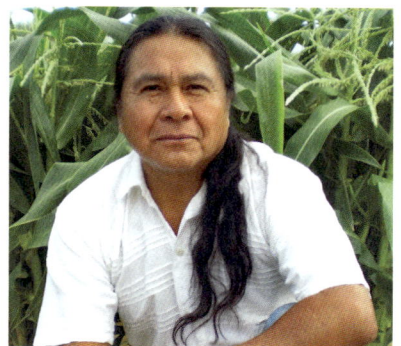

Duwawisioma is profoundly grateful for the early childhood mentoring provided by the elders of Hoatvela Village, where he grew up and continues to live. Primarily it was his Water Coyote Clan mothers and uncles who instructed him. Beyond their community he has been encouraged by a number of friends supporting his position on the tenets of sovereignty, preserving and sustaining the Hopi culture. Now in his seventies he continues to mentor and teach, applying the care for corn plants as a model for his work.

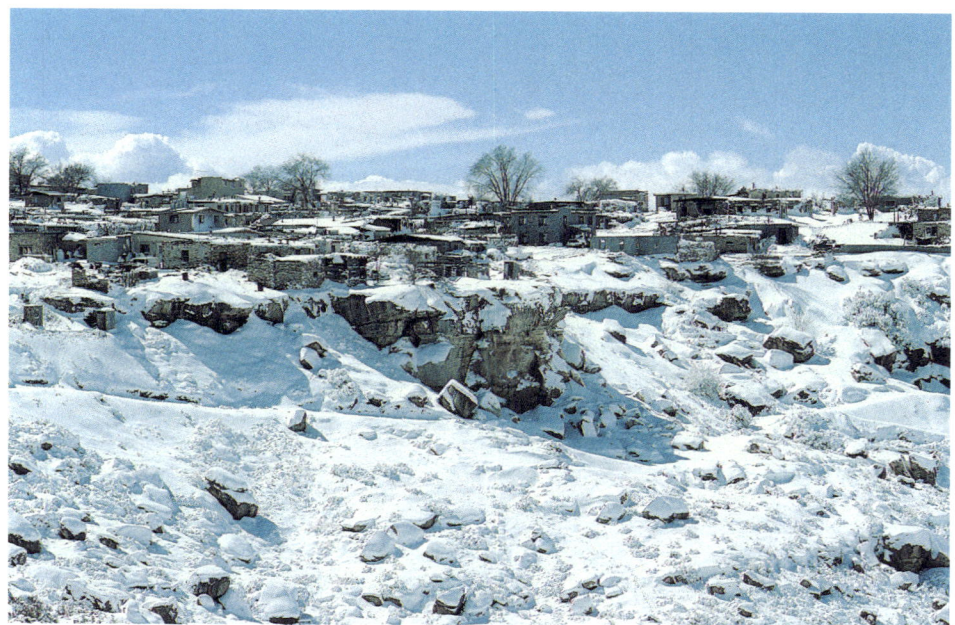

Ka'ila Farrell-Smith
Klamath/Modoc

BORN 1982 IN ASHLAND, OR
LIVES AND WORKS IN MODOC POINT, OR

Ka'ila Farrell-Smith grew up in Eugene and Springfield, Oregon, and went to high school in Wiesbaden, Germany, on a US Air Force base. There she met her first art teacher and chose a path to be a professional artist. She attended Pacific Northwest College of Art as a full-ride Lemelson scholarship recipient and studied archaeology in Greece and art in Cortona, Italy. In addition, she completed an MFA in contemporary art practices from Portland State University.

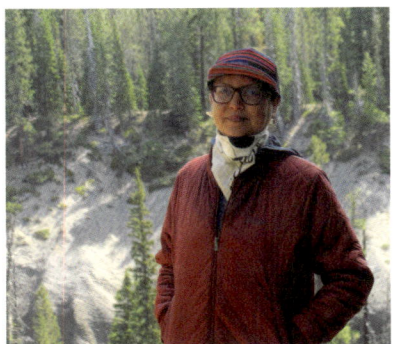

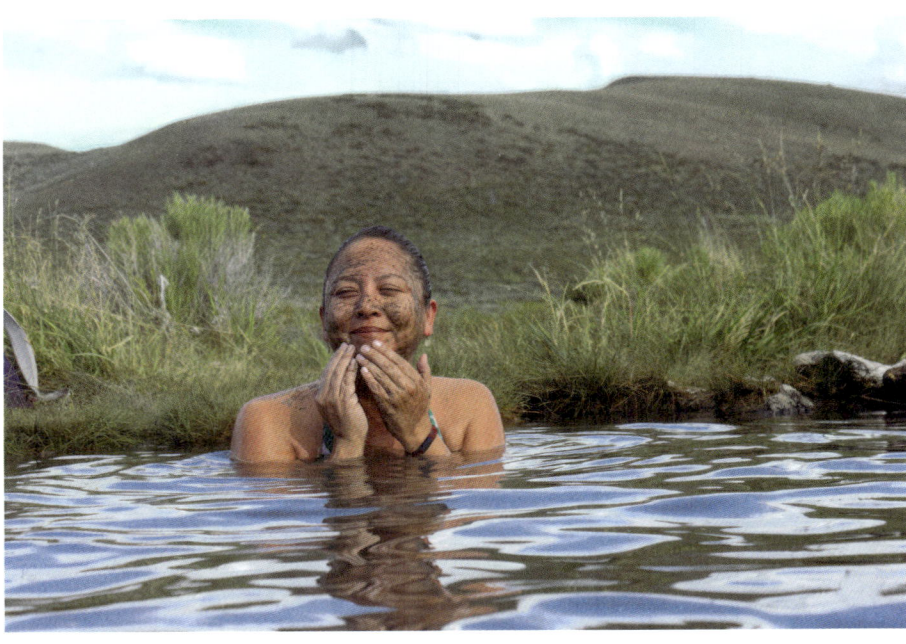

Joe Feddersen
Colville Confederated Tribes

BORN 1953 IN OMAK, WA
LIVES AND WORKS IN OMAK, WA

Joe Feddersen was a faculty member at Evergreen State College in Olympia from 1989 until his retirement in 2009, when he was awarded faculty emeritus status. He received the MoNA Luminaries Legacy Award from the Museum of Northwest Art in La Conner, Washington, in 2018. His work has been included in major exhibitions, such as *Continuum: 12 Artists* (George Gustave Heye Center), *Weaving Past into Present* (International Print Center), *Sharing Honors and Burdens* (Renwick Gallery, Smithsonian Institution), and *Here, Now and Always* (Zimmerli Art Museum, Rutgers University). Feddersen is the subject of a major retrospective exhibition and monograph organized by the Northwest Museum of Arts and Culture in Spokane.

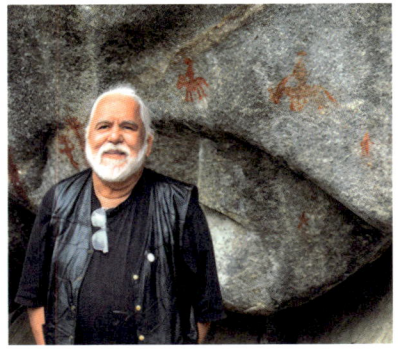

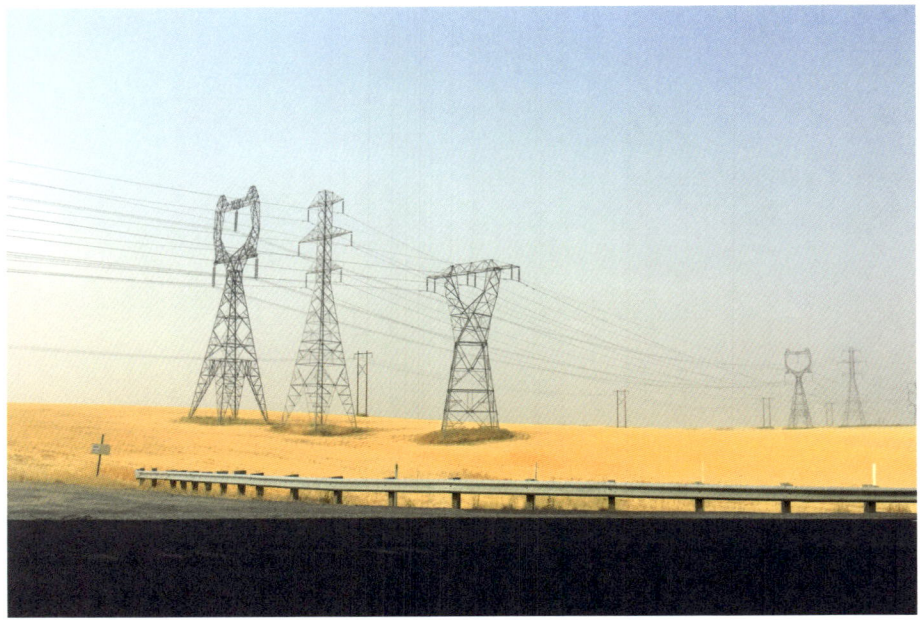

Nicholas Galanin
Lingít/Unangax̂

BORN 1979 IN SITKA, AK
LIVES AND WORKS IN SITKA, AK

Merritt Johnson
Unaffiliated

BORN 1977 IN BALTIMORE, MD
LIVES AND WORKS IN SITKA, AK

Nicholas Galanin engages past, present, and future to expose intentionally obscured collective memory and barriers to the acquisition of knowledge. His works critique commodification of culture, while they contribute to the continuum of Tlingit art. Galanin employs materials and processes that expand dialogue on Indigenous artistic production and how culture can be carried forward. His work appears in numerous public and private collections and is exhibited worldwide. In addition to apprenticing with master carvers, Galanin earned his BFA at London Guildhall University in the UK and his MFA at Massey University in New Zealand.

Born on Susquehannock and Piscataway land, Merritt Johnson currently lives and works with her family on Lingít Aani, her partner's home territory in Alaska. Johnson holds a BFA from Carnegie Mellon University and an MFA from the Massachusetts College of Art and Design.

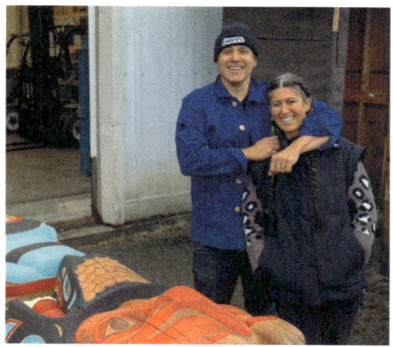

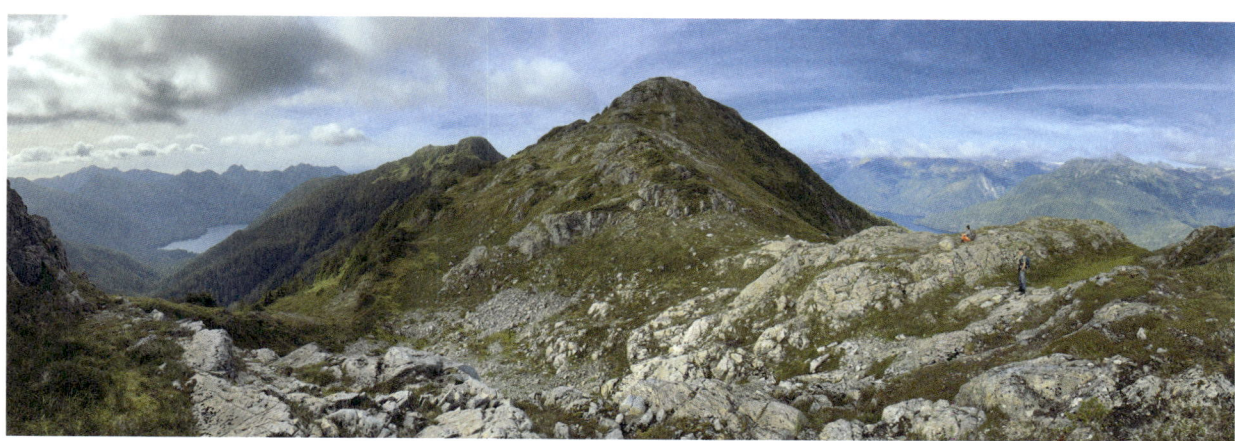

Jeffrey Gibson
Mississippi Band of Choctaw Indians/Cherokee Nation

BORN 1972 IN COLORADO SPRINGS, CO
LIVES AND WORKS NEAR HUDSON, NY

Jeffrey Gibson grew up in major urban centers in the United States, Germany, Korea, and England. He received a bachelor of fine arts in painting from the School of the Art Institute of Chicago in 1995 and a master of arts in painting from the Royal College of Art, London, in 1998.

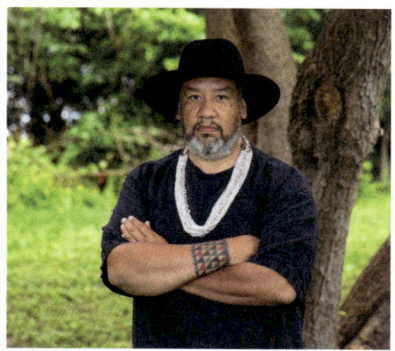

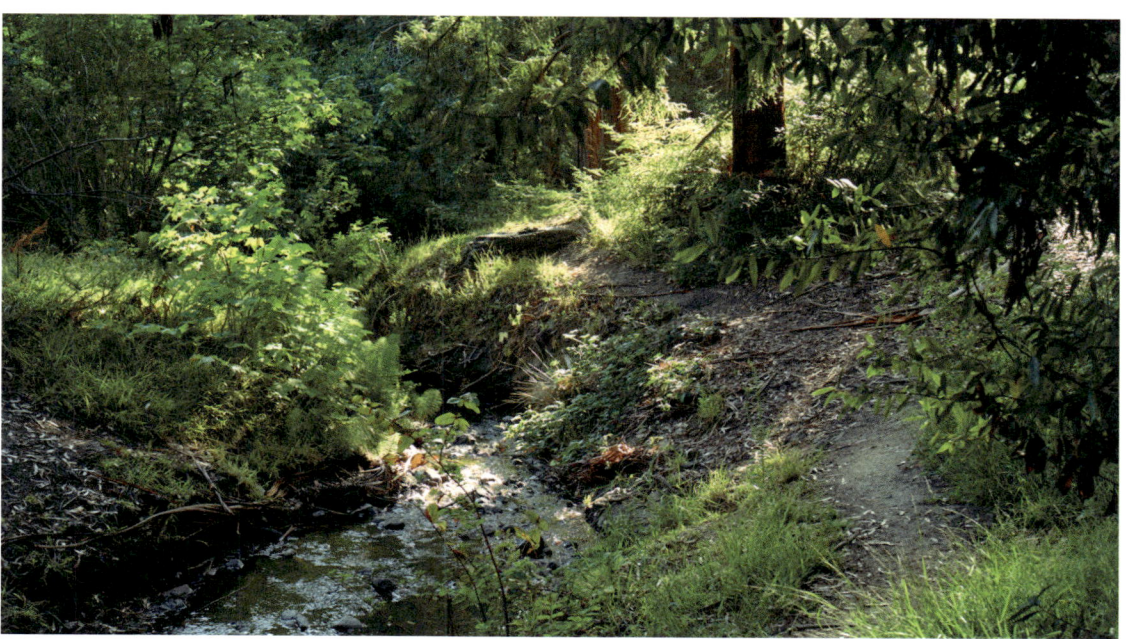

Teri Greeves
Kiowa

BORN 1970 IN LANDER, WY
LIVES AND WORKS IN SANTA FE, NM

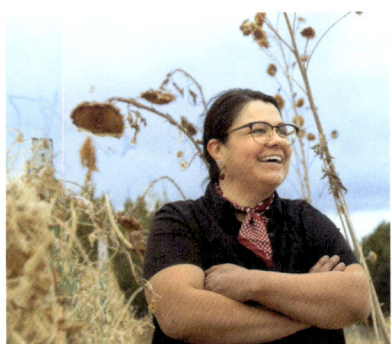

Known for her pictorial narrative beadwork, Teri Greeves has been recognized with the Best of Show award by the Southwestern Association for Indian Arts (SWAIA), a feature in PBS's *Craft in America*, the 2016 United States Artists Distinguished Fellow in Traditional Arts, and designation as a 2022 American Craft Council Fellow. Her beadwork is included in the collections of the Smithsonian's National Museum of the American Indian, British Museum, Heard Museum, Brooklyn Art Museum, and Museum of Arts and Design.

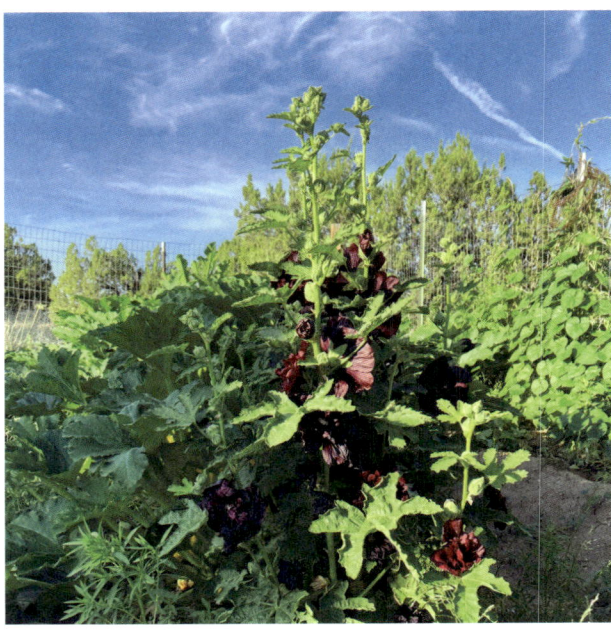

Raven Halfmoon
Caddo Nation

BORN 1991 IN NORMAN, OK
LIVES AND WORKS IN NORMAN, OK

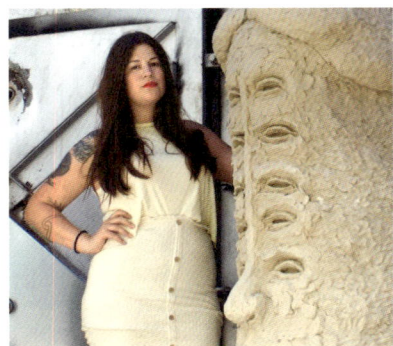

A recent finalist for the Burke Prize at the Museum of Arts and Design in New York, Raven Halfmoon attended the University of Arkansas, where she earned a double bachelor's degree in ceramics/painting and cultural anthropology. She produced a substantial body of monumental work while she was a long-term resident at the Archie Bray Foundation for the Ceramic Arts in Helena, Montana. Halfmoon was also named a Fellow of the Virginia A. Groot Foundation and received top honors from the Eiteljorg Museum in Indianapolis.

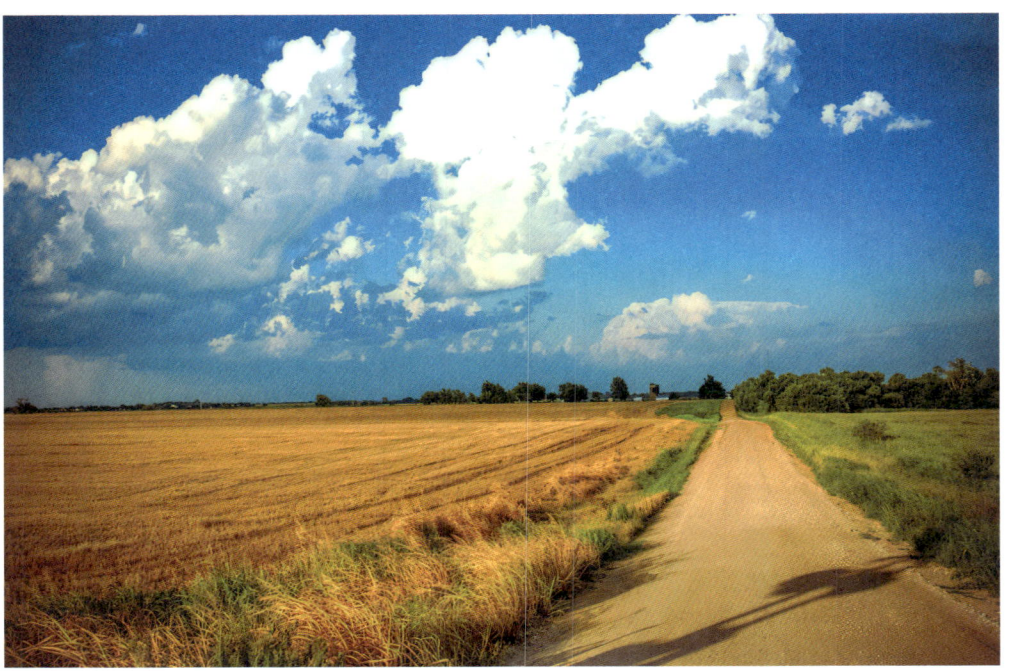

Edgar Heap of Birds
Cheyenne and Arapaho Nations

BORN 1954 IN WICHITA, KS
LIVES AND WORKS IN OKLAHOMA CITY, OK

Works by Hock E Aye VI (Little Chief) Edgar Heap of Birds have been seen in exhibitions around the world, from New York to Cape Town and Hong Kong, and they are now part of numerous museum collections, including the Metropolitan Museum of Art, the Museum of Modern Art, Forge Project, Tate Modern, and the Library of Congress. In 2017, he received an honorary doctorate of fine arts from Emily Carr University of Art and Design in Vancouver. In addition to being an international visiting lecturer, Heap of Birds is now professor emeritus at the University of Oklahoma after 30 years of service in fine arts and Native American studies. He is the grandson of Alice (Lightning Woman) Heap of Birds of Clinton, Oklahoma.

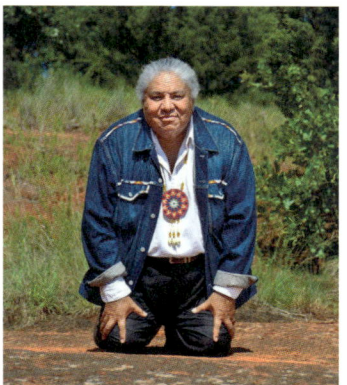

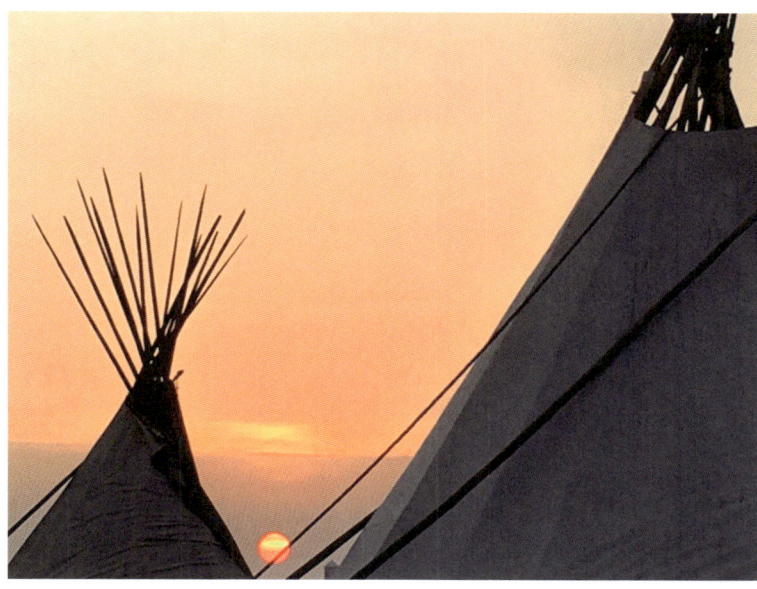

Luzene Hill
Eastern Band of Cherokee Indians

BORN 1946 IN ATLANTA, GA
LIVES AND WORKS IN CHEROKEE, NC

Luzene Hill has lived most of her life in Atlanta. She discovered a passion for drawing at midlife and exhibited her work for the first time at the Santa Fe Indian Market — at the age of 50. Hill recently moved to the Qualla Boundary, traditional Cherokee homeland, in North Carolina. It is important to her to live on sovereign tribal land and to be part of the continuing Indigenous occupation of those lands.

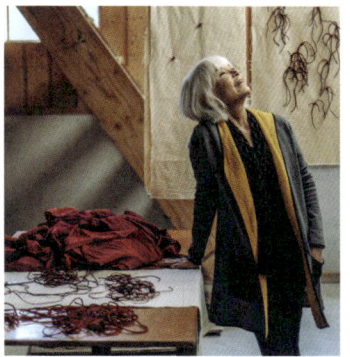

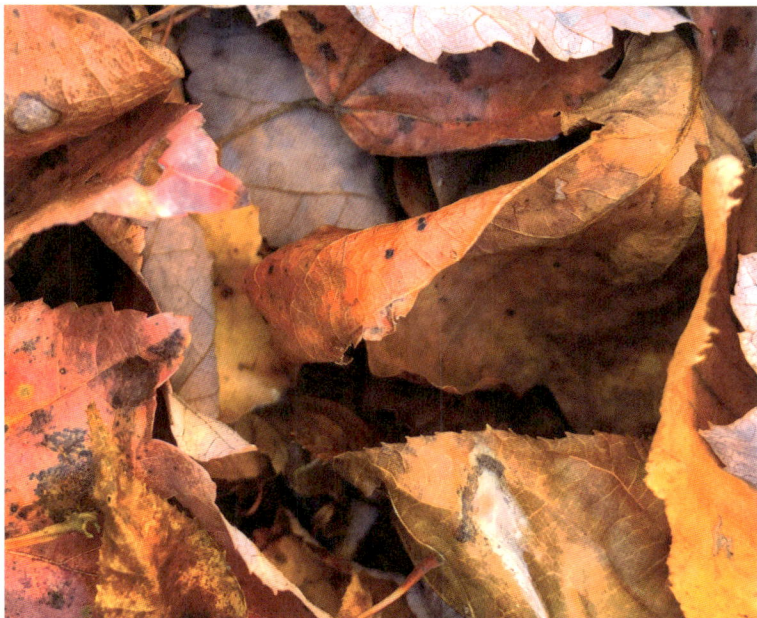

John Hitchcock

Comanche/Kiowa/
European descent

BORN 1967 IN LAWTON, OK
LIVES AND WORKS IN MADISON, WI

An artist and musician, John Hitchcock has taught printmaking at the University of Wisconsin-Madison since 2001. In addition to being a Vilas Distinguished Achievement Professor at the university, he has served as an associate dean for the arts, faculty director of the Studio Learning Community, and graduate chair of the art department. Hitchcock has also taught at the University of Minnesota, Morris, and he holds a master of fine arts degree from Texas Tech University.

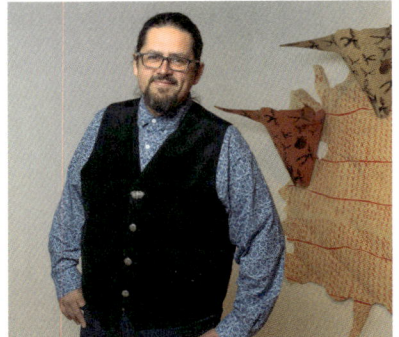

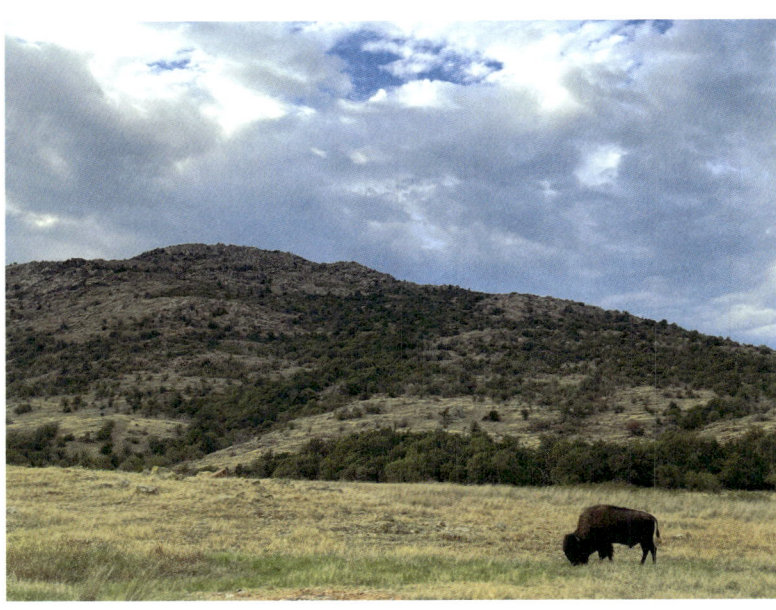

G. Peter Jemison

Seneca Nation of Indians,
Heron Clan

BORN 1945 IN SILVER CREEK, NY
LIVES AND WORKS IN VICTOR, NY

Peter Jemison was born in a farming community near the Seneca Nation Cattaraugus Reservation. While pursuing a degree in art education at Buffalo State College, he studied abroad in Siena, Italy. He did not begin to study Native American art until 1970. Hired by Seneca Nation in 1974 to run its education department, he sought out Seneca people who were maintaining cultural practices, including dance, language, cooking, carving, cornhusk, and beadwork, that were traditionally passed on through families. He also worked with contemporary artists, which in time inspired young members of the community to develop their own artistic expression. Jemison featured the work of Native American artists while he ran the American Indian Community House Gallery in New York City. The founding site manager at Ganondagan and the Seneca Art and Culture Center, Jemison presented the history, art, and cultural traditions of the Onöndowagah for more than 30 years.

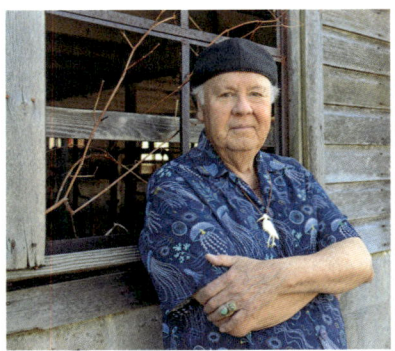

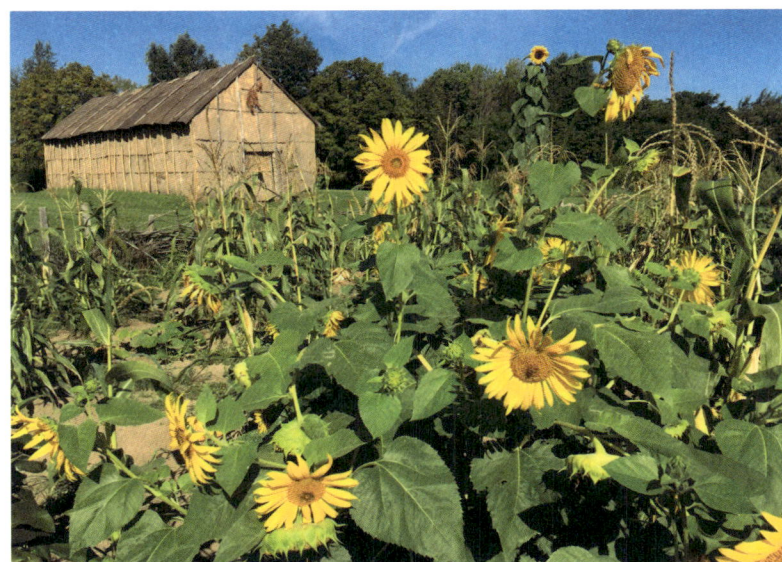

Tom Jones
Ho-Chunk Nation

BORN 1964 IN CHARLOTTE, NC
LIVES AND WORKS IN PRAIRIE DU SAC, WI

Tom Jones is a professor of photography at the University of Wisconsin-Madison. He received a master of fine arts in photography and a master of arts in museum studies from Columbia College in Chicago, Illinois. Jones's artwork is a commentary on American Indian identity, experience, and perception. He continues to work on an ongoing photographic essay on the contemporary life of his tribe, the Ho-Chunk Nation of Wisconsin.

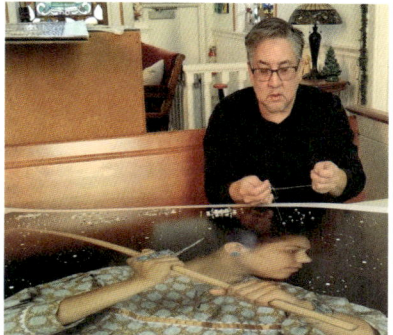

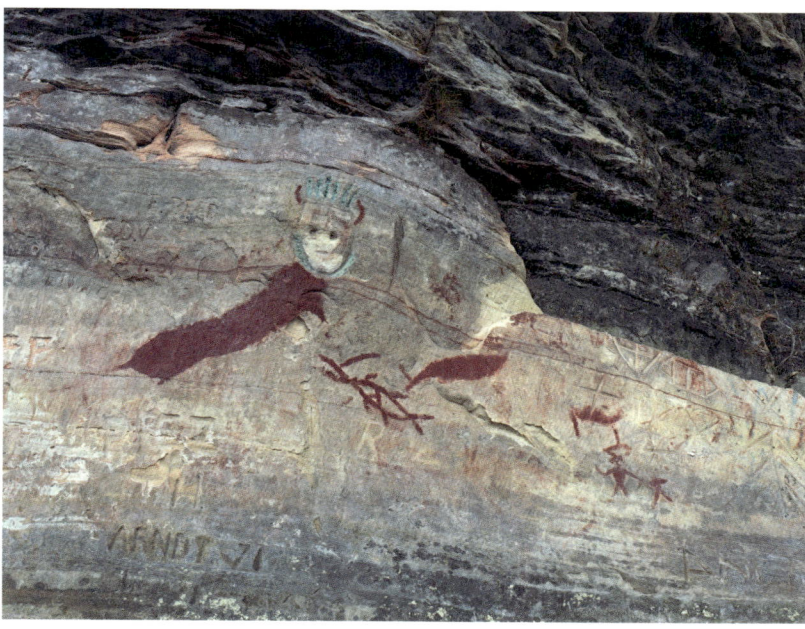

Linda King
Confederated Salish and
Kootenai Tribes

BORN 1952 IN ST. IGNATIUS, FLATHEAD
INDIAN NATION, MT
LIVES AND WORKS IN PABLO, MT

A cultural arts instructor at the Salish Kootenai College near Pablo for 20 years, Linda King is also a traditional tribal dancer. In 1992, she was selected by the state of Montana as a highlighted artist who gave lectures and demonstrations with the traveling exhibition *Bridles Bits and Beads*. King was an invited artist to *Tears of Duk'Wibahl*, an international gathering of Pacific Rim Indigenous visual artists, in 2017 and to *Teaching of the Tree People*, held at the Evergreen State College Long House in Olympia in 2018.

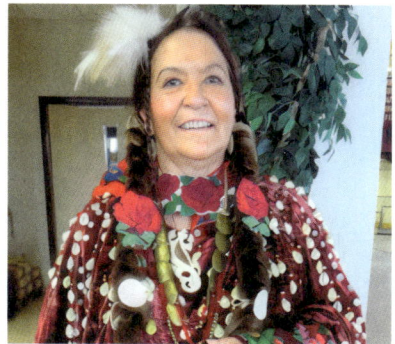

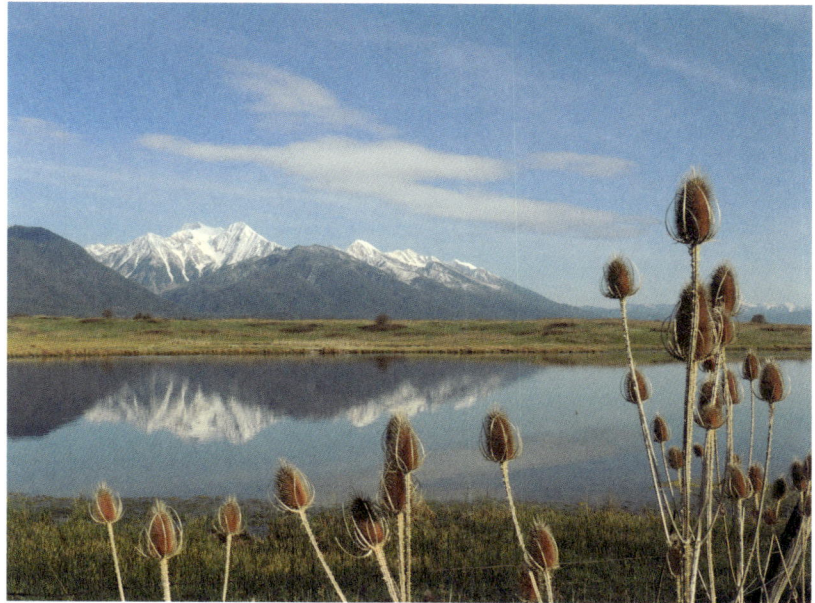

Athena LaTocha

Keweenaw Bay Ojibwe/
Standing Rock Lakota

BORN IN ANCHORAGE, AK
LIVES AND WORKS IN PEEKSKILL AND
NEW YORK, NY

Among Athena LaTocha's many residencies and awards are the Rockefeller Brothers Fund Pocantico Prize for Visual Artists (2022), Eiteljorg Contemporary Art Fellowship and NYSCA/NYFA Artist Fellowship in Painting (2021), the Joan Mitchell Foundation (2019 and 2016), Wave Hill (2018), and the Robert Rauschenberg Foundation (2013). She received her bachelor of fine arts degree from the School of the Art Institute of Chicago and a master of fine arts degree from Stony Brook University, New York. The artist divides her time between New York City and Peekskill, New York.

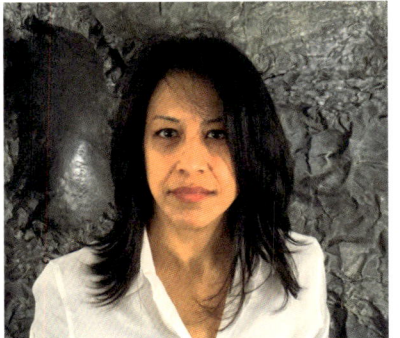

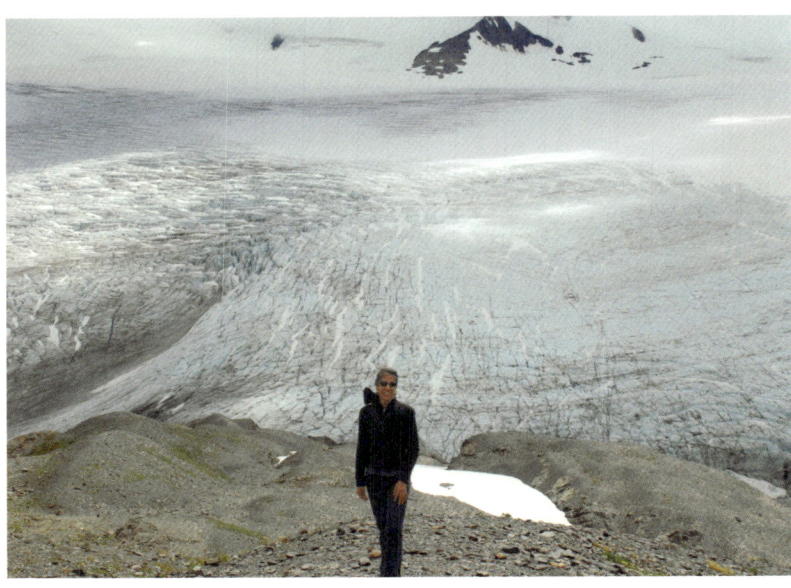

James Lavadour

Confederated Tribes of the
Umatilla Indian Reservation,
Walla Walla

BORN 1951 IN PENDELTON, OR
LIVES AND WORKS ON THE UMATILLA
INDIAN RESERVATION, OR

James Lavadour's life on the Umatilla Reservation in northeastern Oregon led to his profound affection for the mountains and canyons of the vast Columbia plateau country. One of the most important aspects of his prints is that they are created at Crow's Shadow Institute of the Arts, located on the Umatilla Reservation. Lavadour cofounded Crow's Shadow on his homeland in 1992 to provide a creative conduit for educational, social, and economic opportunities for Native Americans through artistic development.

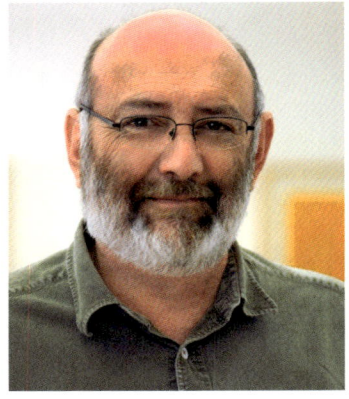

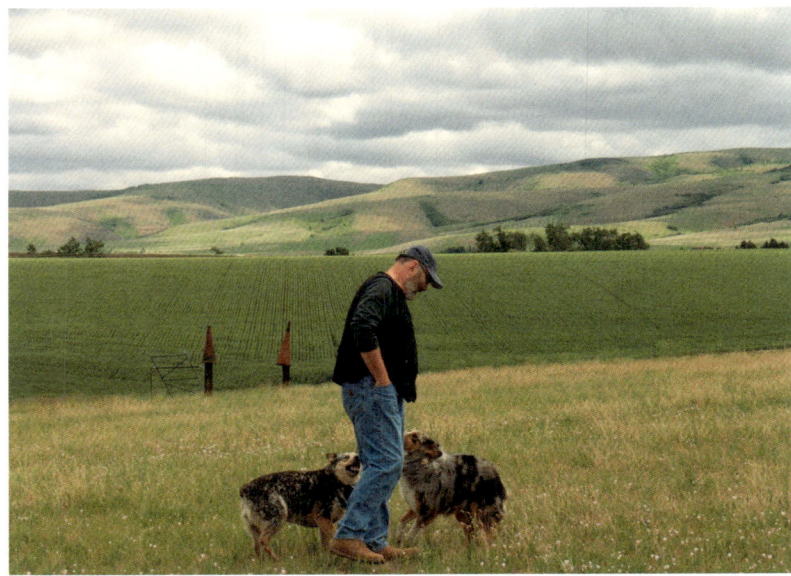

Linda Lomahaftewa
Hopi/Choctaw

BORN 1947 IN PHOENIX, AZ
LIVES AND WORKS IN SANTA FE, NM

In 1962, Linda Lomahaftewa was 15 years old when she left Phoenix to join the first group of Native American youth to study art at the Institute of American Indian Arts (IAIA) in Santa Fe. She later attended San Francisco Art Institute (SFAI) on a full scholarship (1965–1971) and earned her BFA and MFA in painting. Her teaching career includes time at California State University, Sonoma, the University of California, Berkeley, and at IAIA, where she taught until 2017. Lomahaftewa has received honorary doctorate degrees from IAIA (2017) and SFAI (2022).

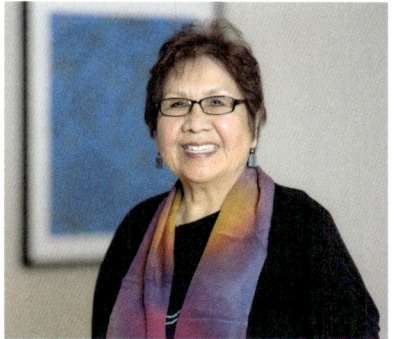

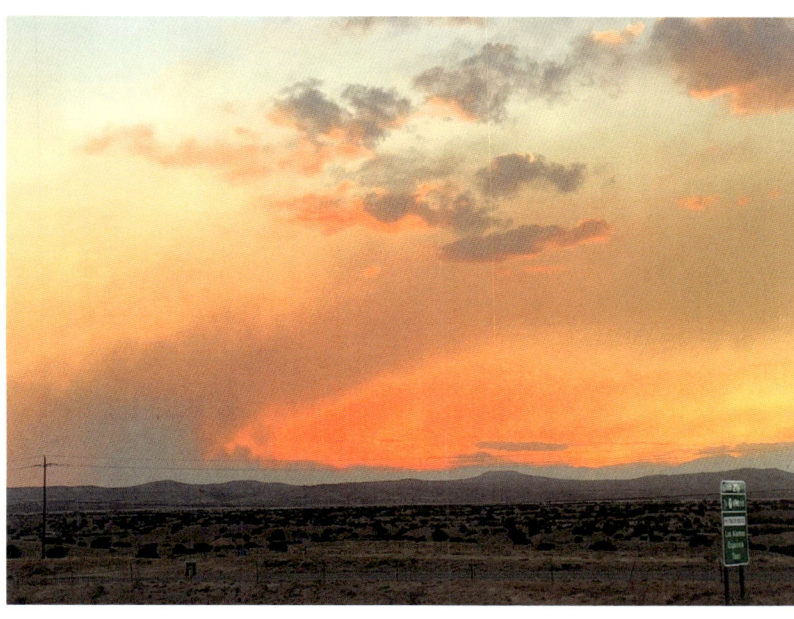

George C. Longfish
Seneca/Tuscarora

BORN 1942 IN OSHWEKEN, ONTARIO
LIVES AND WORKS IN SOUTH BERWICK, ME

George Longfish's early years were spent at Thomas Indian School near Gowanda, New York. After the school closed in 1954, he attended Tuley High School in Chicago. He started at the School of the Art Institute of Chicago in 1963 and graduated with an MFA in 1972. The next year Longfish began working with the Native American department at the University of California at Davis and later served as curator of the C. N. Gorman Museum there. The artist retired in 2003 and moved with his family to Maine.

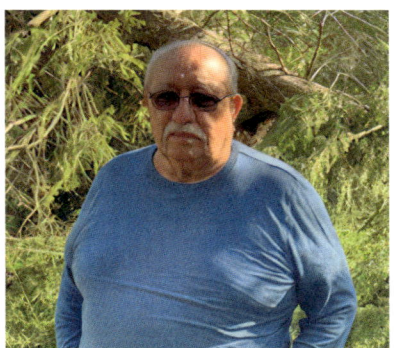

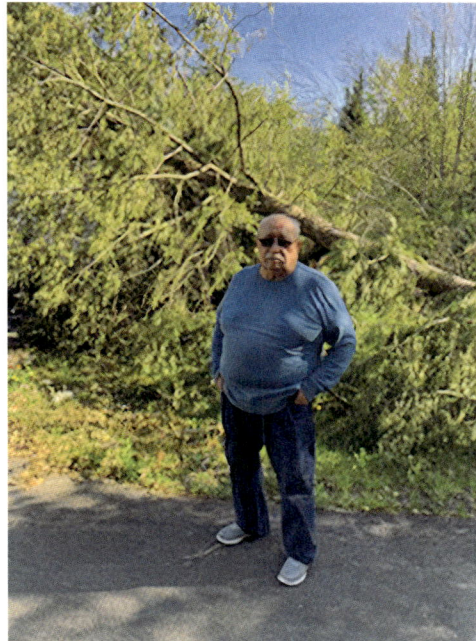

Cannupa Hanska Luger
Mandan/Hidatsa/Arikara/
Lakota

BORN 1979 IN FORT YATES, ND
LIVES AND WORKS IN GLORIETA, NM

Cannupa Hanska Luger uses social collaboration and monumental installations to communicate urgent stories about Indigeneity. Raised on the Standing Rock Reservation in North Dakota, he is an enrolled member of the Three Affiliated Tribes of Fort Berthold. In 2011, Luger received a BFA in studio arts from the Institute of American Indian Arts in Santa Fe. He is a 2022 Guggenheim Fellow and a 2021 United States Artists Fellow. His work has been exhibited at the Metropolitan Museum of Art, the Gardiner Museum in Toronto, and the National Center for Civil and Human Rights in Atlanta.

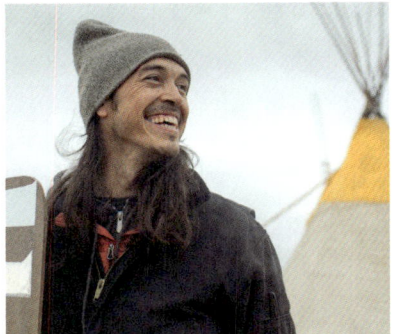

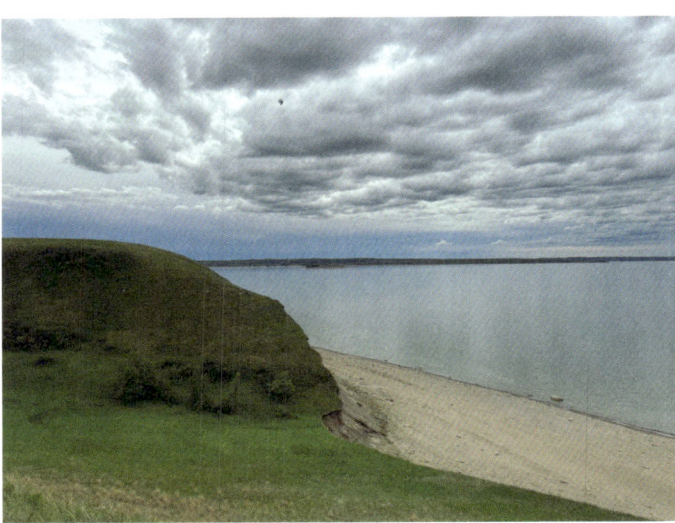

Brenda Mallory
Cherokee Nation

BORN 1955 IN CLAREMORE, OK
LIVES AND WORKS IN PORTLAND, OR

Brenda Mallory earned a BA in linguistics and English from UCLA and a BFA from Pacific Northwest College of Art in Portland. She has received grants from the Oregon Arts Commission, Regional Arts and Culture Council, and the Potlatch Fund. Among her awards are the Eiteljorg Museum Contemporary Native Art Fellowship, Native Arts and Cultures Foundation National Visual Arts Fellowship, Ucross Native Artist Fellowship, and Hallie Ford Fellowship in the Visual Arts. Mallory has enjoyed residencies at Crow's Shadow Institute of the Arts, Jordan Schnitzer Printmaking, Pulp and Deckle, and Bullseye Glass.

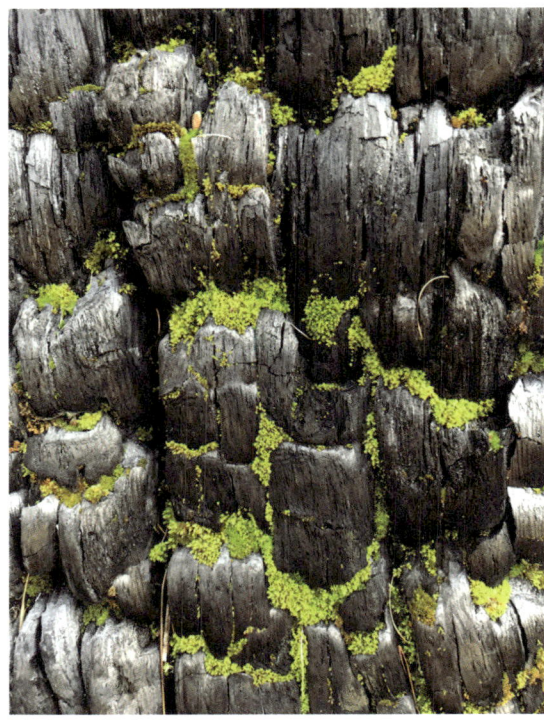

Mario Martinez
Pascua Yaqui Tribe of Arizona

BORN 1953 IN PHOENIX, AZ
LIVES AND WORKS IN BROOKLYN, NY

Mario Martinez grew up in the Yaqui village called Penjamo in Scottsdale. He received a BFA at Arizona State University in 1979 and an MFA at the San Francisco Art Institute in 1985. His work is in the collections of the Heard Museum in Phoenix, Tucson Museum of Art, and the Smithsonian's National Museum of the American Indian (NMAI). Martinez had a midcareer retrospective at the NMAI in New York City in 2005.

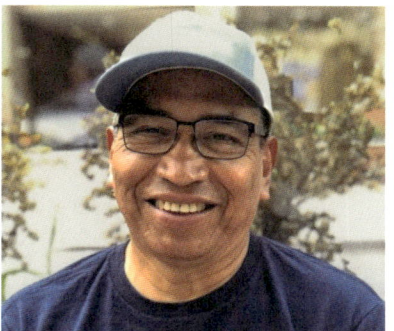

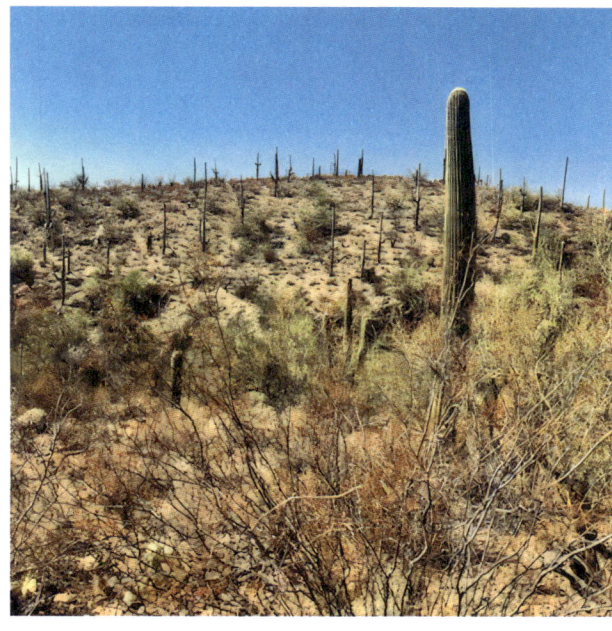

Melissa Melero-Moose
Fallon Paiute-Shoshone Tribe

BORN 1974 IN SAN FRANCISCO, CA
LIVES AND WORKS IN HUNGRY VALLEY, NV

A mixed-media painter with ties to the Fort Bidwell Paiute and Modoc tribes, Melissa Melero-Moose is founder/curator of the art collective Great Basin Native Artists. After she attended the Institute of American Indian Arts in Santa Fe, Melero-Moose received artist fellowships and grants from the Joan Mitchell Foundation, Nevada Museum of Art, School for Advanced Research, Southwestern Association for Indian Arts (SWAIA), Wheelwright Museum of the American Indian, and Institute of American Indian Arts.

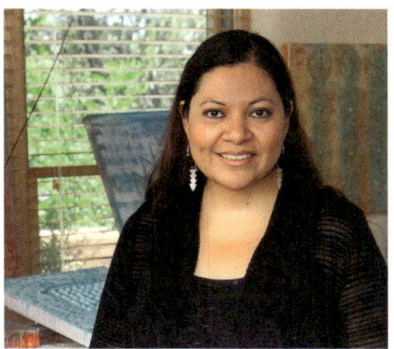

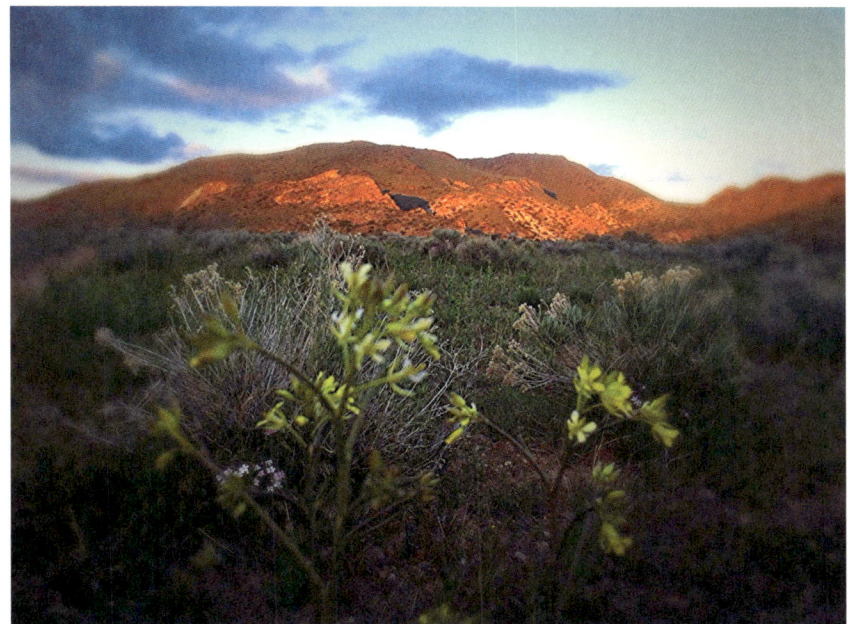

Jamie Okuma
La Jolla Band of Luiseno Indians

LIVES AND WORKS ON THE LA JOLLA INDIAN RESERVATION, CA

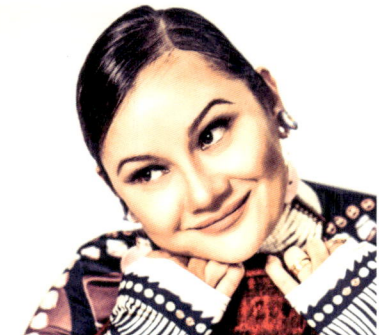

From the age of 18, Jamie Okuma has devoted her professional life to art. Her career began at the age of six, when she entered her first art show and began sewing outfits to dance in at powwows. Okuma, who attended the Institute of American Indian Arts, has exhibited her work at the Heard Museum Guild Indian Fair and Market in Phoenix and at the Santa Fe Indian Market. She has received a total of seven Best of Show awards from these renowned venues. Her work is in the permanent collections of the Minneapolis Institute of Art, the Nelson-Atkins Museum of Art, the Denver Art Museum, the Smithsonian's National Museum of the American Indian, and the Costume Institute of the Metropolitan Museum of Art. An enrolled member of the La Jolla Band of Luiseno Indians, Okuma is also Shoshone-Bannock, Wailaki, and Okinawan.

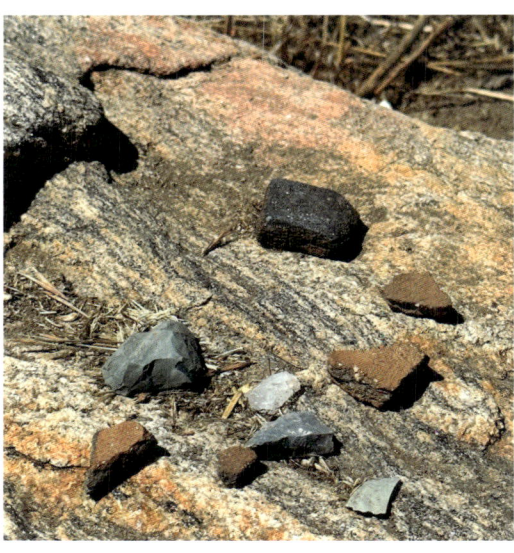

Chris Pappan
Kanza/Lakota

BORN 1971 IN COLORADO SPRINGS, CO
LIVES AND WORKS IN CHICAGO, IL

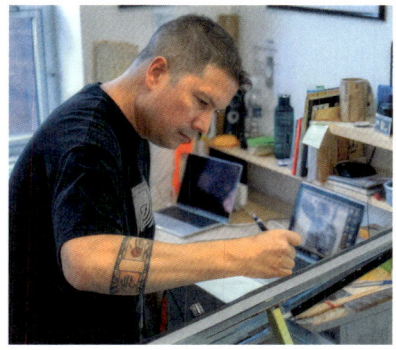

Among Chris Pappan's cited influences are *Heavy Metal* and *Juxtapoz* magazines and the Lowbrow art movement with its cultural roots in 1970s underground comics, punk, and hot rod cultures. His art literally reflects the dominant culture's distorted perceptions of Native peoples and is based on the Plains Native art tradition of ledger art. A graduate of the Institute of American Indian Arts in Santa Fe, Pappan is now a board member of the Illinois State Museum and a cofounder of the Center for Native Futures.

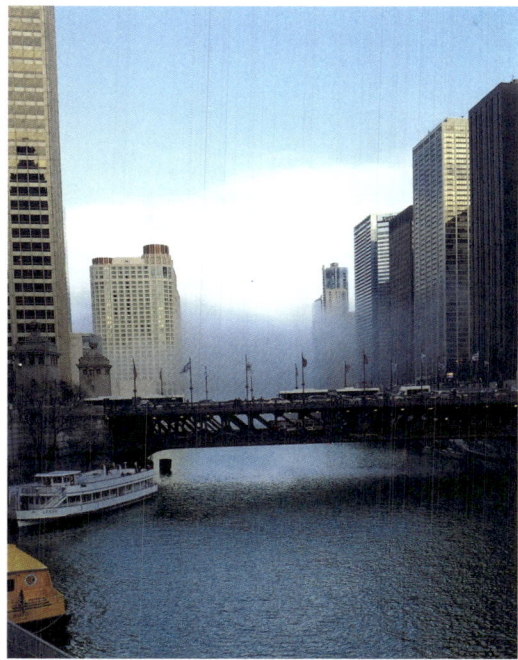

Rose Powhatan
Pamunkey/Tauxenent descent

BORN 1946 IN WASHINGTON, DC
LIVES AND WORKS IN WASHINGTON, DC

Rose Powhatan's extended family once included 29 arts practitioners. Her primary arts mentor was her mother, Georgia Mills Jessup, whose work is in the contemporary collection of the National Museum of Women in the Arts. Powhatan earned both her BFA in painting (cum laude) and MA degrees at Howard University. She also completed graduate studies at Georgetown University, Catholic University of America, and the University of London. A longtime member of the Community Advisory Board at the John F. Kennedy Center for the Performing Arts, she is also cofounder of the intertribal Powhatan Museum.

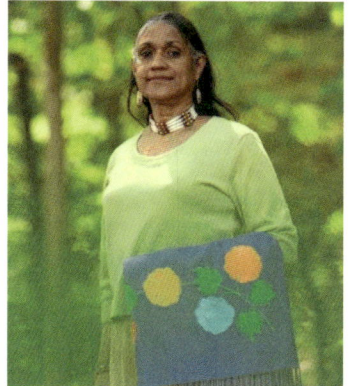

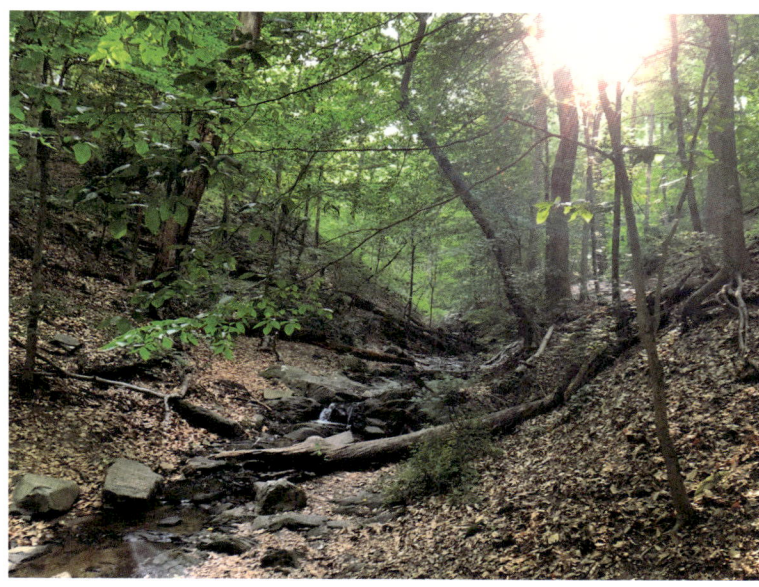

Wendy Red Star
Apsáalooke

BORN 1981 IN BILLINGS, MT
LIVES AND WORKS IN PORTLAND, OR

Raised on the Apsáalooke (Crow) reservation in Montana, Wendy Red Star's work is informed by both her cultural heritage and her engagement with many forms of creative expression, including photography, sculpture, video, fiber arts, and performance. An avid researcher of archives and historical narratives, Red Star seeks to incorporate and recast her research, offering new and unexpected perspectives in work that is at once inquisitive, witty, and unsettling. Red Star holds a BFA from Montana State University, Bozeman, and an MFA in sculpture from the University of California, Los Angeles.

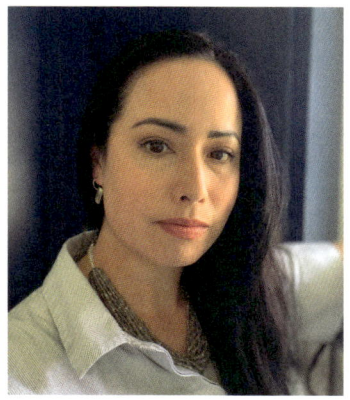

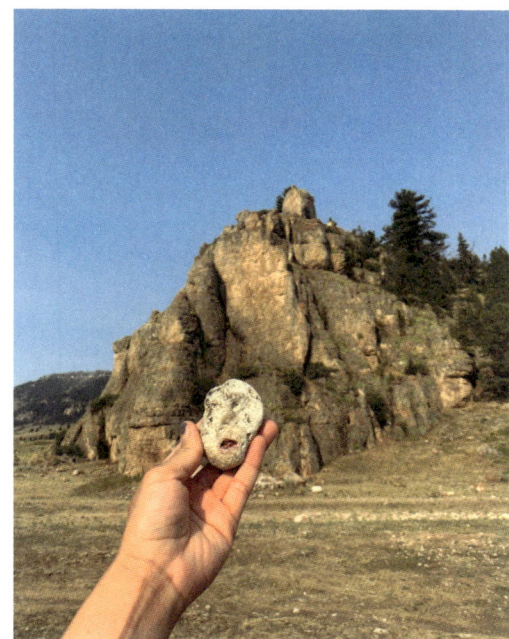

Eric-Paul Riege
Diné

BORN 1994 IN NA'NÍZHÓOZHÍ, GALLUP, NM
LIVES AND WORKS IN NA'NÍZHÓOZHÍ,
GALLUP, NM

Eric-Paul Riege uses a rich array of natural and synthetic materials — including wool, cotton, bone, faux fur, and human hair — to create his signature woven sculptures that reflect the Diné philosophy of *hózhó*. As a practice in everyday life as well as in Riege's own artistic practice, *hózhó* is a worldview that encompasses the values of beauty, balance, and goodness in all things physical and spiritual.

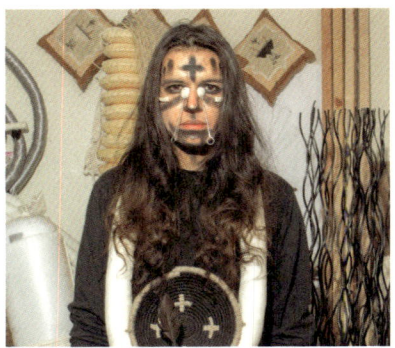

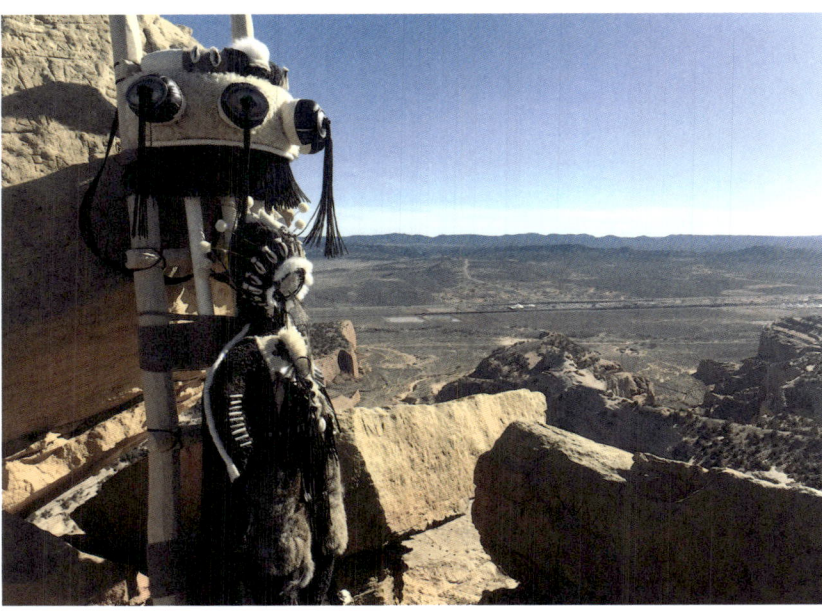

Cara Romero
Chemehuevi

BORN 1977 IN INGLEWOOD, CA
LIVES AND WORKS IN SANTA FE, NM

Growing up in contrasting settings of rural reservation and urban sprawl, Cara Romero now possesses a bicultural Indigenous identity. She pursued an undergraduate degree in cultural anthropology at the University of Houston but became disillusioned by the way Native Americans are portrayed in academia and media. Realizing photography could do more than anthropology did in words, she trained in photojournalism, editorial portraiture, and film, digital, commercial, and fine art photography. Romero travels between Santa Fe and the Chemehuevi Valley Indian Reservation, where she maintains close ties to her tribal community and ancestral homelands.

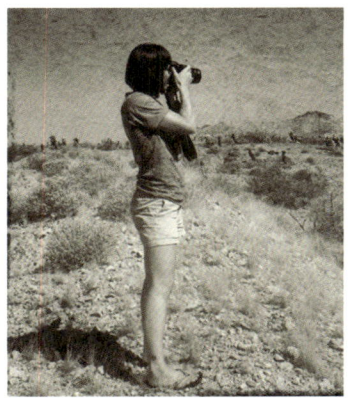

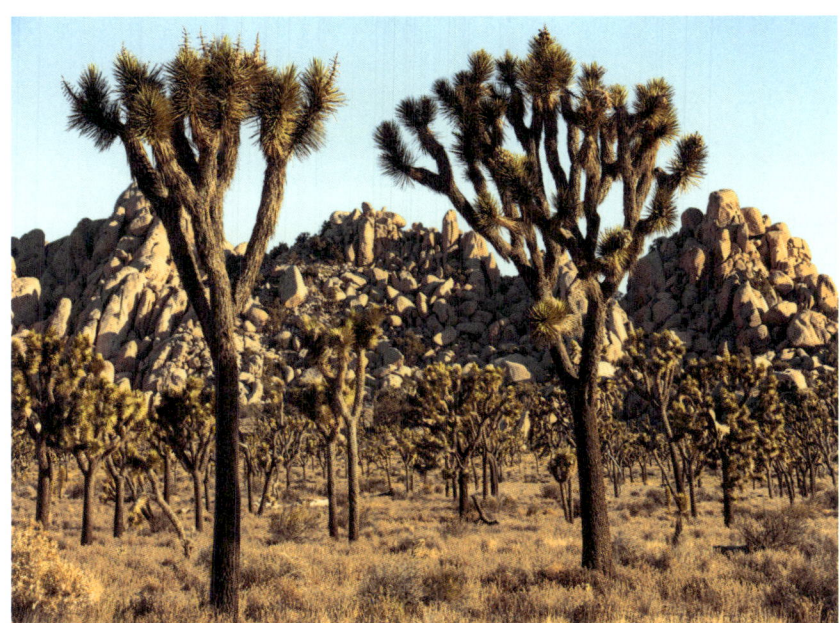

Diego Romero
Pueblo of Cochiti

BORN 1964 IN BERKELEY, CA
LIVES AND WORKS IN SANTA FE, NM

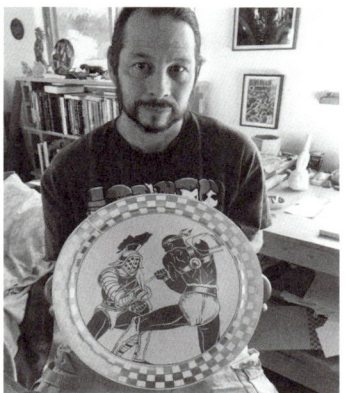

Although raised in Berkeley, Diego Romero spent summers in his ancestral homelands of the Cochiti Pueblo with his paternal grandparents. After finishing high school he settled in New Mexico, where he attended the Institute of American Indian Arts in Santa Fe. He went on to receive his BFA from the Otis College of Art and Design and an MFA from the University of California, Los Angeles. Romero now lives in Santa Fe with his wife, fine art photographer Cara Romero, and their children.

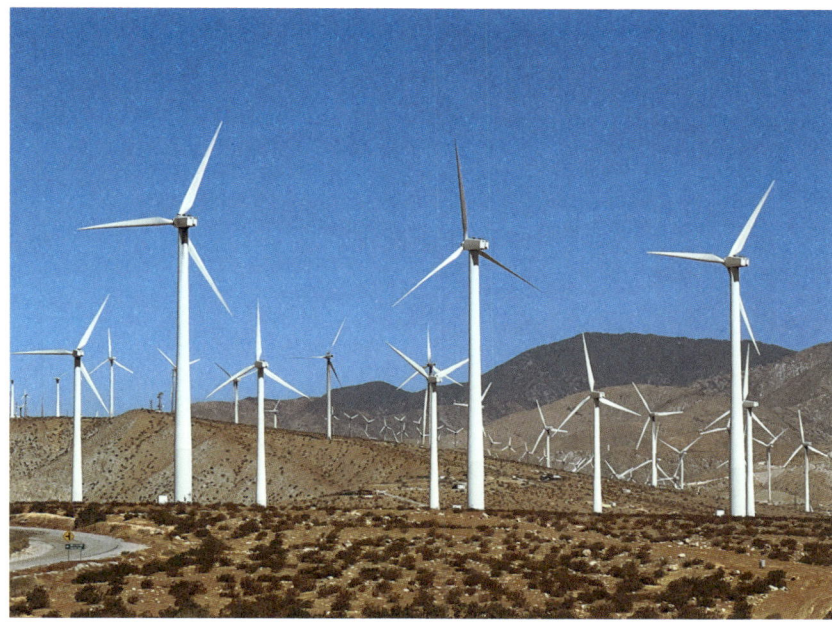

Rose B. Simpson
Pueblo of Santa Clara,
New Mexico

BORN 1983 IN SANTA FE, NM
LIVES AND WORKS IN PUEBLO OF SANTA
CLARA, NM

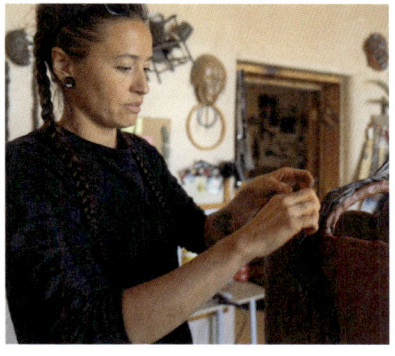

Rose B. Simpson is a mixed-media artist whose work explores the impact of living in a postcolonial world. Belonging to a multigenerational, matrilineal legacy of artists working with clay, her practice is informed by ancestral and indigenous traditions. Simpson has a BFA from the Institute of American Indian Arts (IAIA), an MFA from the Rhode Island School of Design, and an MA in creative writing from IAIA.

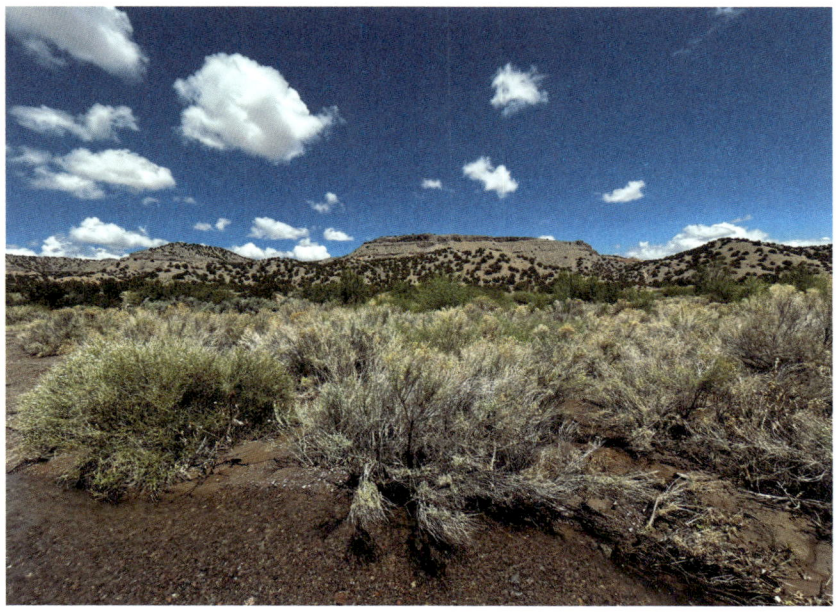

Preston Singletary
Tlingit

BORN 1963 IN SAN FRANCISCO, CA
LIVES AND WORKS IN SEATTLE, WA

Glass sculptures by Preston Singletary deal with themes of Tlingit mythology and traditional designs. His decades of glassmaking began when he attended the Pilchuck Glass School and worked at the glass studio of Benjamin Moore in Seattle. Travel to Sweden in 1993 introduced Scandinavian design into his work. Singletary received an honorary name from elder Joe David (Nuu Chah Nulth) in 2000 and an honorary doctorate degree from the University of Puget Sound (Tacoma, Washington) in 2009. His work is included in museum collections in Boston, Seattle, Stockholm, Edinburgh, London, and Washington, DC.

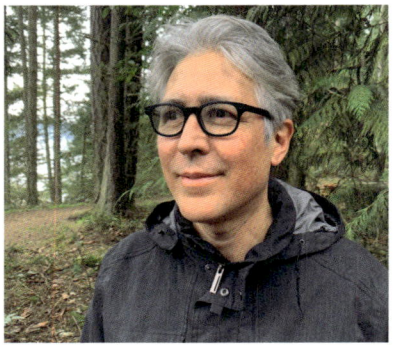

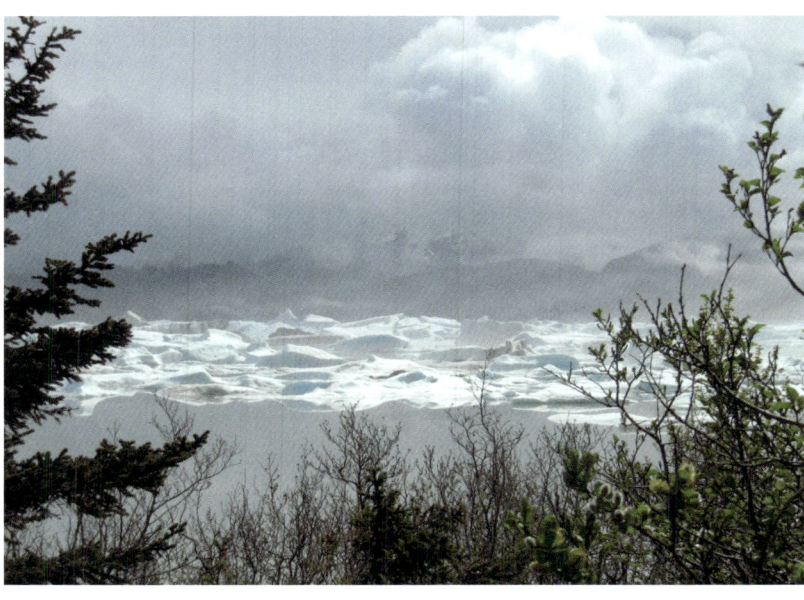

Gail Tremblay
Onondaga/Mi'kmaq descent

BORN 1945 IN BUFFALO, NY
DIED 2023 IN OLYMPIA, WA

Gail Tremblay taught at Evergreen State College in Olympia, Washington, from 1980 to 2018. There she mentored students in the visual arts, creative writing, and Native American studies. She also wrote numerous essays on contemporary Indigenous art. Tremblay's poetry has been published in many anthologies. Her artwork has been widely exhibited and is now included in numerous museum collections.

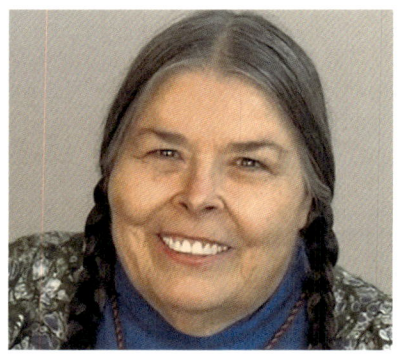

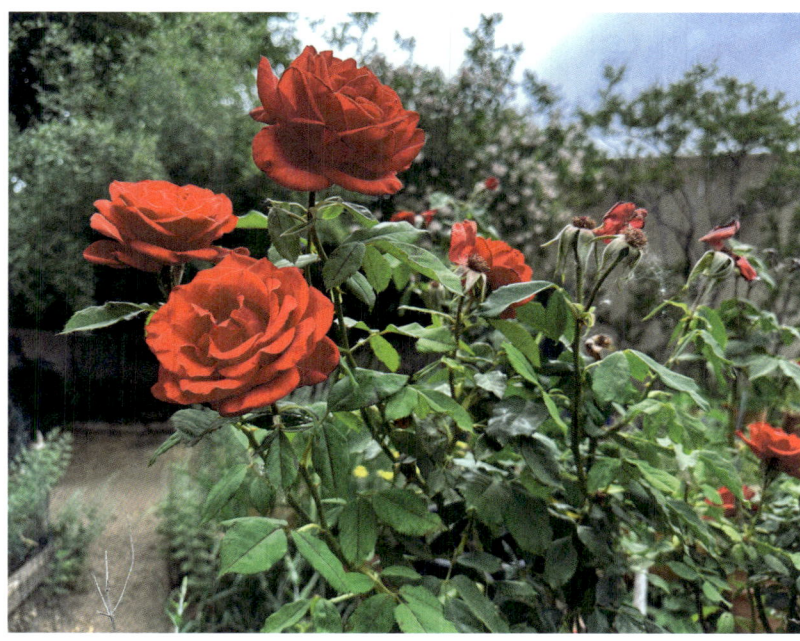

Kay WalkingStick
Cherokee Nation of
Oklahoma/European
descent

BORN 1935 IN SYRACUSE, NY
LIVES AND WORKS IN EASTON, PA

Kay WalkingStick received a BFA from Beaver College (now Arcadia University) in Glenside, Pennsylvania, in 1959 and an MFA from the Pratt Institute in Brooklyn, New York, in 1975. Over a career spanning six decades, WalkingStick's practice has focused on the North American landscape and its metaphorical significances to Native Americans and people around the world.

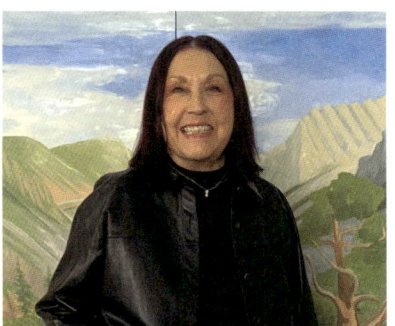

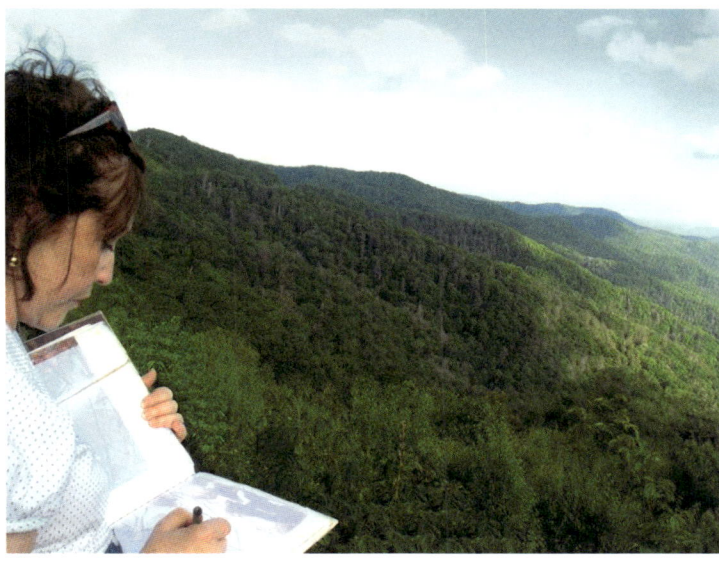

Star WallowingBull
Ojibwe/Arapaho

BORN 1973 IN MINNEAPOLIS, MN
LIVES AND WORKS IN FARGO, ND

Ever since my father, Frank Big Bear, first put a crayon in my hand when I was eight months old, art has been ever-present in my life. I would watch him paint and draw, sometimes for hours at a time, and I took inspiration both from his colorful art and from the experience of visiting museums, art galleries, and artist studios. I began to see that the shapes of ordinary items could present creative possibilities for interpreting ideas.

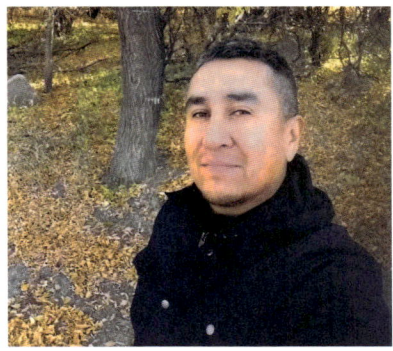

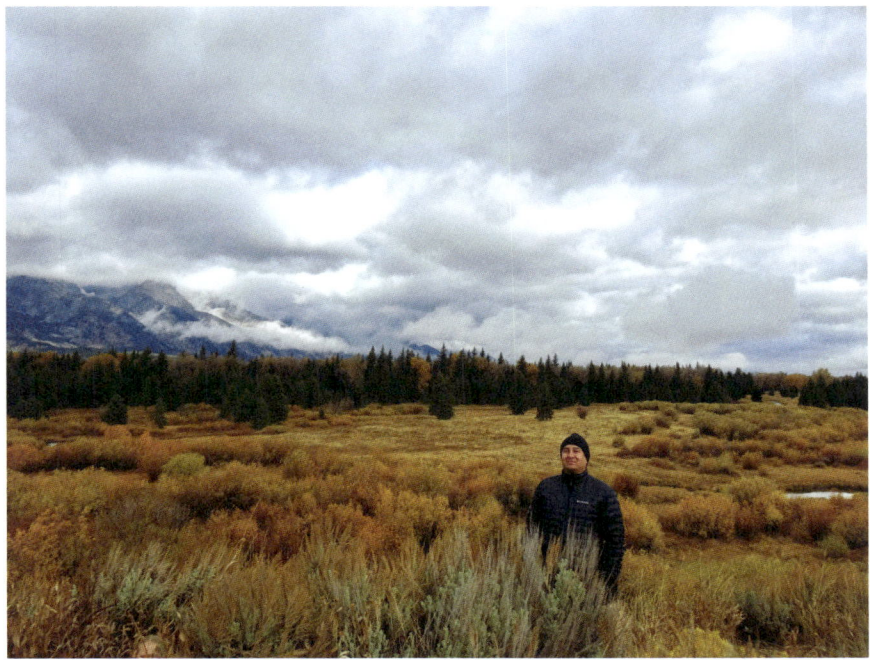

Marie Watt
Seneca Nation of Indians/ European descent

BORN 1967 IN SEATTLE, WA
LIVES AND WORKS IN PORTLAND, OR

Marie Watt's interdisciplinary work draws from biography, conversations across cultures and generations, Hodinöhsö:ni' protofeminism, and Indigenous teachings. In it, she explores the intersection of history, community, and storytelling. She holds an MFA in painting and printmaking from Yale University as well as degrees from Willamette University and the Institute of American Indian Arts. In 2016, she received an honorary doctorate from Willamette University. Watt serves on the board for VoCA (Voices in Contemporary Art), and she joined the board of trustees at the Portland Art Museum in 2020.

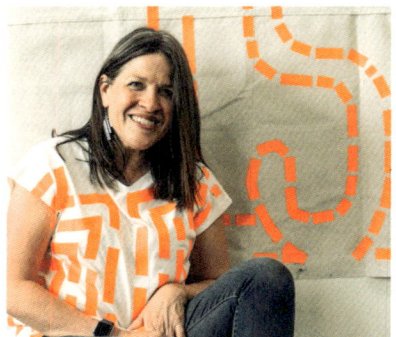

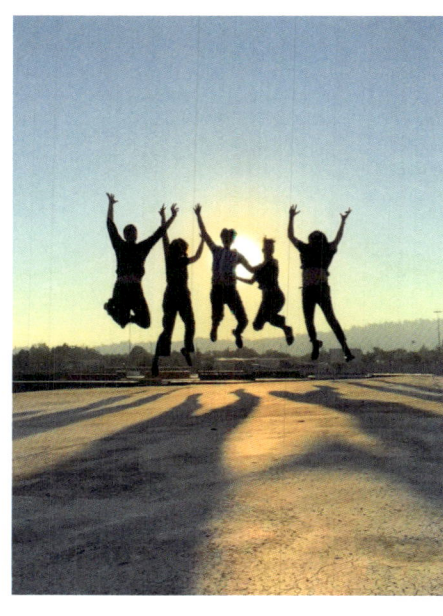

Emmi Whitehorse
Diné

BORN 1957 IN CROWNPOINT, NM
LIVES AND WORKS IN SANTA FE, NM

Emmi Whitehorse grew up in Whitehorse Lake, New Mexico, and attended the University of New Mexico in Albuquerque for her education. She graduated with a degree in art and printmaking. Whitehorse received a master's degree in art in 1982.

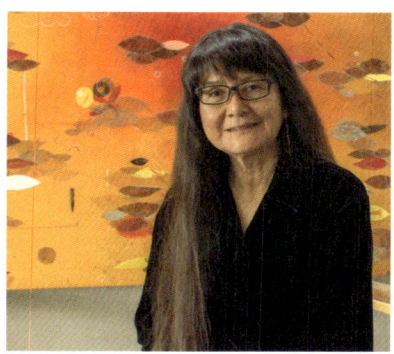

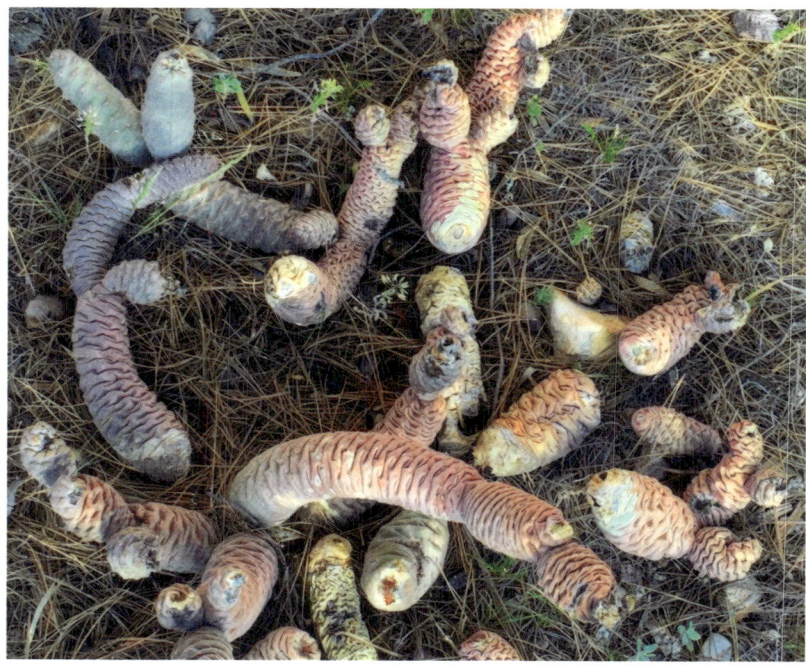

Will Wilson
Diné

BORN 1969 IN SAN FRANCISCO, CA
LIVES AND WORKS BETWEEN SANTA FE,
NM, AND AUSTIN, TX

Will Wilson studied photography, sculpture, and art history at Oberlin College (BA, 1993) and the University of New Mexico (MFA, 2002). He has received the Native American Fine Art Fellowship from the Eiteljorg Museum (2007), the Joan Mitchell Foundation Award for Sculpture (2010), and the Pollock-Krasner Foundation Grant for Photography (2016). In addition to being the 2020 Doran Artist in Residence at Yale University Art Gallery, Wilson has held visiting professorships at the Institute of American Indian Arts, Oberlin College, and the University of Arizona. He received the New Mexico Governor's Award for Excellence in the Arts in 2017.

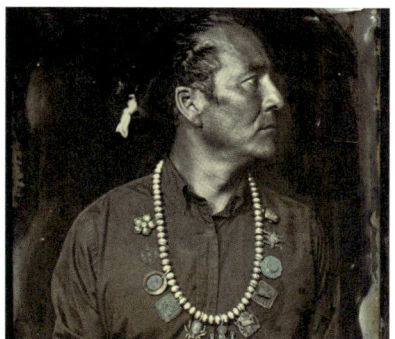

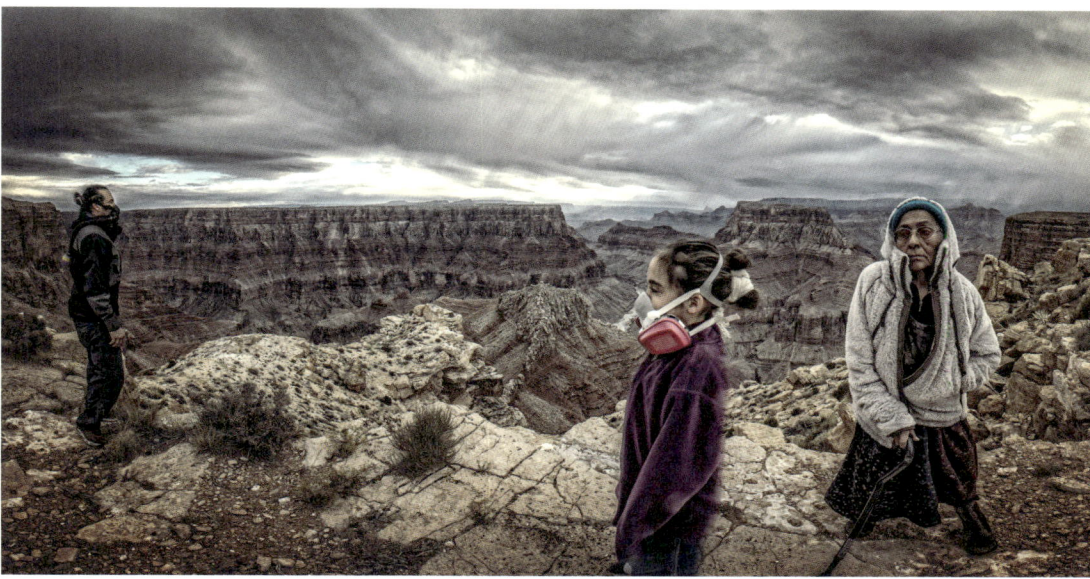

Steven Yazzie
Diné/Pueblo of Laguna, New Mexico/European descent

BORN 1970 IN NEWPORT BEACH, CA
LIVES AND WORKS IN DENVER, CO

A proud member of the Navajo Nation, Steven Yazzie is a veteran of the Gulf War, having served honorably with the United States Marine Corps (1988–1992). He received a bachelor of fine arts degree in intermedia at Arizona State University in Tempe and was named the 2014 outstanding graduate of ASU's Herberger Institute for Design and the Arts. Yazzie also studied at the Skowhegan School of Painting and Sculpture in Maine in 2006.

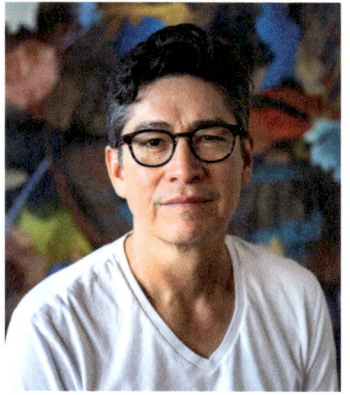

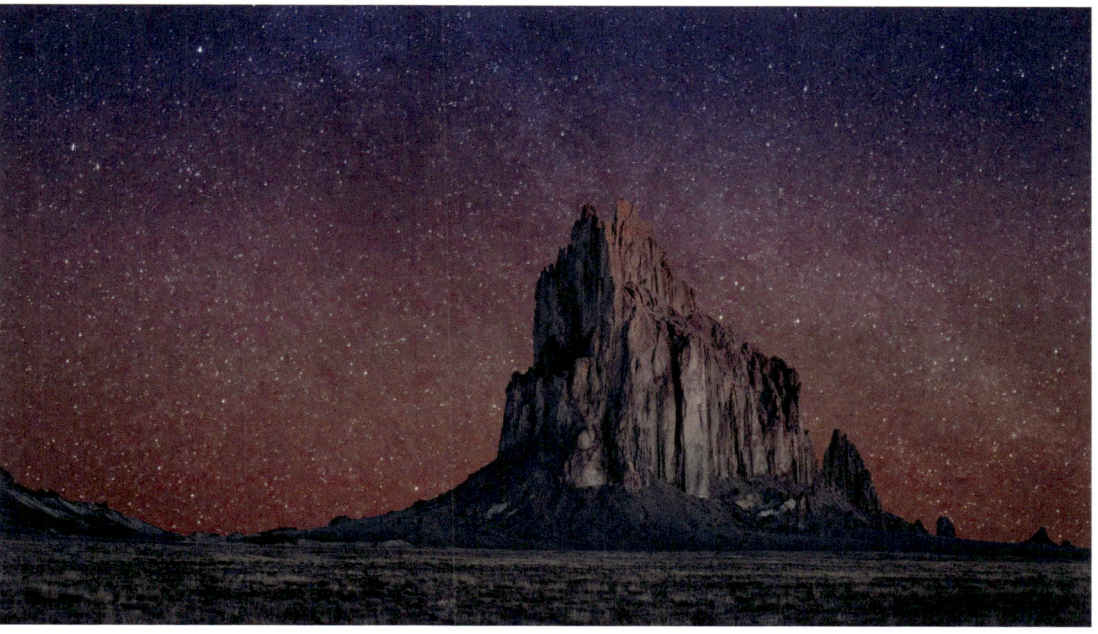

WORKS IN THE EXHIBITION

George Alexander
You found me, you should've never lost me
2022
acrylic on canvas
101.6 × 76.2 cm (40 × 30 in.)
The John and Susan Horseman Collection, Courtesy of the Horseman Foundation, ALEX6.01
page 41

Keri Ataumbi
Kientaddle Baygoon Gah (Dragonflies Dancing)
2021
oxidized sterling silver, 18k yellow gold, brilliant cut diamonds
each 8.9 × 4.5 cm (3 ½ × 1 ¾ in.)
Private collection
page 43

Natalie Ball
Bang bang
2019
elk hide, rabbit fur, oil stick, acrylic, charcoal, cotton, and pine
213.4 × 315 cm (84 × 124 in.)
Rubell Museum, 6358
page 45

Marwin Begaye
Columbia River Custodian
2019
lithograph
71.8 × 56.5 cm (28 ¼ × 22 ¼ in.)
Crow's Shadow Institute of the Arts, CSP 18-101
page 47

Frank Big Bear
Sunflowers in Autumn
2007
Prismacolor pencil on paper
76.2 × 66 cm (30 × 26 in.)
Collection of Plains Art Museum, 2009.003.0001
page 49

Julie Buffalohead
You are on Indian Land
2017
acrylic, ink, and pencil on paper
105.4 × 228.6 cm (41 ½ × 90 in.)
Davis Museum at Wellesley College, Wellesley, Massachusetts, Museum purchase, The Nancy Gray Sherrill, Class of 1954, Collection Acquisition Fund, 2021.4.1.a-.c
page 51

Andrea Carlson
O Cursed Lust of Gold 6
2014
ink and oil on paper
27.9 × 76.8 cm (11 × 30 ¼ in.)
Collection of Mark and Amy Spencer
page 53

Raven Chacon
For Zitkála Šá Series (For Carmina Escobar)
2018
lithograph
27.9 × 21.6 cm (11 × 8 ½ in.)
Crow's Shadow Institute of the Arts, CSP 19-104
page 55

Gerald Clarke Jr.
Native American Art
2019
charred watercolor paper
76.2 × 55.9 cm (30 × 22 in.)
Courtesy of the artist
page 57

Melissa Cody
World Traveler
2014
three-ply wool, aniline dyes, wool warp, and six-ply selvedge cords
228.6 × 124.1 cm (90 × 48 ⅞ in.)
Stark Museum of Art, Orange, Texas, Purchase of the Nelda C. and H.J. Lutcher Stark Foundation, 2014, 2014.1.1
[Washington only]
page 59

Jim Denomie
Edward Curtis, Paparazzi: Chicken Hawks
2008
oil on canvas
88.9 × 101.6 cm (35 × 40 in.)
Loan from the Eiteljorg Museum of American Indians and Western Art, Indianapolis, Indiana, 2009.10.2
page 61

Demian DinéYazhi'
No Place Like Hózhó
2017
six-color lithograph
101 × 76.2 cm (39 ¾ × 30 in.)
Crow's Shadow Institute of the Arts, CSP 17-106
page 63

Duwawisioma (Victor Masayesva Jr.)
Tuwapongya (Earth Altar) Part I
1993
lithograph
image 34.3 × 43.2 cm (13 ½ × 17 in.), sheet 48.9 × 58.4 cm (19 ¼ × 23 in.)
Courtesy Andrew Smith Gallery, Tucson, Arizona
page 65

Duwawisioma (Victor Masayesva Jr.)
Tuwapongya (Earth Altar) Part II
1993
lithograph
image 43.2 × 34.3 cm (17 × 13 ½ in.), sheet 58.4 × 48.9 cm (23 × 19 ¼ in.)
Courtesy Andrew Smith Gallery, Tucson, Arizona
page 65

Duwawisioma (Victor Masayesva Jr.)
Tuwapongya (Earth Altar) Part III
1993
lithograph
image 43.2 × 34.3 cm (17 × 13 ½ in.), sheet 58.4 × 48.9 cm (23 × 19 ¼ in.)
Courtesy Andrew Smith Gallery, Tucson, Arizona
page 65

Duwawisioma (Victor Masayesva Jr.)
Tuwapongya (Earth Altar) Part IV
1993
lithograph
image 43.2 × 34.3 cm (17 × 13 ½ in.), sheet 58.4 × 48.9 cm (23 × 19 ¼ in.)
Courtesy Andrew Smith Gallery, Tucson, Arizona
page 65

Ka'ila Farrell Smith
G' EE' LA
2018
lithograph
55.9 × 38.1 cm (22 × 15 in.)
Crow's Shadow Institute of the Arts, CSP 18-302 (CSPI 1)
page 67

Joe Feddersen
Inhabited Landscapes I
2020
unique print on Rives BFK paper
66 × 50.8 cm (26 × 20 in.)
Courtesy of studio e, Seattle, Washington
page 69

Nicholas Galanin and Merritt Johnson
Creation with her Children
2017
carved wood, fabric, dentalium shells, cast plastic and resin, metal leaf, fish skin leather, carving knife, fringe, plastic tarp, cast hydrocal, rabbit fur, jaw set, paint
157.5 × 213.4 cm (62 × 84 in.)
Courtesy the artists and Peter Blum Gallery, New York
page 71

Jeffrey Gibson
TO FEEL MYSELF BELOVED ON THE EARTH
2020
found punching bag, expanding foam, acrylic felt, plastic beads, glass beads, artificial sinew
144.8 × 38.1 × 38.1 cm (57 × 15 × 15 in.)
Hirshhorn Museum and Sculpture Garden, Smithsonian Institution, Washington, D.C., Joseph H. Hirshhorn Purchase Fund, 2023, TR937
page 73

Teri Greeves
Kiowa Ah-Day
2004
canvas, glass beads, commercial rubber
each 31 × 11 × 15.5 cm
(12 3⁄16 × 4 5⁄16 × 6 1⁄8 in.)
Courtesy of the National Museum of the American Indian, Smithsonian Institution, 26/3325
page 75

Raven Halfmoon
Iichíile (horse | Crow/Apsáalooke)
2021
stoneware, glaze
91.4 × 132.1 × 50.8 cm (36 × 52 × 20 in.)
Collection of Sasha and Charlie Sealy
page 77

Edgar Heap of Birds
Native Host for Washington D.C.
2022
mylar text on metal sign panel with metal post and floor base
45.7 × 91.4 cm (18 × 36 in.)
Collection of the artist
[Washington only]
page 79

Edgar Heap of Birds
Neuf for Modoc
2001
18-color lithograph on Rives BFK white paper
57.2 × 76.2 cm (22 ½ × 30 in.)
Crow's Shadow Institute of the Arts, CSP 01-102
page 32

Luzene Hill
Untitled
2021
ink, charcoal, tea stain, gouache, and colored pencil on Stonehenge paper
38.1 × 55.9 cm (15 × 22 in.)
Courtesy of the artist and K Art
page 81

John Hitchcock
Impact vs. Influence
2023
screen printed felt, paper, and acrylic paint, with contributions by Emily Arthur
dimensions variable
Courtesy of the artist
page 83

G. Peter Jemison
Sentinels (Large Yellow)
2006
acrylic, oil, and collage on canvas
91.4 × 101.6 cm (36 × 40 in.)
National Gallery of Art, Washington, Gift of Funds from Sharon Percy Rockefeller and Senator John Davison Rockefeller IV, 2022.22.1
page 85

Tom Jones
A Hopi Landscape
2013
archival digital print
63.5 × 50.8 cm (25 × 20 in.)
Sherry Leedy Contemporary Art
page 87

Linda King
Teaching of the Tree People
2018
waxed cotton, waxed linen, Red Cedar, and buckskin
height 29.2 cm (11 ½ in.), diam. 22.9 cm (9 in.)
Courtesy of the artist
page 89

Athena LaTocha
Untitled No. 22
2015
sumi and walnut ink and shellac on paper
43.2 × 85.7 cm (17 × 33 ¾ in.)
Collection of RJ and Anne Grissinger
page 91

James Lavadour
Duotone 2
2011
lithograph
38.1 × 28.3 cm (15 × 11 1⁄8 in.)
Crow's Shadow Institute of the Arts, CSP 11-117
page 93

Linda Lomahaftewa
Parrots Prayer Song
1989
lithograph
76.2 × 55.9 cm (30 × 22 in.)
National Gallery of Art, Washington, Gift of Funds from the Roy Lichtenstein Foundation, 2023.22.1
page 95

George C. Longfish
As Above So Below
1997
acrylic on canvas
182.9 × 134.6 cm (72 × 53 in.)
Courtesy of the artist
page 97

Cannupa Hanska Luger
Mirror Shield Project
2016 – ongoing
single channel video and mirror shields
dimensions variable
Courtesy the artist and Garth Greenan Gallery, New York
page 99

Brenda Mallory
The Plural of Nexus
2016
one-color lithograph on Rives BFK white paper
76.2 × 56.8 cm (30 × 22 3⁄8 in.)
Crow's Shadow Institute of the Arts, CSP 16-102
page 101

Mario Martinez
Esoteric Vibration Landscape
2019
colored pencil and oil pastel on paper
61 × 48.3 cm (24 × 19 in.)
Courtesy the artist and Garth Greenan Gallery, New York
page 103

Melissa Melero-Moose
Access Denied
2021
acrylic and mixed media with pine nuts on canvas
91.4 × 122 × 5.1 cm (36 × 48 1⁄16 × 2 in.)
Courtesy of the National Museum of the American Indian, Smithsonian Institution, 27/689
page 105

Jamie Okuma
Peep
2021
antique glass beads, brain-tanned
deer hide, and vintage basket beads on
Casadei boots
each 52 × 21.5 × 12 cm (20 ½ × 8 ⁷⁄₁₆ ×
4 ¾ in.), circum. 39.3 cm (15 ½ in.)
Hood Museum of Art, Dartmouth
College, Hanover, New Hampshire;
Purchased through the Evelyn A. and
William B. Jaffe 2015 Fund, 2021.8.1-2
page 107

Chris Pappan
Atom Heart Mother (Earth)
2016
mixed media on ledger paper
40.6 × 25.4 cm (16 × 10 in.)
Courtesy of Travois
page 109

Rose Powhatan
Fire Warrior Woman
c. 2007
wood, vine, clay, feathers
height 182.9 cm (72 in.), width variable,
base diam. 45.7 cm (18 in.)
Collection of the artist
[Washington only]
page 111

Wendy Red Star
The (HUD)
2010
two-color lithograph with archival
pigment ink photographs on Rives BFK
white paper
76.2 × 56.8 cm (30 × 22 ⅜ in.)
Crow's Shadow Institute of the Arts,
CSP 10-102
page 113

Eric-Paul Riege
jaatłoh4Ye'iitsoh [3–4]
2020
mixed fiber installation
each 335.3 × 45.7 × 15.2 cm
(132 × 18 × 6 in.)
Tia Collection, Santa Fe, New Mexico
page 115

Cara Romero
Indian Canyon
2019
archival pigment print
38.1 × 121.9 cm (15 × 48 in.)
Courtesy of the artist
page 117

Diego Romero
Girl in the Anthropocene
2017
lithograph (printer's proof)
48.3 × 62.2 cm (19 × 24 ½ in.)
Collection of Steven Campbell and
Christina Ziegler Campbell
page 119

Rose B. Simpson
Tonantzin
2021
ceramic and steel, leather, brass
119.4 × 45.7 × 34.3 cm (47 × 18 × 13 ½ in.)
Tia Collection, Santa Fe, New Mexico
page 121

Preston Singletary
Raven Steals the Sun
2017
blown and sand-carved glass
51.4 × 22.9 × 17.8 cm (20 ¼ × 9 × 7 in.)
Collection of Jerry Cowdrey
page 123

Gail Tremblay
*After Global Warming, How Long Will
it Take to Re-Invent a World Where
Everything People Invented Depended
on Snow, Frozen Food, Ice, and Digging
Through it for Cold Water*
2018
16mm film and film leader (blue and
white), silver metallic braid, silver yarn
26 × 16.5 × 16.5 cm (10 ¼ × 6 ½ × 6 ½ in.)
Art Museum of West Virginia University,
2022.7
page 125

Kay WalkingStick
Ute's Homelands
2022
oil on panel in two parts
76.2 × 152.4 × 5.1 cm (30 × 60 × 2 in.)
Courtesy the artist and Hales London and
New York
page 127

Star WallowingBull
Modern Day Indian
2004
lithograph crayon and colored pencil
on paper
56.5 × 76.2 cm (22 ¼ × 30 in.)
Collection Nerman Museum of
Contemporary Art, Johnson County
Community College, Overland Park,
Kansas
page 129

Marie Watt
Antipodes
2020
vintage Italian beads, industrial felt,
and thread
top piece (Skywalker) 137.2 × 160.7 cm
(54 × 63 ¼ in.)
bottom piece (Skyscraper) 135.9 × 151.1 cm
(53 ½ × 59 ½ in.)
National Gallery of Art, Washington,
Gift of Funds from Sharon Percy
Rockefeller and Senator John Davison
Rockefeller IV, 2022.32.1
page 131

Emmi Whitehorse
Fog Bank
2020
mixed media on paper on canvas
129.5 × 198.1 cm (51 × 78 in.)
National Gallery of Art, Washington,
William A. Clark Fund, 2022.41.1
page 133

Will Wilson
Auto-Immune Response no. 2
2004
archival pigment print (digital carbon)
on archival paper
image 43.8 × 68.6 cm (17 ¼ × 27 in.),
sheet 55.9 × 76.2 cm (22 × 30 in.)
Courtesy of the artist
page 135

Steven Yazzie
Orchestrating a Blooming Desert
2003
oil on canvas
121.9 × 152.4 cm (48 × 60 in.)
Collection of Christy Vezolles
page 137

NOTES

FOREWORD AND ACKNOWLEDGMENTS

1. *Art of the American Frontier: The Collecting of Chandler and Pohrt* was on view May 24, 1992 – January 24, 1993. Before that, six other shows featuring Indigenous art were featured at the National Gallery of Art: *Navaho Pollen and Sand Painting* (October 17 – November 14, 1942), *Indigenous Art of the Americas* (April 18 – May 1, 1948), *Contemporary American Indian Painting* (November 8 – December 6, 1953), *Indigenous Art of the Americas* (February 1, 1950 – July 1, 1962), *The Far North: 2000 Years of American Eskimo and Indian Art* (March 8 – May 15, 1973), and *Ancient Art of the American Woodland Indians* (March 17 – August 4, 1985).
2. "Americans," National Museum of the American Indian, Smithsonian Institution. Accessed May 1, 2023. americanindian/si.edu/americans/.

ahtone, "SKY AS PLACE, LAND AS BODY, LANDSCAPE AS SPIRITUAL COMPASS"

1. The author wants to express her gratitude to Jaune Quick-to-See Smith and Shana Bushyhead Condill for their visionary work and steadfast commitment to uplift the Indigenous artists who persistently act on their cultural knowledge and for the invitation to contribute to this book. Further thanks go to Emiko Usui for her encouragement and kindness, as well as the rest of the National Gallery publications team. The comments prepared are inspired by the good work going on in the Indigenous community as we validate our Indigenous knowledge within Western scholarly structures. Thank you to Laura Harjo, who wrote, "The land is not a static object; it is alive, it is kin and the epistemologies from the woodlands of the Southeast are just as alive as renegotiated Mvskoke epistemologies from the southern plains and from the concrete and glass sitting atop the land in Los Angeles." See Laura Harjo, *Spiral to the Stars: Mvskoke Tools of Futurity* (Critical Issues in Indigenous Studies), (Tucson: University of Arizona Press, 2019), 90.
2. The author made these personal notes as a graduate student at the University of Oklahoma's School of Art History in Professor Victor Koshkin-Youritzin's classes on American painting, circa 2004 – 2006.
3. An entire body of literature considers the origins of the biblical creation story. For an accessible discussion, see Mark S. Smith, "Is Genesis 1 a Creation Myth? Yes and No," in *Myth and Scripture: Contemporary Perspectives on Religion, Language, and Imagination*, ed. Dexter E. Callender Jr. (Atlanta: SBL Press, 2014), 71 – 102.
4. The moderate estimate of a population of 18 million in North America at the turn of the 15th century is focused on the land that is now known as the United States, with estimates that nearly 100 million people lived across North and South America prior to contact. Decimated by disease, this population in North America was reduced to 600,000 by 1900, marking an estimated 99.996 percent decrease in population. We, the Indigenous people on this continent today, thrive because of the 0.004 percent who survived.
5. I have appreciated Lavonna Lovern for clarifying that "because of the ability to give life, the title of 'Mother' was a designation of power, not one of sentimentality." See her essay "Women's Roles and Removal," in *Encyclopedia of American Indian Removal*, ed. Daniel F. Littlefield Jr. and James W. Parins, 2 vols. (Santa Barbara, CA: Greenwood, 2011), 268.
6. Many of our tribal stories are recorded in constellations, the sacred knowledge of which has remained protected. The author recommends reading works by Gregory Cajete (Santa Clara Pueblo), David H. Begay and Nancy C. Maryboy (both Navajo), and Annette S. Lee (Lakota), among so many other writers.
7. Kincentricity is a term coined by Dennis Martinez, TEK keeper, in an interview by David E. Hall, "Native Perspectives on Sustainability: Dennis Martinez (O'odham/Chicano/ Anglo)," transcribed by Price McCloud Johnson and Michelle Emery (January 3, 2008), 2. See nativeperspectives. net/Transcripts/Dennis _Martinez_ interview.pdf.
8. Simply stated here, these practices are common among Indigenous peoples and cultures around the world. It is interesting to consider how much of the earth we cannot access when we are restricted to operate within a Western cultural hegemony. I wonder what will be revealed as Indigenous museum workers begin to engage in intercultural discussion and exploration without always reacting to or against the limiting philosophies of Western culture.
9. Emmi Whitehorse has written, "My work is about and has always been about land, about being aware of our surroundings and appreciating the beauty of nature. . . . The act of making art must stay true to a harmonious balance of beauty, nature, humanity, and the whole universe. This is in accordance with Navajo philosophy." See "Native American Heritage: Emmi Whitehorse," blog, Crystal Bridges Museum of American Art, November 2, 2017. Accessed January 28, 2022. crystalbridges.org/blog/ native-american-heritage-emmi-whitehorse/.

Quick-to-See Smith, "LAND/ LANDBASE/LANDSCAPE"

1. This essay is based on conversations between Jaune Quick-to-See Smith and Shana Bushyhead Condill (Eastern Band of Cherokee Indians), executive director of the Museum of the Cherokee Indian in Cherokee, North Carolina. They met on June 2, 2022, at Smith's home in Corrales, New Mexico, and extended their conversation by phone and video calls.
2. Leroy Little Bear, "Jagged Worldviews Colliding," in Marie Battiste, ed., *Reclaiming Indigenous Voice and Vision* (Vancouver: UBC Press, 2000), 82.
3. Eduardo Galeano, *We Say No: Chronicles 1963–1991*, translated by Mark Fried (New York: W. W. Norton, 1992), 179.
4. Dan Wildcat, "Indigenizing Politics and Ethics: A Realist Theory," in Vine Deloria Jr. and Daniel Wildcat, *Power and Place: Indian Education in America* (Golden, CO: American Indian Graduate Center and Fulcrum Resources), 96.
5. Little Bear, "Jagged Worldviews Colliding," 77.
6. César Vallejo, quoted in Galeano, *We Say No*, 146.
7. Joy Harjo, from an undated transcript of her lecture "Native Arts and Culture: Resilience, Reclamation, and Relevance" that she shared with me.
8. This quote is one of many attributed to Chief Crowfoot. See "Chief Crowfoot Quotes." Accessed November 1, 2022. onejourney.net/ chief-crowfoot-quotes/.
9. Rina Swentzell, "An Understated Sacredness," originally published in *MASS: Journal of the School of Architecture and Planning*, University of New Mexico (Fall 1985): 2.
10. Vine Deloria Jr., *God Is Red: A Native View of Religion*, 2nd ed. (Golden, CO: North American Press, 1992), 60.
11. Joseph M. Pierce, "Your Land Acknowledgment Is Not Enough," *Hyperallergic*, October 12, 2022. hyperallergic.com/769024/your-land-acknowledgment-is-not-enough/.

INDEX

CONTRIBUTORS

Jaune Quick-to-See Smith (Citizen of the Confederated Salish and Kootenai Nation) is a noted artist, activist, educator, and curator whose work is the collections of museums around the world.

Joy Harjo (Muscogee [Creek] Nation), the author of two memoirs and several collections of poetry, served as the twenty-third poet laureate of the United States.

heather ahtone (Choctaw/Chickasaw Nation) is director of curatorial affairs at the First Americans Museum in Oklahoma City.

Shana Bushyhead Condill (Eastern Band of Cherokee Indians) is executive director of the Museum of the Cherokee Indian in North Carolina.

CREDITS

Page 10: "Once the World Was Perfect," from *Conflict Resolution for Holy Beings: Poems* by Joy Harjo. Copyright © 2015 by Joy Harjo. Used by permission of W. W. Norton & Company, Inc.

Page 33, fig. 3: Jaune Quick-to-See Smith, *Tongass Trade Canoe*, courtesy the artist and Garth Greenan Gallery, New York

George Alexander
Page 41, plate: © George (Ofuskie) Alexander. Photo by one trip media

Keri Ataumbi
Page 43, plate: Photo by Andy Johnson

Natalie Ball
Page 45, plate: © Natalie Ball. Photo courtesy of Rubell Museum. Photo by Chi Lam

Page 142, artist: Photo by Sam Gehrke Photography

Marwin Begaye
Page 47, plate: © M. Begaye 2018. Photo by Crow's Shadow Institute of the Arts

Page 143, artist: Photo by Patricia Walters

Frank Big Bear
Page 49, plate: © Frank Big Bear. Photo courtesy of Bockley Gallery

Page 143, artist: Photo by Gene Pittman for Walker Art Center

Julie Buffalohead
Page 51, plate: © Julie Buffalohead

Andrea Carlson
Page 53, plate: © Copyright of the artist. Photo courtesy of Bockley Gallery, Collection of Mark and Amy Spencer

Raven Chacon
Page 55, plate: © 2018 Raven Chacon. Photo by Crow's Shadow Institute of the Arts

Melissa Cody
Page 59, plate: © Melissa Cody

Page 146, artist: Photo by Jody Newell

Jim Denomie
Page 61, plate: © Jim Denomie Estate. Photo courtesy of Bockley Gallery

Page 146, artist: Photo copyright Larry McNeil. All rights reserved. Courtesy Jim Denomie Estate

Demian DinéYazhi'
Page 63, plate: © 2017 Demian DinéYazhi'. Photo by Crow's Shadow Institute of the Arts

Page 147, landscape: Photo by Frank T. Dineyazhe II

Duwawisioma
Page 65, plates: © 1993 Victor Masayesva, courtesy Andrew Smith Gallery, Tucson. Photos courtesy of Andrew Smith Gallery

Ka'ila Farrell-Smith
Page 67, plate: © Ka'ila Farrell-Smith. Photo by Crow's Shadow Institute of the Arts

Page 148, landscape: Photo by Emilia Q. Villegas

Joe Feddersen
Page 69, plate: © Joe Feddersen. Photo by R. Johnson - Portland

Nicholas Galanin and Merritt Johnson
Page 71, plate: © Nicholas Galanin and Merritt Johnson. Photo courtesy of IAIA Museum of Contemporary Native Arts (MoCNA)

Jeffrey Gibson
Page 73, plates: Photos courtesy of Jeffrey Gibson

Page 149, artist: Photo by Brian Barlow

Page 149, landscape: Video still from *This Burning World* (still by Michael Barringer and Christine Pfister)

Teri Greeves
Page 75, plate: © Teri Greeves 2004. Photo by NMAI Photo Services

Page 150, artist: Photo by Mary Neiberg

Raven Halfmoon
Page 77, plate: © Raven Halfmoon. Photo by Sean Pathasema

Page 150, landscape: Photo by Jeffrey Osburn

Edgar Heap of Birds
Page 32, fig. 2: © Edgar Heap of Birds. Photo by Crow's Shadow Institute of the Arts

Page 79, plate: © Edgar Heap of Birds. Photo by Shanna Ketchum Heap of Birds

Page 151, artist: Photo by Ted West

Luzene Hill
Page 81, plate: Photo courtesy of the artist and K Art

G. Peter Jemison
Page 85, plate: © G. Peter Jemison

Page 152, artist: Photo by Rikki Van Camp

Tom Jones
Page 87, plate: © Tom Jones

Linda King
Page 89, plate: Photo by Frank H. Tyro

Athena LaTocha
Page 91, plate: © Athena LaTocha

James Lavadour
Page 93, plate: Photo by Crow's Shadow Institute of the Arts

Linda Lomahaftewa
Page 95, plate: © Linda Lomahaftewa. Photo by Gustavo Garcia, Colibri Photography Workshop, Philadelphia, PA

Page 155, artist: Photo by Jason S. Ordaz

Cannupa Hanska Luger
Page 34, fig. 4: Still from *How to Build Mirror Shield for Water Protectors*, 2016. Image courtesy of the artist. Camera/edit and video still by Razelle Benally

Page 99, plate: *Mirror Shield Project* by Cannupa Hanska Luger. Action on November 18, 2016, at Oceti Sakowi Camp, Standing Rock, North Dakota © The artist. Photograph courtesy of the artist and Garth Greenan Gallery, New York

Page 156, artist: Photo by Tomas Karmelo, Indigenous Rising Media

Brenda Mallory
Page 37, fig. 7: *Recollecting Cane*, courtesy the artist and Russo Lee Gallery. Photo by Marion Gallucci

Page 101, plate: © Brenda Mallory. Photo by Crow's Shadow Institute of the Arts

Mario Martinez
Page 103, plate: © Mario Martinez. Photo courtesy the artist and Garth Greenan Gallery, New York

Melissa Melero-Moose
Page 105, plate: © Melissa Melero-Moose. Photo by NMAI Photo Services

The exhibition is organized by the National Gallery of Art, Washington.

The Robert and Mercedes Eichholz Foundation has provided major support for the exhibition.

Additional funding is provided by the Director's Circle and the Tower Project of the National Gallery of Art.

This publication is supported by an endowment for scholarly publications from the Mellon Foundation.

Exhibition dates
National Gallery of Art, Washington
September 22, 2023–January 15, 2024

New Britain Museum of American Art
April 18–September 15, 2024

Tribal affiliations are based on the information provided by each artist.

Produced by the National Gallery of Art, Washington
nga.gov

Designed by Deborah Littlejohn (Eastern Band of Cherokee Indians descent)
Edited by Nancy Eickel
Produced by Brad Ireland and Christina Wiginton
Proofread by Juliet Clark
Indexed by Ian Fry

Typeset in Indivisible by Process Type Foundry

Printed in Italy by Verona Libri on Magno Volume and Munken Polar

10 9 8 7 6 5 4 3 2 1

Published by the National Gallery of Art, Washington, in association with Princeton University Press, Princeton and Oxford

41 William Street
Princeton, NJ 08540

99 Banbury Road
Oxford OX2 6JX

press.princeton.edu

Library of Congress Control Number 2023912738

ISBN 978-0-691-24545-4

Cover: Emmi Whitehorse (Diné), *Fog Bank* (detail), 2020 (p. 133)

Frontispiece: Will Wilson (Diné), *Auto-Immune Response no. 2*, 2004 (p. 135)